The Psychodynamics of Toxic Organizations

Understanding experience at work, especially in toxic organizations, is a multidimensional undertaking that must include all senses. The use of applied poetry has its primary value as an evocative approach to sensing, knowing, and understanding workplace experience. Poetry at its best condenses into relatively few words, metaphors, and images what conventional social science narratives would take much longer to articulate. Where poetry often hints and alludes, narrative seeks to spell out, expound, and complete. Where poetry leaves much mental space for the listener or reader to fill in with one's imagination, narrative fills in the spaces with rich detail. Applied poetry and its contextual stories offer a way of accessing workplace experience that is unique and valuable in terms of understanding lives at work. The use of complementary psychodynamic theories, like all theories, is a way of trying to account for what we have found and experienced and in particular why it happened. "Why," the authors suggest, is critical in terms of understanding the sensing, images, and metaphors evoked by the poetry and stories that may resonate with hearers and readers for reasons that are unconscious and are rooted in the past. These transferences that come forward from life experience into the present are the critical data we work with. These are the data of psychoanalysis. This book both widens and deepens the scope of organizational research offered by other researchers, theorists, and approaches to understanding, interpreting, explaining, leading, and consulting with workplace organizations. Its triangulating integration of applied poetry, experience and stories behind the poetry, and the three psychoanalytic models of explaining life in workplaces is a new and distinct contribution to organizational research, leadership, and consulting efforts to help organization members solve real, underlying problems and not offer simplistic, formulaic solutions based solely on a study of the organization's surface. It will be of interest to researchers, academics, and students in the fields of organizational studies, leadership, and management.

Howard F. Stein is Professor Emeritus in the Department of Family and Preventive Medicine at the University of Oklahoma Health Sciences Center, Oklahoma City, USA.

Seth Allcorn is the former Vice President for Business and Finance at the University of New England in Biddeford, Maine, USA. He has more than twenty years of experience working with physicians, hospitals, and academic medical centers and is an organizational consultant specializing in the management of change, strategic planning, and organizational restructuring.

Routledge Studies in Management, Organizations and Society

This series presents innovative work grounded in new realities, addressing issues crucial to an understanding of the contemporary world. This is the world of organised societies, where boundaries between formal and informal, public and private, local and global organizations have been displaced or have vanished, along with other nineteenth century dichotomies and oppositions. Management, apart from becoming a specialized profession for a growing number of people, is an everyday activity for most members of modern societies.

Similarly, at the level of enquiry, culture and technology, and literature and economics, can no longer be conceived as isolated intellectual fields; conventional canons and established mainstreams are contested. **Management, Organizations and Society** addresses these contemporary dynamics of transformation in a manner that transcends disciplinary boundaries, with books that will appeal to researchers, student and practitioners alike.

Recent titles in this series include:

Organizational Culture and Paradoxes in Management
Firms, Families, and Their Businesses
Saulo C. M. Ribeiro

The Democratic Organisation
Democracy and the Future of Work
Thomas Diefenbach

Management and the Sustainability Paradox
David M. Wasieleski, Paul Shrivastava and Sandra Waddock

The Psychodynamics of Toxic Organizations
Howard F. Stein and Seth Allcorn

For more information about this series, please visit: www.routledge.com/history/series/SE0246

The Psychodynamics of Toxic Organizations
Applied Poems, Stories and Analysis

Howard F. Stein and Seth Allcorn

Routledge
Taylor & Francis Group

NEW YORK AND LONDON

First published 2020
by Routledge
605 Third Avenue, New York, NY 10017

and by Routledge
2 Park Square, Milton Park, Abingdon, Oxon, OX14 4RN

First issued in paperback 2022

*Routledge is an imprint of the Taylor & Francis Group, an
informa business*

Publisher's Note
The publisher has gone to great lengths to ensure the quality of this
reprint but points out that some imperfections in the original copies
may be apparent.

Library of Congress Cataloging-in-Publication Data
A catalog record for this book has been requested

ISBN 13: 978-0-367-50743-5 (pbk)
ISBN 13: 978-0-367-44235-4 (hbk)
ISBN 13: 978-1-00-300955-9 (ebk)

DOI: 10.4324/9781003009559

Typeset in Sabon
by Apex CoVantage, LLC

Contents

Authors

Howard F. Stein, PhD (University of Pittsburgh, 1972), an applied, medical, psychoanalytic, and organizational anthropologist; psychohistorian; organizational consultant; and poet is Professor Emeritus in the Department of Family and Preventive Medicine, University of Oklahoma Health Sciences Center, Oklahoma City, where he taught for nearly 35 years (1978–2012). He was a group facilitator of the American Indian Diabetes Prevention Center in Oklahoma City from 2012 to 2017. He is Poet Laureate of the High Plains Society for Applied Anthropology. He is author, co-author, or editor of 32 books, of which 10 are books or chapbooks of his poetry. His most recent scholarly books are *Listening Deeply* (2nd Edition, University of Missouri Press, 2018) and *The Dysfunctional Workplace*, co-authored with Seth Allcorn (University of Missouri Press, 2015). His most recent poetry books are *Centre and Circumference* (2018) and *Light and Shadow* (2nd edition, 2018). He has also published a book of clinical poetry, *In the Shadow of Asclepius: Poems from American Medicine* (2011). He and Seth Allcorn, longtime friends and colleagues, have co-authored numerous papers, chapters, and books.

Seth Allcorn, PhD, MBA is the former Vice President for Business and Finance at the University of New England in Biddeford, Maine. Dr. Allcorn has more than twenty years of experience working with physicians, hospitals, and academic medical centers. He has served as a financial and administrative Assistant Dean at the Texas Tech School of Medicine and as Associate Dean for the Stritch School of Medicine, Loyola–Chicago. He has also managed two departments of internal medicine for the University of Missouri–Columbia and University of Rochester. He has twenty years of experience as an organizational consultant specializing in the management of change, strategic planning, and organizational restructuring. Dr. Allcorn is the author or co-author of 13 books, 9 book chapters, and over 90 papers that have appeared in scholarly and practitioner journals. He is a founding member of the International Society for the Psychoanalytic Study of Organizations.

Preface

Sun, Sand, and Water

Howard F. Stein and Seth Allcorn

A lifetime of poems washed ashore—
a beautiful shell here,
a wonderfully colored and smooth stone there,
a long-lost toy, weathered and rusty but of so much value.
We dare not overlook a single treasure,
as the ocean's surface splashes gently on the sand,
while sandpipers and gulls mine the beach for food.
So it is we who also harvest the possibilities of the poems.
What do they mean?
How can we use them?
How should we arrange them in the larger universe?
As the bright overhead sun shines brightly on them, an order emerges.
Yes, this shell, that stone, this long ago lost treasure:
There is order in the chaos and meaning in the universe.
We here share our beach with you in all its amazing beauty and grace.
There is meaning in life to be discovered.
Meaning can also be found in our lives at work.

Books have to start with a single keystroke, a word, a sentence, and a paragraph. They have to start with inspiration, an idea, and a vision—something that excites the writer to make the effort to write. Writing books is both fun and exciting, and stressful hard work that turns to labor that challenges us to make clear our fleeting thoughts and images. For this book, the first keystroke was actually another book—inspired in turn by books of poetry—in which we focused on telling workplace *stories* that you could not make up[1]. These unbelievable stories defied the much-preferred image of organizations as rational, calculating, and professionally run. This book brings the original inspiration full circle to a book that incorporates *applied poetry* as a starting point to find meaning in our lives at work.

The opening poem was inspired by the process used to construct the framework for this book—our lives at work. A great many poems related to the workplace, or indirectly so, were considered for inclusion in the book. Much like a walk on a beach, these poems were gradually reduced down to those most fitting to use in terms of providing workplace insights. These poems were further divided up by the *themes* in the poems to create book chapters. Finally, they were sequenced within the chapters to provide a sense of a narrative and dramatic arc, where the poems move the reader along on a journey through the workplace. The stories behind the poems were then written and the poems and stories explored using psychodynamically informed perspectives. We hope the triangulation of poems, stories, and analysis provides readers many insights into toxic organizational dynamics and your experience at work.

Note

1. Allcorn, S. & Stein, H.F. (2015). *The dysfunctional workplace: Theory, stories, and practice*. Columbia, MO: University of Missouri Press.

Acknowledgements

We owe so much to the many people who helped us to bring this book into fruition. We begin by acknowledging the deep friendship and long collaboration we co-authors, Howard F. Stein and Seth Allcorn, have had that has brought us to this point. Most of the time, so rich were our conversations that we ultimately could not discern who had any given idea originally—and it did not matter. Likewise, in countless conversations since the early 1990s—in person, on the telephone, in e-mails, and most recently in Skype visits—Seth Allcorn would often say, as we were discussing some experience or idea in organizational dynamics, "You know, Howard, there might be a poem in there." And in most instances, there was.

We are grateful to our longtime friend and colleague, Dr. Michael Diamond, who has been supportive of and encouraged this project from the outset. Dr. Mindy Duncan devoted much time and effort in bibliographic searches for us, both online and in libraries. We are likewise indebted to Drs. David Lotto and Peter Petschauer for reading and critically commenting on an earlier draft of this book. Howard also wishes to express his gratitude to his wife and colleague, Rev. Dr. Nance Killough Cunningham, who lived through the long development of this book—and who insisted that he now and then get up from in front of the computer and rest.

Dr. Johanna Shapiro has long encouraged and advocated for Howard's poetry in *Family Medicine* journals and beyond. Dr. Peter Petschauer has long advocated Howard's poetic voice as well as his scholarly one. Likewise, Dr. Warren Holleman and Dr. Paul Fischer have made a home for Howard's applied medical poetry in *The Journal of Family Practice*. Dr. Paul Elovitz and Dr. David Lotto have published many of Howard's organizational, cultural, and historical poems in *Clio's Psyche* and the *Journal of Psychohistory* respectively. Dr. Maria Vesperi graciously made a place for Howard's poetry in *Anthropology Now*.

Howard wishes to acknowledge the encouragement given to him by the High Plains Society for Applied Anthropology, of which he is Poet Laureate; the International Psychohistorical Association; the *Journal of*

Psychohistory; *Clio's Psyche*; *The Applied Anthropologist*; *Families, Systems and Health*; *Family Medicine*; *Anthropology Now*; *Harp-Strings Poetry Journal*; *Songs of Eretz Poetry Review* (of which he is a frequent contributor; Steven Gordon, MD, Editor); the International Society for the Psychoanalytic Study of Organizations; and the Poetry Society of Oklahoma. They have made a place for his applied poetry. Several fine poets and poetry editors have been mentors of Howard throughout his development as a poet: among them, Maxine Austin, Madelyn Eastlund, Vivian Stewart, and Margaret Touhey.

Howard wishes to thank his 14-year-old cat, Luke, for his comforting presence during Howard's long hours of work at the keyboard and with pen and pad in a recliner.

Permissions

The Applied Anthropologist

Permission from Peter Van Arsdale, Chairman, Publications Committee, High Plains Society for Applied Anthropology.
Includes permission for:
The Corporate Table. *The Applied Anthropologist* 35(1)2015: 39;
Good Enough. *The Applied Anthropologist* 35(2)2015: 56.
How Things Work Around Here. Appears In: The Routing Slip. *The Applied Anthropologist* 34(1–2)2014: 42

The Healing Muse

"One time rights" only. No need for permission.
Appointment at the Doctor's. *The Healing Muse* 10(1)2010: 115–116;
Medical Records. *The Healing Muse* 13 (October 2013): 24.

The Journal of Psychohistory

Permission from Susan Hein, Managing Editor.
Stewardship. *The Journal of Psychohistory* 45(2)Fall 2017: 148–149.
Psychohistory.com website. Reprinted with permission.

Anthropology Now

"Transformational Leadership" in:
Howard F. Stein (2015) Poetry, *Anthropology Now*, 7:1, 129–130, DOI: 10.1080/19492901.2015.11728314. Taylor & Francis. Reprinted by permission of the publisher Taylor & Francis Ltd, www.tandfonline.com/
"Where Is the Blood?" in:
Howard F. Stein (2017) Poetry, *Anthropology Now*, 9:1, 139, DOI: 10.1080/19428200.2017.1291060. Taylor & Francis. Reprinted by permission of the publisher Taylor & Francis Ltd, www.tandfonline.com/

"Invisible" in:

Howard F. Stein (2015) Poetry, *Anthropology Now*, 7:1, 129–130, DOI: 10.1080/19492901.2015.11728314. Taylor & Francis. Reprinted by permission of the publisher Taylor & Francis Ltd, www.tandfonline.com/

The Journal of Family Practice

Schizophrenic. Reprinted with permission from *The Journal of Family Practice®*. 2002 Jun; 51(6):529. © 2002, Frontline Medical Communications, Inc.

Gulf. Reprinted with permission from *The Journal of Family Practice®*. 1998 Nov; 47(5):391. © 1998, Frontline Medical Communications, Inc.

Case Report: Caged. Reprinted with permission from *The Journal of Family Practice®*. 2000 May; 49(5):406. ©2000, Frontline Medical Communications, Inc.

Conflict Avoidance. Reprinted with permission from *The Journal of Family Practice®*. 2001 February; 50(2): p. 144. © 2001, Frontline Medical Communications Inc.

Families, Systems and Health

A Quiet Place. From Stein, H.F. (1998). Two Poems. *Families, Systems and Health* 16(3)Fall 1998: 321. http://dx.doi.org/10.1037/h0092895 Copyright © 1998 American Psychological Association. Reproduced with Permission.

ABC-CLIO LLC and Copyright Clearance Center

Nothing Personal, Just Business. Howard F. Stein. Westport, CT, 2001. Permission granted by ABC-CLIO Inc. and Copyright Clearance Center.

Without Windows, Without Light.

Journal for the Psychoanalysis of Culture and Society

Journal for the Psychoanalysis of Culture and Society. 4(2) Fall 1999: pp. 209–227. Permission letter from Tony Sanfilippo, Director, The Ohio State University Press.

Title of article containing poems: "Downsizing, Managed Care, and the Potlatching of America: A Study in Cultural Brutality and Its Mystification."

Story Telling, or Flawed Narrative. (pp. 220–221)

Survivor's Wound. (p. 213).

Friday's Poems/*Ascent Aspirations Magazine*

Boxes Everywhere. Published 9/2/2016. Friday's Poems. *Ascent Aspirations Magazine.* www.davidpfraser.ca/fridays-poems.html Accessed 2 September 2016 Reprinted with permission.

CLIO's Psyche

Thaw in the Ice. p. 20(2) September 2013: 219. Reprinted with permission.

Mindmend Publishing

Howard F. Stein. (2017). Centre and Circumference. New York: MindMend Publishing, 2017. p. 37. Copyright © Howard F. Stein. 62 Conventions. p. 37. Reprinted with permission.

Center for the Study of Organizational Change

Company Man. Permission from Michael Diamond, Founding Director of CSOC, e-mail 9/10/19. Originally published in 2015, by Center for the Study of Organizational Change, University of Missouri, Columbia, MO. Retrieved on April 28, 2015 from http://csoc.missouri.edu/company-man/.

Poems published in poetry books of Howard F. Stein and in journals/magazines currently in print:

*Raisins and Almonds**

Georgetown, KY: Finishing Line Press, 2014.
The Wrong Ending. p. 4.

*From My Life**

Georgetown, KY: Finishing Line Press, 2005.
Seeing Far Enough. p. 23.
Stay Beneath the Smoke. p. 19.
Badges. p. 20.
Art Form. p. 22.

*Poems from *Raisins and Almonds* and *From My Life* have been reprinted with the permission of The Permissions Company, LLC on behalf of Finishing Line Press, www.finishinglinepress.com

Blood and Thunder: Musings on the Art of Medicine

A literary journal of the University of Oklahoma College of Medicine
Why We're Here. p. 8(Fall 2008): 76. Reprinted with permission.

Floyd County Moonshine

The Box. p. 7(2) Summer 2015: 64–65. Reprinted with permission.

Light and Shadow

Howard F. Stein. Yukon, OK: Doodle and Peck Publishing, 2016.
Reprinted with permission of Marla Jones, Publisher.
Who We Are. (no page number)

Poems in Order of Appearance

Acknowledgments

The journals, magazines, and poetry books by Howard F. Stein, in which the following poems were originally published, are no longer being published and are long out of print. We list the poems in aggregate after the name of the journal, magazine, or book.

Evocations. Howard F. Stein. Pittsburgh: Dorrance, 1997. Copyright © Howard F. Stein. Book long out of print. Copyright belongs to HF Stein. Permission not needed.

Poems reprinted:

Downsizing the Company, or the Perfect Bureaucrat
Thought's Geography
Speak Your Mind
On Forgetting Your Place
Telephone Salutation
Importance
Business Meeting Agenda
Gulf
The Order
That Look

Learning Pieces. Howard F. Stein. Pittsburgh: Dorrance, 2000. Copyright © Howard F. Stein. Book long out of print. Copyright belongs to HF Stein. Permission not needed.

Poems Reprinted:

Car Ride
Progressively
Bullring at the Office
Business Meeting, Good Friday
Office Space
Imagine You
Caulking the Wall
Overdressed

Harp-Strings Poetry Journal (Defunct)

Songs and Dances of Death. p. 21(3) Winter 2010: 18.
Reply to Adorno. p. 18(2) Autumn 2006: 17.
Baggage. p. 20(3) Winter 2009: 16–17.
Downsizing. p. 18(4) Spring 2007: 18–19.
Music Director. p. 19(4) Spring 2008: 20.
Those Who Clean Up After Us. p. 22(1) Summer 2010: 15.
Bartender. p. 19(1) Summer 2007: 21.

Mediphors: A Literary Journal of the Health Professions (Defunct)

Office and Theater. p. 4(Fall/Winter 1994): 167.

Manna (Defunct)

Job Description. p. 9(4) Winter 1995: 4.
Caulking the Wall. p. 12(3) Fall 1998: 4.

AHEC News

(Northwest Oklahoma Area Health Education Center): Defunct.
Rain Upon Our Corporate Roof. p. 4(3) November 1996: 16.
Poems published in poetry books of Howard F. Stein and in journals/
    magazines currently in print:

Unpublished Poems by Howard F. Stein

Corporate Greed: A Fantasy
Alone
Taking It Personally
Anonymous People, Nameless People
Poor Aim
Inquiry at the Office
Exit Visa
Getting Lost
Impaired Vision
Rush Hour Definition
The End of the World
The Door

Unpublished Poem by Howard F. Stein and Seth Allcorn

Sun, Sand, and Water

1   Introduction

The applied poetry we explore in this book is a way to communicate, at a higher level than academic narrative, about workplace experience in an emotionally destructive organization. We share the first author's long history of writing *workplace poetry* that has been published in books of poetry; scholarly, literary, and practitioner journals; presented at meetings; and used to make workplace interventions. The poems are grounded in *lived experience* of leaders, groups, and organizations—the workplace. They are about real events, real experience, and real thoughts and feelings.

An example of applied workplace poetry is the opening poem. It emerged from the work and bears witness to the process of discovery that is the method of arriving at the book's themes and chapters. The poem is an *applied* poem that peels back the lived experience of writing this book. It offers insight into the nature of work not readily apparent from the written words that are this book as a narrative.

In this book, we explore the inner (intrasubjective) and intersubjective workplace through applied poetry and the stories behind the poems. This use of "applied poetry"—that is, poetry meant to be useful—helps organizations to identify and solve problems in the workplace. This book addresses the issue of how organization members and consultants together can access and make use of this inner and intersubjective world in their work as revealed in recurrent themes, metaphors, and images. The authors use applied poetry to illustrate and evoke workplace experiences for inspection that become the subject of research and consulting. The poems became the co-created and reflective space discussed in the Chapter 13 summary. More broadly, the arts in all their forms can help to create psychological space both internally and between organization members, researchers and consultants. In this new space, filled with latent potential, the interior worlds of leaders and followers, clients and consultants, become available for creative organizational problem-solving.

In this book, we take the creative workplace potential of the applied poems several steps further. We share the *context* that inspired the poems—the story within the poems. To this we add a relatively new way to understand organizational experience and dynamics. We use three *psychoanalytically informed perspectives* to explore in greater depth the applied poems, but also the conscious and unconscious experiences, thoughts, and feelings that they represent. We hope that this *triangulation* of applied poems, stories, and analysis will provide new insights and a method for the study of organizations and workplace experience.

Studying Toxic Organizations

The tyranny that is often present in our organizations leads to a sense of organizational darkness and inconsolability, pervasive death imagery, the suffocating feeling of organizational pollution or miasma, the death of the spirit, the murder of the individual and group spirit, a feeling of chronic vulnerability, and lack of a sense of safety.[1] The presence of this tyranny is underscored by this book, although within organizations it is often cloaked in logic and the use of words to conceal it.

The pervasive and deceptive language of euphemism (*downsizing, reengineering, restructuring, reengineering,* and *off-shoring*) conceals a world of corporate violence expressed in psychological brutality and the dehumanization of workers.[2] The slogan "nothing personal, just business" belies just how personal corporate decisions can become when implemented.[3] The reality of this toxicity is all too often denied by pseudo-rationality and the invocation of economic necessity. Top-down leadership in rigid, hierarchical workplaces leads to organizational totalitarianism, and with it, traumatic change and psychological atrocity.

For the authors, these many perspectives condense into the experience of "organizational toxicity," the pervasive sense that one is being spiritually poisoned in a polluted workplace ostensibly meant for the accomplishment of *work*. The "psychological contract" between employer and employee was long ago nullified and replaced by the pursuit of stockholder value by corporate executives and their boards. Employees—workers—have become exploited and disposable objects. Our use of applied poetry, stories, and psychoanalytically informed analysis will illuminate these soul-stripping aspects of our toxic organizations.

What This Book Is and Is Not About

This book is a contribution to the psychoanalytic study of organizations. Its specific contribution is the research "instrument" the authors use to conduct that study: *poetry about the lived experience of organizational life and the stories behind the experiences that inspired the poetry.* Applied poetry serves as the research tool that offers access into the psychological reality of workplaces, what Michael Diamond refers to as the "unconscious life of organizations."[4] This role of poetry as an instrument of research will be explained in Chapter 2. We use psychoanalytic theory to explore and interpret the poems and stories from which the poetry arises. Three psychoanalytic models (object relations; group relations; and Karen Horney's perspective of movement toward, away from, and against others) are discussed in Chapter 3 and serve as a theoretical template for interpreting the poems and stories starting with Chapter 4.

What is *new* about this book is the use of applied poetry as an instrument of organizational research paired with the triangulation of poetry/stories/psychoanalytic theories to add depth of understanding. Stated differently, we believe that the elaboration of how to apply psychoanalytic theory to the lived experience represented by the applied poetry and stories is an informative example of how to think psychodynamically about the workplace. It is also one of the book's major contributions.

The authors wish to make clear at the outset that this book is *not* a book of poetry-for-poetry's-sake. Rather, poetry in this book is instrumental and a means to a wider end. It is "applied poetry," which the authors use as a research tool (1) to explore organizational life; (2) to offer the reader a means of recognizing themselves within the workplace and their emotional experiences of their workplaces; and (3) perhaps to provide some degree of healing to readers through thought and reflection. With this approach, we hope to convey to the reader: You are not alone in having had these experiences. The poetry itself is a *means* toward these ends. Our use of applied poetry as an instrument of engagement, for helping people to feel understood, to deepen their own insights through reflection, and to solve problems in the real world is worthy of thoughtful inspection.

In conclusion, our use of applied poetry can be seen as an addition to other approaches used in qualitative methodology to plumb the depths of human experience of the workplace. In particular, we use applied organizational poetry as both a qualitative research instrument and a way to represent research data. It complements other approaches for understanding organizations as *a different way of knowing*. As both method and data, applied poetry constitutes a form of organizational research, distinct from conventional narrative inquiry and quantitative methods. Applied organizational poetry resonates with listeners and readers in ways that standard academic narratives cannot. Also to be appreciated is that the interpretive and explanatory framework of psychoanalytically informed interpretation provides an instrument for making sense of applied workplace poetry and of the organizational life behind it.

In Sum

In this book, the applied poems, together with the stories about how the poems came to be written, are the *research data*. They are our "case studies," written by a poet who, as an organizational member and consultant, lived the experience. The book connects this personal journey to wider organizational, historical, and cultural contexts, and then *interprets* these contexts through the conceptual lens of *psychoanalytic theory*.

Applied organizational poetry, we underscore, serves the *dual* function of constituting a qualitative research method that reveals findings as data to be "sensed" and analyzed. The method of *triangulating* poem, story, and psychodynamic analysis creates insight for understanding our complex organizations and leaders and the presence of workplace toxicity. We also hope that the poems and contextual stories will *draw the reader into* the conceptual and emotional space of the authors' organizational experience and promote reflection on that experience by learning how to use psychoanalytic theories to explore their own unconscious nature.

Why Is This Book Important? Contributions of This Book

With so much written about workplace organizations based on empirical positivistically-rooted research, what could poetry, contextual stories, and a psychoanalytic informed perspective possibly add to what is already known about organizations? Whatever is known about workplaces by relying on conventional empirical research methods must be considered to be opaque to the lived experience of work. It provides at best only a superficial understanding of life at work. Applied poetry, in contrast, by accessing unconscious processes, fills the chasm left by empirical methods. Simply put, positivist-based empirical research methods do not access the heart of "what it is like to work here," that is, to the meaning of workplace experience.

In this book, we hope that the applied poems, the stories about their origins, and the psychodynamically-informed analysis that are grounded in the inner and intersubjective world of work will resonate with the experience of the reader in his or her own organization. This book breaks this silence and gives a liberating voice to employees' lived experiences. Poetry, like stories, tells the listener and reader "what it is like to work here" as an employee—not management's viewpoints of "what it is supposed to be like to work here" (as in corporate brochures and financial reports, strategic planning, promotional videos, and procedures manuals for workers). Conceivably, the reader could be moved to write poems creating a sense of healing and mastery that might also contribute to better organizational functioning. It is therefore important to appreciate that a key to both the book's perspective and making sense of what can be learned from this perspective is the role of applied poetry—the poetry of witness to the darkness of much of organizational life.

Applied Poetry and Poet as Witness

The applied poems in this book belong to a genre of what Carolyn Forché calls "poetry of witness."[5] It is a category of writing that is neither objective nor subjective, neither individual nor political. Rather, the poet and the poem bear witness to an extreme, terrible human situation and testify that "this really happened." Taken further, it will soon become apparent to the reader that the applied poems, the contextual stories behind them, and the psychodynamic interpretations *all* entail the process of bearing witness and communicating to the world what one has seen, heard, and felt.

The applied workplace poems in this book are largely of a character that what they describe, evoke, and make real would be officially denied as having happened. Like other poems of witness, they take a stand "against forgetting"—which includes officially enforced forgetting—in our dark times, organizational and beyond. This book is then in part an effort by the authors to join with the readers in not forgetting toxic organizational events and bearing witness to their at-times devastating personal and group outcomes. The *entire book*—and not only the poems—bears witness to the at-times unimaginable toxicity with our organizations.

This process of bearing witness leads us to offer some suggestions for you, the reader, about how to read this book. Following Thomas Ogden, we ask you to be aware of your resonance with *your own work experience* as you read of the work experience presented in the poems and stories.[6] Simply put, as you read and hear the words in this book, allow your mind to drift and pay attention to where that drifting takes you. In this way of listening both to the voices of the poetry together with your own voice as you read, you may come to have a mirroring experience and more fully appreciate the poet who listened to himself while listening to the voices in the workplace, and from that listening, wrote the poems.[7]

Finally, let us provide a "roadmap" of the book so that the reader can begin to imagine the book as a whole.

Organization of This Book

Chapter 1 Introduction

In this chapter we introduce our use of poems, stories, and psychoanalytically informed perspectives to explore toxic organizations in greater depth. Better understanding of work life in toxic organizations is essential not only in terms of personal survival but also in improving our organizations. The many stressful events that occur in the workplace must be acknowledged to have happened in order to begin to address their underlying organizational dynamics, of which they are often unaware.

Chapter 2 Applied Poetry and Storytelling

This chapter introduces the basic approach of the book, which uses three key perspectives: the triangulation. Applied workplace poems, the story of the workplace experience that inspired each poem, and the use of three different psychoanalytic insights into the workplace provide a challenging context for understanding the nature of the complexity of work experience in organizations. Each of the perspectives is explored for its contribution to the triangulation. Poetry, paired with the contextual stories and interpreted using three psychoanalytically informed perspectives, offers a new in-depth approach to understanding what it means to work within large organizations that often contain destructive dysfunctions.

Chapter 3 Understanding Psychoanalytic Theory

Psychoanalytic theory embraces many different types of theorizing. In this book three theories that we have found to be especially applicable to the workplace will be used to interpret and analyze the workplace poems and the stories that describe what inspired the poems. Object relations theory offers many insights into the psychodynamics of the interpersonal world and intersubjectivity.[8] How do we come to know others, groups, and organizations? Object relations theory offers many helpful approaches. The tripartite theory of Karen Horney (movement toward, away, and against others) provides a readily accessible set of perspectives that are easily identified as explaining workplace dynamics. The work of Wilfred Bion and the group relations community is also used here. Understanding group and intergroup dynamics at work is complex and challenging. Group relations theory offers a third important approach to understanding the workplace. Additional theories drawn from other psychoanalytic approaches will be used as appropriate. In sum, these three theoretical perspectives can be combined to illuminate poetry inspired by the workplace.

Chapter 4 Leaders and Followers in the Workplace

This chapter begins our work of using applied workplace poetry to experience and understand organizational life. We begin by giving an account of organizational leadership, followership, and alienation in organizations. Our use of the triangulation of applied poetry, stories, and analysis in this chapter evokes the psychological brutality of leaders who are hired to turn-around-the-organization and who ruthlessly execute their task. Likewise, the triangulation also portrays what it is like to be an employee under these circumstances.

Chapter 5 Downsizing the Workplace

This chapter continues our triangulation of the workplace by illuminating the experience of organizational downsizing, RIFing, restructuring, reengineering, deskilling, outsourcing, and other euphemisms of "managed organizational change" in America since the early 1980s. The chapter portrays the story of dehumanization, demoralization, and chronic fear of "waiting for the next shoe to fall" in American workplaces. Beneath the touted corporate benefits of rapid organizational change by consulting firms and staffing ratios lies the story of unconsciously driven traumatization. With the aid of the triangulation, this chapter opens for inspection the dark side of massive organizational change.

Chapter 6 Alienation and Bureaucracy at Work

This chapter explores how people in workplace bureaucracies come to treat others as inanimate objects. The chapter gives voice to the soul-destroying and surreal experience of alienation, bearing witness to and validating the experience that "this really happened." Our use of triangulation helps to probe the world of how seemingly innocuous material such as routing slips, identification badges, old computers, and boxes serve as powerful metaphors for the dark side of organizational life where people are reduced to numbers on spreadsheets.

Chapter 7 Loss of Self: Disappeared Into Anonymity

This chapter explores the experience of organizational employees who are transformed into "human resources" and what it is like to be de-selfed in bureaucracies, becoming little more than an anonymous cog in a machine. Our triangulation attests to what the dissolution of self feels like, an experience often the result of being objectified by supervisors and leaders.

Chapter 8 Conflict at Work

This chapter is an exploration of institutionalized and interpersonal aggression in the workplace—despite widespread corporate-sponsored seminars and workshops on "the angry worker" and "conflict management." Usually no attention is given to unconscious sources of aggression and conflict. In this chapter, applied poetry helps to reveal that the supposedly rational workplace is filled with war metaphors, splits into us/them factions, and employees who become "collateral damage" during periods of traumatic change.

Chapter 9 Life at Work in Hospitals and Clinics: Modern Medicine and Us

Both authors have spent their careers in healthcare institutions. With the aid of applied poetry, this chapter approaches healthcare as an organization, albeit a special kind of organization that addresses what most people wish to keep far from themselves: infirmity, disease, suffering, decline, and death. The applied poetry and the triangulation uncover some of the organizational dynamics behind such slogans as "managed healthcare" and "cost-contained medicine."

Chapter 10 Meetings at Work

Meetings, formal and informal, are ubiquitous in organizations. Much goes on beneath the surface of printed agendas and rational decision-making. This chapter identifies the unconsciously driven undercurrents that are rarely acknowledged. Through our use of triangulation it becomes clear that participants in tedious, autocratically conducted meetings often wish not to be there at all, and they develop defensive ways of expressing this sentiment.

Chapter 11 The Psychogeography of Work

In this chapter, applied poetry identifies the use of organizational objects and space itself as profound metaphors of "what it is like to work here." Desks, doors, tables, coffee machines, office equipment, and office placement are all about undiscussable issues of power, control, priorities, values, and narcissism. This chapter helps to make clear that workplace space utilization and objects are not only about utilitarian, task-related concerns, but they may also symbolically embody statements about workplace relationships and their significance. Objects and space can be used by leaders to intimidate, control, exclude, and include people.

Chapter 12 Playing With Perspective: The Workplace on the Stage

This chapter is a culmination of the previous chapters. It is written by the first author in the form of a play about an organizational consultant who makes soliloquies punctuated by some of the poems in this book. The poems function like a Greek chorus or commentary. The consultant despairs over the overwhelming darkness of the organizations in which he works, wondering whether his work does any good at all. In fact, through monologue and poetry he bears witness to the psychological destruction and destructiveness and to the suffering in American organizations. Although many of the poems in the play appeared earlier in the book, their inclusion in the play is not mere repetition. Rather, they are "reframed" in a new context and have a new purpose.

Chapter 13 In Conclusion: Knowing and Feeling in the Workplace

What may be learned from the experiment that is this book—from applied workplace poetry; from the stories of the context from which poetry emerges; from using psychoanalytic theory to understand workplace poetry and our shared experiences of our workplaces? This final chapter reviews what was learned, including the parallelism that unfolded in writing about our experience of writing poetry, experiencing the workplace, and using psychoanalytic theory to gain workplace insights. In our experiment, we found the unexpected re-experiencing of our individual and shared workplace traumas in the process of exploring the nature of toxic organizations. We realized that understanding the poem and poet in an intersubjective context, and bearing witness to the dark side of our organizations and work experience, are liberating and healing. The triangulation metaphor as the book's central organizing method for understanding life at work proved to be a strong construction. We conclude the book by suggesting that the reader engage in a similar process of discovery, creation, and analysis.

In Sum What This Book Is About

The book offers the triangulation of applied poetry, organizational experience, and psychodynamically informed analysis to create insight into organizations and our lives at work. Each of the three perspectives informs and complements the others to access the inner experience of toxic American workplaces. In doing this work, we illumine the dark side of our workplaces and the individual and group destructiveness that contribute to the structural violence that degrades our lives at work.

Notes

1. Allcorn, S. (2002). *Death of the spirit in the American workplace*. Westport, CT: Quorum Books; Gabriel, Y. (2012). Organizations in a state of darkness: Towards a theory of organizational miasma. *Organization Studies*, 33(9), 1137–1152; Stein, H.F. (2007). The inconsolable organization: Toward a theory of organizational and cultural change. *Psychoanalysis, Culture and Society*, 12, 349–368.
2. Stein, H.F. (1998). *Euphemism, spin, and the crisis in organizational life*. Westport, CT: Quorum Books; Stein, H.F. (2005). Corporate violence. In C. Casey & R. Edgerton (Eds.). *A companion to psychological anthropology*. Malden, MA: Blackwell. pp. 436–452.
3. Stein, H.F. (2001). *Nothing personal, just business*. Westport, CT: Quorum Books.
4. Diamond, M. (1993). *The unconscious life of organizations*. Westport, CT: Quorum Books;Diamond, M. (2017). *Discovering organizational identity*. Columbia, MO: University of Missouri Press.
5. Forché, C. (1993). Twentieth century poetry of witness. *American Poetry Review*, 22(2), March–April, 17. www.english.illinois.edu/maps/poets/a_f/forche/witness.htm
6. Ogden, T. (1999). 'The music of what happens' in poetry and psychoanalysis. *The International Journal of Psychoanalysis*, 80, 979–994.
7. Stein, H.F. (1994). *Listening deeply: An approach to understanding and consulting in organizational culture*. Boulder, CO: Westview Press; Stein, H.F. (2017). *Listening deeply: An approach to understanding and consulting in*

organizational culture (2nd ed.). Columbia, MO: University of Missouri Press.

8. Greenberg, J. & Mitchell, S. (1983). *Object relations in psychoanalytic theory*. Cambridge, MA: Harvard University Press.

2 Applied Poetry and Storytelling

This book is an experiment, an exploration of an interdisciplinary frontier. Exploring how applied poetry, stories, and psychoanalytic theory inform understanding the workplace is new. The use of psychoanalytic theory to understand human behavior in organizations is relatively recent, largely arising post-WWII and with substantially more development since the 1980s. The use of applied poetry and stories to understand the toxic workplace as put forward here is also new.[1] In this book, applied poetry and the contextual stories of the poems offer workplace insights that speak to the darker side of organizational life. The three discussions when combined offer a way to study toxic organizations and organizational dysfunctions. They allow for insight and imagination to interplay with the often harsh realities of the workplace.[2]

In this book, we begin our work of *triangulating* (1) applied poetry, (2) workplace stories, and (3) psychoanalytic theory by first exploring each separately. To locate meaning and to understand our lives at work, it is important to understand each before combining them in triangulation. This important sense-making in all of its complexity is essential in terms of knowing and understanding ourselves at work, our fellow workers and colleagues, the groups we work within, and our local organization as well as the larger organization as a whole. We begin with a brief examination of the workplace with its rationalized structures and processes and an appreciation that the people at work are not always rational and all too often introduce the dark side of human nature, creating a toxic workplace.

The Workplace

Organizations, whether small or large, are complex primarily because of the people who create them every day they come to work. There are many fundamental organizing principles all organizations share such as hierarchies, reliance upon professions and professional skill sets, and a necessity to organize and coordinate work. This usually boils down to bureaucracy that may range from minimally present to oppressive. It is not our purpose to explore this side of organizational life that is presumably based on rigorous logic, rational decisions, and near-mathematical precision in execution of work. We do, however, appreciate that this book cannot entirely avoid these considerations. They are resident in all aspects of organizational life and workplace experience.

Our purpose here is to focus on the "soft side" of organizations where people and their thoughts, feelings, and emotions reside. Individuals and groups continually interact to create a vast indeterminate stew of outcomes that are hard to know, predict, and manage. It is indeed the case that it is much easier to manage the organization without having to deal with human nature—the earlier-described attributes. A leader could, for example, continually reorganize the hierarchy or production process without resistance to change if there are few or no employees—a much-fantasized outcome of all those in leadership roles.

However, barring fantasy fulfillment, we are left with the challenging and time-consuming matter of managing ourselves, each other, groups, and the organization as a whole—filled with the people who animate its existence. This appreciation, as mentioned, introduces thoughts, feelings, and emotions into workplace dynamics and, also to be appreciated, irrationality that may dwarf any thoughts that the workplace is governed by rationality.[3] In fact, the applied poetry, contextual stories, and psychodynamic framework used here will show how much organizations are influenced by irrationality.

Understanding the Irrational Workplace

Organizations are preferably thought of as running with clock-like precision. Production processes, whether operated by people, computers, or machines often *appear* to approach this level of precision. They are carefully engineered to do so. Much the same can be said of other business processes such as marketing, finance, and sales, including order-taking and order-fulfillment. These processes, however, are often much more dependent on imperfect people, especially in those situations where clients and customers must be dealt with. There are, in sum, a vast range of complexities and even chaos involved with running any organization where, in particular, human nature and all of its variability are present. This appreciation necessitates understanding the underlying psychodynamics of organizational life.

Good management is often equated with good *control* of operating processes, resources, information, and people. Gabriel, however, notes:

> How can we control others when we can hardly control ourselves? How can we manage organizations when we can hardly manage our own unconscious desires? How can we remain organized in the face of crises, turmoil and unpredictability?[4]

These questions lead Gabriel to suggest:

> Actions which appear on the surface to make perfectly good sense can turn out to serve ends which have little to do with organizational efficiency and rationality. Such action may in the end turn out to be better understood by reference to motives which some organizational members may not openly acknowledge or may prefer not to understand.[5]

William Czander is also aware of the contribution irrationality, unconscious psychodynamics, and the darker side of human behavior makes to the workplace. These are difficult to comprehend in terms of why many things happen at work that are hard to explain and not clock-like in their essence. Czander writes:

> Although one must gaze in wonderment at the accomplishments of these hierarchical modern organizations and the improvements they have made in the world, one hopes perhaps there could be a "better way." Theorists and teachers of business are constantly responding to this hope, and they do so by continuously proposing new and exciting organizational structures, procedures, technologies, programs, and processes to make the organization more effective and efficient and at the same time to increase commitment and esprit. Invariably they come up short. Perhaps the reason is their lack of understanding of the conscious and unconscious forces that bind people together and stimulate motivations for work and achievement, or perhaps they do not adequately understand the "dark" forces that underlie human behavior.[6]

Manfred Kets de Vries also emphasizes that participants in organizational life have come to accept that there are limitations to logical decision-making.[7] There are many less than fully rational forces that influence leadership and followers, organizational structure, strategy, and culture. Better appreciating the presence of unconscious fantasies and out-of-awareness behavior in organizations is a necessity.

Manfred Kets de Vries underscores this appreciation by noting:

> Too often, the collective unconscious of business practitioners and scholars alike subscribes to the myth that the only thing which matters is what we see and know (in other words, that which is conscious). That myth is grounded in organizational behavior concepts of an extremely rational nature—concepts based on assumptions about human beings made by economists (at worst) or behavioral psychologists (at best). The social sciences, ever desperate to gain more prestige, seem unable to stop pretending to be natural sciences;

they cannot relinquish their obsession with the directly measurable. For far too many people, the spirit of the economic machine appears to be alive and well and living in organizations. Although the existing repertoire of "rational" concepts has proven time and again to be insufficient to untangle the really knotty problems that trouble organizations, the myth of rationality persists.[8]

These authors make clear why this book matters in terms of seeking out and illuminating the darker unconscious recesses of what we are calling *toxic* organizational life. Our use of the triangulation of applied poetry, contextual stories, and psychologically informed organizational analysis offers insight into the infinite complexity that resides within the unconscious side of the workplace. Before continuing to discuss the three elements of the triangulation, some academic context setting is necessary.

Situating This Book in the Larger Picture of Organizational Analysis

At the outset of this book's journey, let us summarize our approach to understanding the psychodynamics of toxic organizational life. Our broadest possible question is: *What is/are the appropriate methodology(ies) for studying human subjectivity anywhere?* The instrument of measurement must suit what and who are being studied ("measured"). The wrong yardstick will yield false and misleading data.

Our approach to answering this methodological question is qualitative rather than quantitative. Each approach is scientific, if used properly, but in a different way. We do not begin with hypotheses to test. Our starting point is observation of others, of ourselves, and of our relationships. Our interpretations and explanations are deductive, not only in the sense of logic, but in the use of unconsciously rooted creative imagination to make sense of what all we see, hear, and feel (sense). Our *data* here take the form of poetry and the stories behind the poems. In this book, we have selected poems and stories to describe and evoke various organizational themes in emotionally destructive workplaces.

Three complementary psychoanalytic theoretical perspectives (Chapter 3) are then used to gain insight into the poems and stories. They help us to learn something new about the unconscious life in workplaces that inspired the poems and stories. We do not use these poems and stories to prove a point but rather to illuminate and evoke an experience of the workplace readers might have also experienced. Psychodynamic theories, like all theories, are ways of trying to account for what we have found and experienced.

The matter of *gender* arises with respect to the applicability of the poems in this book. Who might the poems speak to? Does the gender of the poet limit the range of empathy? The poet and storyteller co-author

(Howard) is male. However, his poems and the stories behind them have, over many decades, resonated with and spoken to both female and male readers, fellow employees and managers, and participants in organizational consultations and professional meetings. While the poet is a man, his poems do not only "speak to" workplace male experience.

The matter of the first author (Howard) being a member of a minority group, as he is Jewish, is also an important feature of this book. At times the poems surface for inspection the experience of being an alien "other" in the midst of a group—another singled out for differential treatment and discrimination. We suggest this element of the book provides considerable insight if not empathy for all those members of disparaged minority groups who are singled out as different in what is often now seen as a white-male dominated society.

In sum, just as stories can help us to understand poems, applied organizational poetry also uses methods and has data that are distinct from, and go beyond, narrative forms. This will be addressed in greater detail later in this chapter. We now turn to a discussion of the elements of the triangulation. We note that we focus here on the use of applied poetry and the contextual stories and defer discussion of the use of psychoanalytic theory as the third element to Chapter 3.

Applied Poetry at Work

With so much written about workplace organizations based on empirically, positivistically-rooted, narrative research, what could applied poetry and stories, combined with a psychoanalytic perspective, possibly add to what is already known about organizations? Understanding experience at work is a multidimensional undertaking that must include all our senses. Our use of applied poetry, we suggest, has its primary value as an evocative approach to sensing, knowing, and understanding workplace experience. Applied poetry offers a way of accessing workplace experience that is unique, and we believe is valuable, in terms of understanding our lives at work. Organizational poesis *complements*, not replaces, other ways of knowing workplaces, and, when combined with stories and psychoanalytic theory, offers greater awareness at work.

Applied poetry offers a royal road to the "unconscious life of organizations."[9] Just as for Sigmund Freud dreams were the "royal road" to the individual unconscious, applied poetry offers a unique form of access to the inner experience of our lives at work.[10] Applied poetry takes us beneath the surface experience of organizational charts, job descriptions, mission statements, and strategic plans. Throughout this book we use applied poetry and the accompanying contextual stories of the poems to explore American workplaces and in particular, the dark side of workplace experience.[11] Applied poetry helps us to remain honest about "what it is really like to work here." As organizational researcher Eda

Ulus writes, applied poetry offers a "portrayal of what we are encountering in this work world;" a poet can "express through poetry what we are living."[12]

Whatever is known about workplaces by conventional empirical theory and method, the results cannot comprehend the *lived experience* of work. The former is superficial, in the sense of providing understanding on the surface; the latter draw from the depths of human experience. Applied poetry and stories, allied with attention to unconscious processes, fills the chasm left by what empirical methods cannot fathom. Simply put, positivistically based empirical research methods do not have access to the heart of "what it is like to work here."

As methodological and philosophical correctives to this often-hollow way of approaching workplace life, there is a burgeoning literature on how applied poetry can illumine organizational experience.[13] Its authors address key issues such as meaning and meaninglessness, chaos and order, emotions, imagery, the senses, self, role, values, and workplace spirituality.[14] They reveal organizational life to be human—and often inhuman— rather than mechanistic and entirely rational. Applied poetry, we suggest, can access and convey the inner world of the workplace in ways that go beyond linear description and interpretation.[15]

Further, in this book we shall argue that *outsiders* such as researchers and consultants, as well as organizational members, can write articulate poetry about the organization and their experience of the workplace. Researchers and consultants are often *immersed* in the workplace they are studying and trying to help. Through empathy and identification, as well as participant observation and other tools of fieldwork, they can *imagine* what it is like to be a member of the organization. That is, they take into their minds and internalize their relationships and experiences.[16] One can think of the-organization-in-the-poet.

Where, then, does the poem exist? Through this intersubjective alchemy, the poem emerges and belongs *simultaneously* to the poet and to the people in the workplace. It exists in the transitional and intersubjective space between them, in the unconscious reciprocity of their relationship. Even though "I" am the poet, the poem is in a sense both mine and theirs—ours. Like all researchers, we *together* discover the reality of the workplace.

We emphasize that applied poetry serves at once as a way of knowing, a way of representing social reality, a way of bringing people's experience to life (in the form of "research findings"), and *a way of helping people to reflect both on their own and on others' experiences and in turn to create the possibility of new solutions to problems.*[17] This is especially relevant for improving the performance of our large and complex toxic organizations. Piercy and Benson write that "[W]e believe that traditional qualitative (and quantitative) researchers should consider alternative ways to present their findings that connect with various audiences on emotional as well as intellectual levels, and reflect the experiences of their research participants."[18] We draw attention to Piercy and Benson's words *connect(ion)* and *reflect(ion)*, which are two of the functions of applied poetry. Understanding the contribution applied poetry makes to leading and managing toxic organizations is the goal of this book. Further, the specific type of applied poetry used here is a *poetry of witness*, where poetry serves the purpose of validating people's traumatic experiences and consequent suffering, affirming that "this really happened."[19]

We now further explore poetry as a research methodology and as a way of representing research findings that create new insights.

Poetry as Research: Toward Organizational Poetics

Just as psychoanalysis makes the unconscious conscious, poetry makes the invisible visible and the unspeakable spoken. Poetry tells us what we already know but didn't know that we knew. It makes the strange familiar. Where narrative expounds, poetry condenses and distills. The language of poetry has the ability to articulate, evoke, and embody the depths of human experience. It inspires resonance in the inner world of the listener and reader. It creates intersubjective space for new possibilities to emerge. Poetry is an unparalleled way of listening, hearing, and being heard. Poetry evokes rather than describes, shows rather than tells. There are many ways of knowing, not limited to a single, linear, positivism.[20] *Research poetry* we suggest is a form of qualitative inquiry that promotes understanding. This is made clearer by the work of the following researchers, whose work helps to ground our own contribution.

Poetry as a Research Methodology

In the field of arts-based research, applied poetry can be seen as a research method, a form of inquiry, a form of research data, and a method of representing research findings.[21] Poetry both is a *form* of research and a way of *representing* research data. It is an alternate way of knowing.[22] Poetic voice and poetic approach have a vital place in qualitative research inquiry. In a sense, they begin where narrative approaches leave off. Where narrative is opaque, poetry is transparent. Poetry is a unique mode of representation, compensating for the inadequacy of standard narrative to capture and evoke a hidden, inner dimension of lived reality.[23]

Louise Grisoni writes that "By immersing in the experience of organizational life through poetry, customary ways of making sense are suspended, and new insights into encountered reality become possible. Poetic expression therefore grasps at a newly discovered reality."[24] Poetry is a form of knowing through emotional engagement.[25] Through poetry, one connects with the subjects of research at a deeply personal level.[26] "[P]oems can be a powerful narrative tool to further empathy and understanding and can serve education and advocacy goals."[27] Research poetry gives voice to the unsayable as well as the sayable. It shapes the researcher and consultant's experiences into stanzas.[28] Poetry offers us insights that feel like sudden revelations.[29]

Poetry as Research Finding Representation

Poetry becomes an alternate form of *representing* research interviews and data from participant observation. For instance, Poindexter writes that:

> I continually feared that I would not be able to sufficiently give voice to the respondents' stories and not be able to translate their experiences in a way that would be useful and meaningful to readers. I was aware that the respondents were counting on me to tell their stories, but I did not feel that I had the language at that time to express their experiences.[30]

Sherry and Schouten likewise recognize that "Traditional or conventional prose articles seem increasingly insufficient as vessels for representing our understandings and experiences."[31] Poetry represents and points toward lived truth in ways that the linear language of traditional social science narrative cannot fathom.[32] The artist-researcher is a necessary supplement to the scientist-researcher. Poetry is thus as capable of representing research as is narrative science.

Emotional communication between the researcher poet and the listener and reader can be likened to the resonance between two tuning forks tuned to the same pitch. The resonance makes understanding possible by evoking the listener and reader's own world, as if to say, "I've had experiences like that." Poetry helps to diminish the distance between researcher, subject, listener, and reader. The language of poetry helps us to get closer to the lived inner experience of others.[33]

Poetry complements, not replaces, conventional narrative approaches to research. It deepens the researcher and consultant's access to the lived, inner world of people. Personal experience is thus not tangential or a barrier to understanding of others, but instead it constitutes valuable research data, often in the form of autoethnographic poetry.[34] Of particular significance for this book, it brings toxic organizations and their wider cultures to life.

Applied Poetry Creates Insights

Workplace organizations are places of meaning and emotion, belonging and alienation, not only of task and function, job and paycheck. This dimension of work life is well represented, articulated, and evoked by poetry.[35] Workplaces are steeped in value and devaluation, in hope and disappointment, experiences well suited to the language of poetry. These dimensions and poetry about them draw our attention to the spiritual dimension of the workplace.[36]

Through applied workplace poetry, we can discover life at work if we are open to it, not merely confirm what we already knew—or thought we knew. By letting go of control, we give imagination free reign, and emergent solutions rather than rigid strategic plans become possible. Applied poetry is an instrument of this possibility. Applied poetry helps us to stand back and think and reflect about work, not simply uncritically act.

Applied poetry as a means of research and research finding representation creates *bridges* in the mind, in workplace relationships, and in problem-solving, leading in turn to discovery of links between conscious and unconscious, between implicit and explicit, between what we already knew and what we might come to know. Applied poetry may then be understood to help organizations create new knowledge, to develop virtuous upward spirals rather than vicious downward spirals.[37] Stated differently, applied poetry facilitates double-loop learning in contrast to the repetitiveness of single-loop learning.[38]

Yet another way to appreciate applied poetry as a research methodology is to recognize that poets create poetic portraits that explore context and voice, complexity and subtlety.[39] These poetic portraits in turn help communicate research findings. Applied poetry alludes rather than strives to "tell all," thereby giving the listener and reader room for imaginative, creative thought. Vivid poetic portraiture describes and evokes the depth and range of the inner world and of relationships in organizational life— a picture of "what it is like to work here."

In sum, applied poetry offers the possibility of a multi-dimensional image of the workplace. Applied poetry as a form of research reveals the emotional complexity of workplaces and simplifies and reduces that complexity into emotionally rich images and metaphors.[40] Organization members, researchers, and consultants who use applied poetry (and other arts) to explore the inner life of workplaces create pathways of discovery to heretofore unconscious and underappreciated workplace dynamics that all too often are toxic.[41]

Poetry Versus Applied Poetry

These research-based considerations about applied poetry lead us to make an essential distinction. Poetry of and from the workplace, and the stories that led to the poetry, constitute the "database" in this book for the study of toxic organizations. The type of poetry included here is "applied poetry," in contrast to the "pure poetry" that has largely dominated the American academic cultural scene since the 1970s. What we are identifying as pure poetry has occupied the pages of the most respected literary journals and the discourse on poetry in universities.

This genre is often characterized as academic, abstract, abstruse, complex, convoluted, difficult to understand, opaque, clever, impersonal, and often self-indulgently cunning in language construction. Pure poetry is a genre of poetry-for-its-own-sake, that is, often removed from ordinary experience and emotions.

The most recent and currently dominant use of the term *pure poetry* consists of poems written by and largely for poets in the institutional cultures of academia, "ivory towers," poetry published in over 127 literary journals affiliated with MFA (Master of Fine Arts) programs.[42] These pure poems and their poets are situated within the academy and are written largely for the academy. "Pretense and pretentiousness" characterizes their predominant style.[43] Rosemarie Dombrowski cites a common example of their preference for the word *loam* over *dirt* or *soil*.[44] By contrast, pure poetry in the *older, non-academically institutionalized sense* is written to make a difference in and speak to people's lives, to be available and emotionally accessible to listeners and readers, and to plumb the musicality of language to help people to both understand their experience and to feel understood, affirmed, and less alone and isolated.

Applied poetry is steeped in the unkempt world of life. Poets who write with this approach strive to be emotionally available and depict everyday life—such as in workplace organizations—with a hope of helping listeners and readers to make sense of their experience. Readers of this genre of poetry often feel understood, less alone, their lives and experiences affirmed, and are often able to say, "I recognize myself and my world in that poem. I've had that experience too." Applied poetry helps people to feel less isolated.

The idea of applied poetry refers to the poet's wish to be socially useful, practical, and helpful (1) in addressing a concern; (2) in illuminating something kept in the dark; (3) finding a solution to a problem; (4) in thinking, reflecting, and feelings in new ways; and (5) in reaching out to listeners and readers in such a way that the poet's voice and experience come to resonate with the voice and experience of listeners and readers. Applied poetry directs the listener and reader beyond itself. Although poetry is a form of language and the poet is always concerned with craft—*ars poetica*— applied poetry should never be about showing how cunning the language can be but rather about how *we discover ourselves and the world through the language of poetry and are moved to do something with what we have learned*. Language should be a means to an end, not an end itself.[45]

Applied organizational poetry helps us to recognize *unintended consequences* and new connections and imagine novel worlds and solutions, to "think outside the box," to create inner and interpersonal creative space that in turn makes room for new approaches to organizational problem-solving and everyday management. In David Whyte's words, what we are calling *applied poetry* helps us to have "courageous conversations" that lead us to taking the next step in addressing workplace operating problems and issues.[46]

In particular, it is important to appreciate that, "[T]he intense empathy developed by so many poets is a skill essential to those who occupy executive suites and regularly need to understand the feelings and motivations of board members, colleagues, customers, suppliers, community members, and employees."[47] With imagination, empathy, and identification, one can walk into poems, making us the subject of the poem and making it come alive for us. This added depth to our knowledge and understanding help us to be able to "walk into" others' worlds in the workplace. The expression "walking a mile in another's shoes" speaks to this powerful sense of empathy. There is a translation of experience into awareness, translation of the awareness into thought, translation of the thought in words, and translation of words to poems (and stories) that in turn help others translate their own experience into "*Yes, I know that! That's right.*"

In sum, applied workplace poetry helps listeners and readers to recognize and tell their own stories, if not also to conceptually write their own poems. This is because readers may have "lived" the poems themselves. In telling his or her own story, the poet evokes the listener or reader's own story. This "resonance" retrieves the listener or reader's story, creating a shared emotional experience. It brings what was unconscious back into conscious awareness.

A Reflection on the Relational Subjectivity of Poetry

The nature of this book resides in our effort not only to evoke on the part of the reader consciousness of the workplace but also to tap the deeper levels of unconsciousness that influence who we are and how we think and feel. This work, it must be appreciated, has an underlying psychological complexity explored by Thomas Ogden.[48] Ogden emphasizes the joining together of the poet with the reader or listener. The writing or speaking of a poem (or story) reverberates with the reading or listening to create a relational subjectivity (a co-creation or co-construction).

The poem exists in this interpersonal space between the poet and reader or listener with all its creative potential.[49] The poem becomes a shared creation in a transitional and potential space in the moment that transcends both. Most fundamentally the poet comes to experience and know him- or herself by *reading aloud* the poetry and *listening* to his or her voice recite the poetry, not merely seeing the words. Similarly, the reader or listener comes to know him- or herself by creating anew the poem and its meaning in mind. Paradoxically, then, the shared intersubjective experience allows each person to emerge from the experience with a greater sense of separateness and self, in addition to a greater sense of authentic sharing of experience and meaning.[50]

Ogden sums this appreciation up by noting:

Creating a voice with which to speak or write might be thought of as a way, perhaps the principal way, in which an individual brings himself into being, comes to life, through his use of language. This conception of voice applies to all forms of language usage, whether in poetry, in fiction, in prose, in drama, in the analytic dialogue, or in everyday conversation.[51]

The poetry provided in this book may then be appreciated to be an effort *to bring to life one's experience of self at work.* Some of the poems and subjects may have more resonance than others, but we suggest all have their creative potential to bring to life one's work experience within this shared co-created context of poet and reader. Ogden suggests that multilayered meanings of poetry arise from reveries that surface from the unconscious that comes to life in the movement of feelings, thoughts, images, bodily sensations, and language that lie at the heart of poetry.[52] With respect to the linkage between psychoanalysis and poetry, Jeanine Vivona has even argued that psychoanalysis *is* poetry.[53]

At one level, all applied organizational poetry is *personal* and reflects and expresses the unconscious as well as conscious life of the researcher/ consultant poet. At the same time, it also expresses what could be called *the-organization-in-the-poet.* This corresponds to the internalization, resonance, articulation, and putting outside oneself the (countertransference) experience of being there and emotionally absorbing, processing, and thinking about that experience. The researcher/consultant's poem *embodies* the organization. It is not entirely "subjective." It is *intersubjective.*[54] That is, it is the product of the dance of the unconscious of the researcher/consultant and the unconscious of leaders, managers, and employees as *individuals* and as *members of a group* called an "organization." Thus, the triad of contributions of this book are: (1) applied workplace poetry, together with (2) their stories, and (3) the psychodynamic approach to making sense of the poetry, the poet, and the situation. These contributions together offer a new perspective on workplaces.

In sum, the reader or listener to poetry is not a passive receptacle of a poem. The "voice" of the reader or listener is in conscious and unconscious dialogue with the voice of the poet. The meanings of the poem exist in the creative potential space between poet and reader or listener.[55] Thus, the workplace experience of the reader of this book is as important as the poet author's workplace experience. In fact, to use a visual metaphor, one refracts the poem and poet's experience through one's own prism of experience. We hope this work creates some shared meaning as well as meaning to one's self-experience. We have tried to tap this creative potential by providing the poems that open for inspection, discussion, and analysis the all-too-often darker side of our workplaces.

The Context-Setting Stories of the Poems

In this book, the stories that provide the settings for the poems, and the exposition of psychoanalytic theory to help understand the unconscious process the poems reveal, are also narratives. At their best, poems and narratives both bring a subject to life. Poetry at its best condenses into relatively few words, metaphors, and images what conventional social science narratives would take much longer to articulate. Where poetry often hints and alludes, narrative seeks to spell out, expound, and complete. Where poetry leaves much mental space for the listener or reader to fill in with one's imagination, narrative fills in the spaces with rich detail.

The relationship between applied poetry and narrative bears some clarification. For one thing, poetry and narrative are not necessarily opposite, even opposing, forms. There are many types of narrative. There is often poetic attention to language in many short stories and novels. Many organizational ethnographies and psychoanalytic accounts (much like applied poetry) evoke, bring to life, the world of workplaces and of analyst-patient (or consultant-client) communication. In fact, it is commonplace in ordinary English language usage for a journalist, book reviewer, clergy-person, or teacher to say or write that a particularly beautiful or emotionally powerful passage in a short story, novel, scholarly article or book, or the entire work, or even for a political speech, is *poetic*. It is meant as one of the highest compliments a narrative form can receive.

Where do poems and stories come from? Stories, like poems, are born from the writer's *immersion* in and *relationship* with another person or group's world, a historical era or culture, or the natural world. That deep relationship is then processed, unconsciously as well as consciously, by poet and storyteller, and emerges in the symbolic shape of a poem or story—or, in the example of this book, both. To write an emotionally compelling poem or story, one in which the reader is drawn into the writer's world, the writer must first be an astute and compassionate *listener* and *observer*—of other people, of him- or herself, and of the space between them.

Just as poets and storytellers write for other people, these others in turn become listeners and observers, ultimately of their own lives as poems and stories reawaken them. The reader in turn bestows the gift of presence to the poem and poet, story and storyteller. The reader wants to hear and to try to contain what the poem or story is saying, and behind it, the writer who is not entirely absent. The reader and listener now, in turn, offer affirmation to both poet and storyteller, as if to say, "I know that what you wrote really happened because it also happened to me." When a poem or story truly "works," the writer contains the reader, and the reader contains the writer.

Applying this perspective to workplace organizations, stories and poems give the lie to widely shared and enforced fantasies about workplace reality—that rationality governs executive decision-makers and relationships with their employees. Poets and storytellers who write about workplaces reveal the irrationality and emotional cruelty of the darker side of organizational life. They speak the unspeakable truth, the forbidden. Through stories as well as poems, the unimaginable becomes imaginable—they validate the reality of their own experience.

In this book the relationship between applied poems and stories/narratives can be imagined as two tuning forks that *resonate* with each other, being "tuned" to the same "pitch" of experience. One can listen to them both separately and together. Applied poem and story complement each other, much as—to use a different metaphor—surveyors determine the same point in space but from different vantage points.

Further, on the surface, the applied poem might seem to be "foreground," and the accompanying story might seem to be "background" or "backdrop" to the poem. In fact, both story and poem can be understood and experienced as *alternating* between being foreground and background, figure and ground, to each other. In yet another image or metaphor, poem and story can be experienced as *amplifying* each other, each *intensifying* the experience which both poem and story separately evoke—both the poet's and storyteller's workplace experience and the reader or listener's own work life, which story and poem re-awaken.

In this book, the applied poet's poems and stories come from several ways of "processing" emotionally and physically overwhelming traumatic workplace experiences. In one type of poem/story pair, the poet's writing, reading, and listening to the poem and story feel like a *memory* of some *past* event in time and space, that is, looked back upon as separate in time and space from the poet's current reality.

A second type of poem/story set does not feel as if the experience it relates has the *distance* in space and time that memory confers. Instead, the poet/storyteller feels a frightening *immediacy*, as if the writer were back inside the event, *reliving* it in words, with a blurring of past and present. From inside that moment, past is present. To the writer, it feels as if the traumatic experience were happening now, recurring, as though he or she were once again "possessed" by it, re-living it over and over.

A third type of poem/story pair draws upon a writer's sense of there being a *recurrent*, even *timeless*, *type* of event and experience of it. Memory for this is not for a specific, distinct moment that seized the poet/storyteller's soul, but of a long, *repetitive sequence* of events that, in terms of content and structure, are virtually interchangeable. Over time the writer may no longer be able even to pinpoint when they began. There is an oppressive sameness about them. Thus, the poem and story, even if the poet writes as if he or she were recounting an individual moment, describe, evoke, and bear witness to the *emotional experience of changelessness and timelessness amid relentless organizational (and societal) change.*

In all three of these scenarios, the story is never a "poor second" or afterthought to the poem, although the poem was written first. The process of storytelling and the story itself are equal partners with the writing, reading, and listening to the poems. As such, they have equal importance and emotional weight on the two points they occupy on the equilateral.

In sum, there is then much that is shared between applied poetry and stories, where each creative form complements and enhances the other. It is our goal and hope that this book captures their contribution to understanding toxic organizations.

Psychoanalytic Theory at Work

For decades many authors have explored the use of psychoanalytically informed perspectives not so much to understand *what* happened but *why* it happened? Why did she do that? Why did he say that? Why did others react the way they did? We are therefore primarily focused on the *why* of the journalist's motto—who, what, where, when, and why. Very often in the news the *why* of what happened becomes the ultimate goal of reporting and for many, in the event of a tragedy such as a mass shooting or bombing, an obsession. We have used psychoanalytic theory over the many years to understand "why" because it offers many good insights not available from any other perspective. Chapter 3 is devoted to articulating three psychoanalytic theories and perspectives that we have found to be valuable in terms of interpreting and explaining toxic organizational life.

We hope to show that a psychodynamic perspective makes intuitive sense to the reader as we travel together on this journey. We leave it to the reader's judgment to decide whether a view of organizations from the inner life makes emotional as well as intellectual sense because the reader can identify with the organizational experience of the poet and his story. Thus, the ultimate litmus test of the poems, their stories, and the use of psychoanalytic theory is whether they resonate with you the reader, as if to say: "That happened to me, or it could have happened to me, and I realize there are ways of understanding *why* it happened to me and my response to what happened."

Exploring the Nature of the Triangulation

In this book, we use psychoanalytic theory *triangulated* with two other dimensions of organizational understanding—workplace poems and stories. We use the word *triangulation* with a specific intent. First, it underscores our tripartite approach to understanding the workplace in this book. Second, and more fundamentally, it offers a way of understanding and representing the complexity of our approach that needs to be highlighted.

A triangle, as a geometric structure, has all its corners clearly set apart but also implicitly in communication with each other. The corners—the applied poetry, the workplace stories, and psychoanalytic theory—are linked together, creating a synergistic whole. It is this nature of a systemic conceptual linkage that we wish to emphasize, even though the constituent parts are, to coin a new word here, *interconceptual*. We believe that these paradigms of knowing the workplace, when taken together, create a bold new way to study, know, and understand our lives at work. Embracing this sense of a whole, where (1) poetry and stories inform experience, and psychoanalytic theory informs analysis, and (2) the three are placed into the context of toxic organizations and the workplace, is essential to understanding organizations and workplace experience. We approach our work in the balance of this book with this metaphor in mind.

We believe that this approach offers the opportunity to sense the workplace and to reflect upon and understand this experience, using perhaps the only approach that we have to understand not only who, what, where, and when, but also *WHY*. "Why," we suggest, is critical in terms of understanding the sensing, images, and metaphors evoked by poetry and stories that often deeply resonate with hearers and readers for reasons that are unconscious and are rooted in the past. These *transferences* that come forward from life experience into the present are the critical *data* we wish to work with. These are the data of psychoanalysis.

The applied workplace poetry provided here confirms that much of organizational life is driven by irrational, often destructive, unconscious forces, rather than by techno-rational, objective decision-making, informed by enlightened self-interest. This appreciation makes clear that bureaucratically structured workplaces with their dysfunctional as well as functional organizational dynamics are not simply logical creations but are creations permeated with unacknowledged unconscious desires and motivations. Life at work does not always make sense until it is, we suggest, examined through the conceptual lens we provide in this book.

Conclusion

The triangulation of applied poetry, context setting stories, and psychoanalytic theory that we use serves as an instrument for making sense of workplaces, and we suggest that together they can help workplaces to heal. We hope that you as reader will find this approach to be engaging, thought provoking, and informative. More than anything else, we have written this book in order to make its ideas more accessible and useful to the reader.

Chapter 3 provides descriptions of the three complementary psychoanalytic theoretical perspectives we have found to be especially informative in terms of using them to understand toxic organizations, their dynamics, and the work experience of their members. Starting with Chapter 4, the analyses offer many insights into how the theory may be used to understand toxic organizations and the applied poetry that they inspire.

Notes

1. Whyte, D. (1996). *The heart aroused: Poetry and the preservation of the soul in corporate America* (rev. ed.). New York: Crown Business; Allcorn, S. & Stein, H.F. (2015). *The dysfunctional workplace: Theory, stories, and practice.* Columbia, MO: University of Missouri Press.
2. Stein, H.F. (2007). *Insight and imagination.* Lanham, MD: University Press of America.
3. Allcorn, S. & Stein, H.F. (2016). Storytelling: An approach to knowing organisations and their people. *Organisational & Social Dynamics,* 16(1), 19–38; Stein, H.F. (2017). *Listening deeply: An approach to understanding and consulting in organizational culture* (2nd ed.). Columbia, MO: University of Missouri Press.
4. Gabriel, Y. (1999). *Organizations in depth.* London: Sage. p. 280.
5. Gabriel, Y. (1999). *Organizations in depth.* London: Sage. p. 1.
6. Czander, W. (1993). *The psychodynamics of work and organizations.* New York: Guilford Press. p. 1.
7. Kets de Vries, M. (1991). *Organization on the couch.* San Francisco, CA: Jossey-Bass.
8. Kets de Vries, M. (2006). *The leader on the couch: A clinical approach to changing people and organizations.* San Francisco, CA: Jossey-Bass. p. 2.
9. Diamond, M. (1993). *The unconscious life of organizations.* Westport, CT: Quorum Books.
10. Freud, S. (1900/1958). *The interpretation of dreams: The standard edition of the complete psychological works of Sigmund Freud.* Volumes 4 and 5. London: Hogarth Press. pp. 1–625.
11. Stein, H.F. (2001). *Nothing personal, just business.* Westport, CT: Quorum Books; Gabriel, Y. (2012). Organizations in a state of darkness: Towards a theory of organizational miasma. *Organization Studies,* 33(9), 1137–1152.
12. Personal communication to Stein, 5 March 2017, quoted with permission.
13. *This literature places our book in a wider context.* Armitage, A. (2015). The dark side: The poetics of toxic leadership. *Advances in Developing Human Resources,* 17(3), 376–390; Fraiberg, A.M. (2010). With edges of rage and despair: Anger and the poetry of office life. *Journal of Management Inquiry,* 19(3), 96–207; Whyte, D. (1996). *The heart aroused: Poetry and the preservation of the soul in corporate America* (rev. ed.). New York: Crown Business.
14. Allcorn, S. (2002). *Death of the spirit in the American workplace.* Westport, CT: Quorum Books.
15. Diamond, M. (1993). *The unconscious life of organizations.* Westport, CT: Quorum Books.
16. Duncan, C.M. & Diamond, M.A. (2011). *One foot in, one foot out: The paradox of participant observation.* 6th International Conference on Interdisciplinary Social Sciences, July 11–13. Center for the Study of Organizational Change. University of Missouri, Columbia.
17. Piercy, F.P. & Benson, K. (2005). Aesthetic forms of data representation in qualitative family therapy research. *Journal of Marital and Family Therapy,* 31(1), 107–119.
18. Piercy, F.P. & Benson, K. (2005). Aesthetic forms of data representation in qualitative family therapy research. *Journal of Marital and Family Therapy,* 31(1), 107–119.

19. Forché, C. (1993). Twentieth century poetry of witness. *American Poetry Review*, 22(2), March–April, 17. www.english.illinois.edu/maps/poets/a_f/forche/witness.htm; Forché, C. (Ed.). (1993). *Against forgetting: Twentieth-century poetry of witness*. New York: Norton.
20. Stein, H.F. (2003). The inner world of workplaces: Accessing this world through poetry, narrative literature, music, and visual art. *Consulting Psychology Journal: Practice and Research*, 55(2), 84–93.
21. Hanauer, D.I. (2010). *Poetry as research: Exploring second language poetry writing*. Amsterdam: John Benjamins Publishing Company; Knowles, J.G. & Cole, A.L. (2008). *Handbook of the arts in qualitative research*. Thousand Oaks, CA: Sage Publications; Faulkner, S.L. (2007). Concern with craft: Using Ars Poetica as criteria for reading research poetry. *Qualitative Inquiry*, 13(2), March, 218–234; Faulkner, S.L. (2016). *Poetry as method: Reporting research through verse*. New York: Routledge; Cahnmann, M. (2003). The craft, practice, and possibility of poetry in educational research. *Educational Researcher*, 32(3), April, 29–36; Bochner, A.P. & Carolyn, E. (Eds.). (2001). *Ethnographically speaking: Autoethnography, literature, and aesthetics*. Walnut Creek, CA: Altamira Press; Richardson, L. (1990). *Writing strategies: Reaching diverse audiences*. Newbury Park, CA: Sage.
22. Piercy, F.P. & Benson, K. (2005). Aesthetic forms of data representation in qualitative family therapy research. *Journal of Marital and Family Therapy*, 31(1), 107–119.
23. Faulkner, S.L. (2007). Concern with craft: Using Ars Poetica as criteria for reading research poetry. *Qualitative Inquiry*, 13(2), March, 218–234.
24. Grisoni, L. (2009). Exploring organizational learning and knowledge exchange through poetry. Chapter 7. In D. Jemielniak & J. Kociatkiewicz (Eds.). *Handbook of research on knowledge-intensive organizations*. Hershey, PA: IGI Global. pp. 98–115. www.irma- international.org/viewtitle/20848/https://pdfs.semanticscholar.org/9891/2d94e6307161ab9e5 92daa1f26ea4cffc506.pdf
25. Lapum, J., Ruttonsha, P., Church, K., Yau, T. & David, A.M. (2011). Employing the arts in research as an analytical tool and dissemination method: Interpreting experience through the aesthetic. *Qualitative Inquiry*, 18(1), 100–115.
26. Lapum, J., Ruttonsha, P., Church, K., Yau, T. & David, A.M. (2011). Employing the arts in research as an analytical tool and dissemination method: Interpreting experience through the aesthetic. *Qualitative Inquiry*, 18(1), 100–115.
27. Poindexter, C.C. (2002). Research as poetry: A couple experiences HIV. *Qualitative Inquiry*, 8(6), 707–714.
28. Poindexter, C.C. (2002). Research as poetry: A couple experiences HIV. *Qualitative Inquiry*, 8(6), 707–714.
29. Faulkner, S.L. (2007). Concern with craft: Using Ars Poetica as criteria for reading research poetry. *Qualitative Inquiry*, 13(2), March, 218–234.
30. Poindexter, C.C. (2002). Research as poetry: A couple experiences HIV. *Qualitative Inquiry*, 8(6), 707–714.
31. Sherry, J.F. Jr. & Schouten, J.W. (2002). A role for poetry in consumer research. *Journal of Consumer Research*, 29, September, 218–234.
32. Piercy, F.P. & Benson, K. (2005). Aesthetic forms of data representation in qualitative family therapy research. *Journal of Marital and Family Therapy*, 31(1), 107–119; Sherry, J.F. Jr. & Schouten, J.W. (2002). A role for poetry in consumer research. *Journal of Consumer Research*, 29, September, 218–234.

33. Langer, C.L. & Furman, R. (2004). Exploring identity and assimilation: Research and interpretive poems. *Forum: Qualitative Social Research*, 5(2), Article 5, May, no page numbers.

34. Cahnmann, M. (2003). The craft, practice, and possibility of poetry in educational research. *Educational Researcher*, 32(3), April, 29–36; Lahman, M.K.E., Geist, M.R., Rodriguez, K.L., Graglia, P.E., Richard, V.M. & Schendel, R.K. (2010). Poking around poetically: Research, poetry, and trustworthiness. *Qualitative Inquiry*, 16(1), 39–48.

35. Whyte, D. (1994). *The heart aroused: Poetry and the preservation of the soul in corporate America*. New York: Knopf Doubleday Publishing Group; Burrell, L. (2007). A larger language for business. Poet David Whyte on conversational leadership. *Harvard Business Review*, 85(5), May, 28; Seddio, M. (n.d.). *Poetry and the soul in the workplace?* An interview with David Whyte. www.corptalkonline.com/custom/uploads/news/articles/article-david_whyte.pdf.

36. Whyte, D. (1994). *The heart aroused: Poetry and the preservation of the soul in corporate America*. New York: Knopf Doubleday Publishing Group.

37. Grisoni, L. (2009). Exploring organizational learning and knowledge exchange through poetry. Chapter 7. In D. Jemielniak & J. Kociatkiewicz (Eds.). *Handbook of research on knowledge-intensive organizations*. Hershey, PA: IGI Global. pp. 98–115. www.irma-international.org/viewtitle/20848/https://pdfs.semanticscholar.org/9891/2d94e6307161ab9e592daa1f26ea4cffc506.pdf

38. Argyris, C., Putnam, R. & Smith, D. (1987). *Action science: Concepts, methods, and skills for research and intervention*. San Francisco, CA: Jossey-Bass.

39. Hill, D.A. (2005). The poetry in portraiture: Seeing subjects, hearing voices, and feeling contexts. *Qualitative Inquiry*, 1(1), February, 95–105.

40. Coleman, J. (2012). The benefits of poetry for professionals. *Harvard Business Review*, November 27. https://hbr.org/2012/11/the-benefits-of-poetry-for-pro

41. Stein, H.F. (2003). The inner world of workplaces: Accessing this world through poetry, narrative literature, music, and visual art. *Consulting Psychology Journal: Practice and Research*, 55(2), 84–93.

42. Burrell, L. (2007). A larger language for business. Poet David Whyte on conversational leadership. *Harvard Business Review*, 85(5), May, 28, 58.

43. Dombrowski, R. (2014). *Academia vs. poetry: How the gatekeepers of contemporary literature might be killing it*. www.thereviewreview.net/publishing-tips/academia-vs-poetry-how-gatekeepers-contempor

44. Dombrowski, R. (2014). *Academia vs. poetry: How the gatekeepers of contemporary literature might be killing it*. www.thereviewreview.net/publishing-tips/academia-vs-poetry-how-gatekeepers-contempor

45. Faulkner, S.L. (2007). Concern with craft: Using Ars Poetica as criteria for reading research poetry. *Qualitative Inquiry*, 13(2), March, 218–234.

46. Burrell, L. (2007). A larger language for business. Poet David Whyte on conversational leadership. *Harvard Business Review*, 85(5), May, 28, 58.

47. Coleman, J. (2012). The benefits of poetry for professionals. *Harvard Business Review*, November 27. https://hbr.org/2012/11/the-benefits-of-poetry-for-pro

48. Winnicott, D.W. (1945/1958). Primitive emotional development. In M.M.R. Khan (Intro.). *Through pediatrics to psychoanalysis: Collected papers*. New York: Basic Books. pp. 243–254.

49. Winnicott, D.W. (1945/1958). Primitive emotional development. In M.M.R. Khan (Intro.). *Through pediatrics to psychoanalysis: Collected papers*. New York: Basic Books. pp. 243–254.

50. Ogden, T. (2002). *Conversations at the frontier of dreaming.* New York: Karnac. p. 47.
51. Ogden, T. (2002). *Conversations at the frontier of dreaming.* New York: Karnac. p. 47.
52. Ogden, T. (2002). *Conversations at the frontier of dreaming.* New York: Karnac.
53. Vivona, J.M. (2013). Psychoanalysis as poetry. *Journal of the American Psychoanalytic Association,* 61(6), 1109–1137.
54. Vivona, J.M. (2013). Psychoanalysis as poetry. *Journal of the American Psychoanalytic Association,* 61(6), 1109–1137;
55. Ogden, T. (2002). *Conversations at the frontier of dreaming.* New York: Karnac. p. 47; Vivona, J.M. (2013). Psychoanalysis as poetry. *Journal of the American Psychoanalytic Association,* 61(6), 1109–1137; Ogden, T. (1989). *The primitive edge of experience.* Northvale, NJ: Jason Aronson.

3 Understanding Psychoanalytic Theory

Various schools of psychoanalytic theory are used to understand leaders, organization members, and organizational dysfunctions at the individual, group, and organizational level. These uses of the theory include executive coaching, management consulting, and use by management practitioners. There are a number of psychoanalytic theories. Three theoretical perspectives are commonly used. These are object relations theory, group relations theory, and to a lesser extent the theoretical work of Karen Horney. We will use these three perspectives, supplemented as appropriate by others, to analyze and interpret the nature of toxic organizational life that is revealed in the applied workplace poems.

We note that there is a growing literature on the use of these three perspectives. We will provide references for each at the beginning of each of their respective sections. The reader is encouraged to consider exploring these theoretical perspectives. We will, however, provide sufficiently accessible definitions and descriptions of the theories to promote understanding them as they are subsequently used.

Object Relations Theory

Management, leadership, and followership have been discussed from many perspectives. In this section, we will examine how object relations theory can be used to examine the workplace. This psychodynamically informed perspective as applied to organizations has been evolving for the past fifty years, and there is a growing literature on the subject. We will use here the work of a few of the more established authors.[1]

We begin by introducing the concepts of denial, splitting, projection, projective identification, and transference. Every effort is made to keep the theory accessible and grounded in concrete examples.

Denial

Denial is a common psychological defense mechanism that disposes of distressing experience relative to one's self or one's group by suppressing awareness. Awareness, however, is not entirely banished by denial, and the individual must invest some conscious effort in maintaining the denial especially when the "facts" become progressively harder to ignore and deny. Denial is often spotted by others and perhaps pointed out to the person in denial. This can be problematic, reinforcing efforts to maintain the denial.

Denial is such a common psychological defense that further explanation is perhaps not needed. We may observe denial in others and in organizations where the individual, management, and employees act as though the distressing situation is not happening or a problem does not exist. Denial is an integral part of splitting and projection, and it is further discussed in the next sections.

Splitting

Splitting is an unconscious psychological defense. It divides one's self or a representation of another individual or group formulated in one's mind into good and bad. This usually results in one's sense of self as good and the representation of the other as bad. It is a response to distressing self-experience, making it a defensive response to anxiety. Splitting includes denial of the distressing experience that is to be split off from the self. We may, for example, deny we are feeling concerned or threatened by what is going on. At the same time, we may locate these same thoughts and feelings in another person (in our minds) who is then thought to be anxious. We feel calmer because the anxiety is now suppressed from awareness. An individual may appear anxious but deny it. Another individual may be thought of as anxious but not appear to be anxious.

The sequence is this: first the distressing self-experience is denied, and then it is split off, creating the possibility of locating (projecting) the experience in someone else, at least in one's mind. I am not afraid; you are. Splitting, it may then be appreciated, creates the basis for projection and projective identification to be discussed. Theoretically it is important to consider splitting and projection as occurring together as in this discussion.

Splitting is complex enough to merit more discussion. Splitting is an unconscious mental process that can be shared with others, given that there is a shared distressing experience. I or we are good and being attacked by a bad other person or group. This process is so common and natural that we do not pay much attention to these dynamics in our lives at work or outside of work. We simply feel we are being attacked or victimized by another individual or group. The world becomes divided into a black and white landscape, often with little to no middle ground. The world can become filled with evil empires, axes of evil, and polarization. Within organizations the finance department and its mission to manage costs can create an oppressive and limiting experience for other departments that need resources to do their work.

Splitting may also happen in the reverse. For example, we might see ourselves as weak and ineffective and therefore unworthy. We may also see someone else or a group as better and acting effectively. The other person or group is then worthy of admiration and respect, and we or I are not. For example, when we are in the presence of a powerful senior executive, we might feel anxious, diminished by comparison, and vulnerable. The executive is in our minds bigger than life, and we are small and weak.

Splitting combined with projection occur frequently enough that they affect how we experience ourselves and others. The splits are durable in part because they are out-of-awareness. As a result, they are not particularly open to self-inspection unless something happens that challenges this defensive pattern. It may be the case that the splits are defended and evidence to the contrary ignored.

In sum, splitting is common and degrades accurate reality testing. We create in our minds a context that is not accurate, but it is comforting. The split context in our minds helps us to cope with distressing anxiety in the moment. It is also important to appreciate that splitting promotes thinking and feeling that can lead to actions that can be destructive of others or groups. Others may become despicable and should be destroyed. It is this dynamic that creates hostile takeovers where members of the other organization are seen as incompetent and disposable. Splitting also readily forms the basis for interpersonal dominance and submission, and for cultural dislocations such as genocide and ethnic cleansing, which unfortunately are common.

An Example

In this example the focus is on splitting. However, as noted, it cannot be entirely understood without also considering denial and projection (discussed next).

Sarah owns a food service company with nearly 50 employees. It is easy to see she is admired and respected. She founded the company with the vision of serving a niche market for French cuisine. As a result, her company occupies a narrow but safe market with no other major competitors, and the employees feel secure. They enjoy their work, feel appreciated, and they are reasonably well compensated.

Almost everyone feels she is a superior leader, and she basks in this warm glow of employee approval. Thomas, a new employee, based on experience, is not too eager to join in this shared admiration. He needs to see that the admiration is merited. He is not willing to deny and split off his experience of himself as competent or deny and split off aspects of Sarah that do not support idealizing her. Many of his colleagues are aware of his unwillingness to join with them in idealizing her. He is also aware of pressure from others and from Sarah to validate these psychodynamics.

One way to understand this context is that it contains collusion and coercion. It is easily observed that Sarah acts in ways to draw positive projections. She has split off those aspects of herself that are less than admirable and projected them onto others, leaving her feeling competent and perhaps at times arrogantly so. Thomas' sense of these dynamics is that Sarah encourages (pulling projections) but also merits some conscious and unconscious positive and idealizing splitting and projection onto her mental representation. This is how her employees think of her and see her in life. She is also omnipresent in her organization because she does closely monitor the quality of the work and service. This bigger-than-life presence and her attention to quality encourage the splitting and projection.

In sum, employees are encouraged to some extent to split off and project some of their competencies onto their mental representation of Sarah. Sarah, being aware of this at least to some extent, encourages them to do so. This dynamic makes her feel better about herself by receiving the projections, but she also splits off and projects any sense of her lacking competencies onto her employees. They need her close oversight, training, and supervision.

Projection

Projection arises when denial and splitting are present. Projection as discussed disposes of denied and split off distressing self-experience by creating a representation in one's mind of the other individual(s) or group and locating the denied experience in this representation. The representation is then available to be manipulated at will in one's mind. We often "know" others and groups in this way. This is natural and happens out of awareness. Denial, splitting, and projection are not particularly open to reflection but can be acknowledged if pointed out to the individual perhaps in therapy but also at work. These mental representations are unique to each person, yielding different views of one individual (or group) who may be "known" by others in many different ways—some good and some bad.

Projection can alter one's sense of self but also one's sense of another individual or group, with both often happening concurrently. Projection may occur when a hard-to-resolve internal conflict arises where we become aware that we have good and bad qualities or self-experience and wish to be rid of usually the bad qualities or experience. This may also occur as mentioned relative to our good qualities and experience, depending on the circumstances of the moment.

Denial, splitting, and projection may also occur relative to others as mental representations. When we are aware of another person having both good and bad qualities, we might split the individual and, for example, only come to know his or her good or bad qualities. This then furthers the splitting and projection, allowing us to feel good about ourselves and feel that the other person is bad as a result of what we have put into the mental representation, but also what we have removed by denying the good parts of the other. Most often projection involves experiencing oneself as good or as a victim and the other person as bad or the victimizer. This outcome leads to an unconscious commitment to maintaining the splits and projections. Information that does not support this dynamic may not be attended to (selective attention and recall) or denied, bending reality to one's own needs.

It is also important to appreciate that splitting and projection that take place in one's mind leak out into the interpersonal world, leading to our acting in ways relative to the other person consistent with the splits and projections relative to the other person. This person who is the focus of the projections may sense that he or she is thought to be a certain way (as bad or a victimizer) that may not be consistent with his or her own self-conception. This is common in of interpersonal and intergroup relations. And since it occurs at the margins of awareness, it is not particularly open to discussion. Challenging this dynamic by the individual or group that is being targeted may paradoxically validate that the person is bad, reinforcing the splits and projections.

An Example

Continuing with the previous example, organization members often feel inferior to Sarah and act as though this is true and accurate. They tend to assume roles of dependency on her, and she does not discourage this. Sarah feels more important due to the constant press of leaked projections. Others often wait for her to make decisions, and their waiting encourages her to make them. This is a subtle process that, while observable, is usually unacknowledged. To the extent that she fulfills their expectations, she completes what amounts to interpersonal contracting and collusion. On those occasions when Thomas has called this into question, others defend their conception of Sarah, seeing Thomas as bad for raising questions.

Projective Identification

Projective identification takes splitting and projection to a new level: that of trying to *control* the other person by getting him or her or the group to *become like the projections*. The subject is actively encouraged to feel, think, and act in accordance with the projections. The goal of projective identification is to have the other person or group accept (take in or introject) the projections. The outcome is that the other individual or group begins to act out the projections, confirming their accuracy.

For the recipient of the projective identification, the constant pressure to become like the projected content can be subtle but also distressing, in that others make clear the individual is not meeting their expectations. This sense of pressure is diminished by embracing the projections, relieving the anxiety associated with resistance. Of course, if the projections are positive the person or group may welcome and embrace them.

It is important to emphasize that all of this is very natural and that these dynamics are going on all of the time. Think for a moment of a father and daughter. The father in his mind wants to see his daughter as sweet and innocent. He acts as though she is the perfect little girl and actively encourages her to feel this way. She is of course punished when she fails to fulfill this mental representation of her. With time and persistence, the other person or group often becomes as desired. All is well as the gradual reshaping of the other fulfills our projections. To be noted, the opposite of an idealizing dynamic may occur where projective identification creates a bad "other" person or group that is continually coached (baited) into acting in bad ways consistent with the projections, such as victimizing others.

An Example

Continuing with the example, Sarah is idealized by employees. Why not? She created the company. This idealization is in part based on projective identification. Sarah often acts, thinks, and feels like her employees imagine her to be. This reduces anxiety about meeting their expectations, and it reduces their anxiety by providing them some sense of control over her. They know what to expect from her.

The employees often do more than merely wait for Sarah to make decisions. They often encourage her to feel that she is the only person capable of making them. She is complimented and carefully coached into becoming the leader who they desire. She makes all the major decisions, sheltering everyone from distressing operating problems. This constant press of projections is eventually accepted, leading Sarah to experience herself as not only an outstanding manager and leader, but also the only person who can make the important decisions.

It must also be appreciated that in order for Sarah to believe that she has to make most of the decisions, she must eliminate self-experience that is not consistent with being able to do so. Her imperfections and limitations may be split off and projected onto her marginally capable employees, who are actively encouraged to feel less than capable. As a result, they have to be managed (micro-managed), fulfilling their vision of her and hers of them. Many of the employees may accept this view of themselves as Sarah evacuates her own imperfections and limitations, locating them in her employees.

The employees feel less than capable and need her to take charge of the work and organization. The dynamic is a collusive interpersonal transaction, where the competence rests with Sarah and the incompetence with the employees. Sarah must assume most of the responsibility for operations, which is also stressful for her, promoting anxiety and psychological regression that may lead to denial, splitting, and projection to defend against it.

Thomas needs to be careful. He might easily evoke anxiety in others by questioning these dynamics directly or indirectly by pointing out Sarah's imperfections and unresolved operating problems. Everyone is at some level easily threatened by anyone who does not support their splitting and projection. Denial of Sarah's imperfections is essential in terms of maintaining the idealization. If something goes wrong, it is most likely the employees who will think they are at fault.

Transference

The workplace is filled with many thoughts and feelings not related to work or the present moment. Transference involves the unconscious transfer of past experience and the accompanying feelings onto the present, creating confusing distortions of relationships. A manager who resembles an abusive, manipulative, or emotionally unavailable parent or past authority figure may evoke unconscious feelings that are consistent with this past experience. The manager unwittingly evokes transference by his or her behavior or even appearance.

Splitting and projection contribute to this dynamic. The manager is simply experienced as familiar, since he or she has been created in one's mind, and the mental representation evokes overly strong thoughts and feelings not necessarily consistent with the nature of the manager's self or actions. The response to a bad representation is disproportionate, leading to overly fearful, submissive, enraged, or withdrawn reactions. In the case of a good representation, transference may include idealization and adoring and loving feelings. The manager may be left to wonder what happened.

Transference blurs reality in conjunction with splitting and projection. The manager is created in one's mind via splitting and projection, perhaps taking the form of past authority figures. From a psychological perspective, it must be appreciated that the pattern of splitting, projection, and transference is an unconscious defensive response learned by trial and error by the child or adult to cope with abusive and un-nurturing parental figures or other managers. This often-stable defensive pattern of splitting, projection, and transference "normalizes" what is a powerful and unconscious coping response to manage anxiety in interpersonal relationships, groups, and organizations.

An Example

Sarah is a much-admired leader who created the company. She has benefited from her employees' idealization of her in ways that are not always consistent with accurate reality testing. She has also over time accepted many of her employee projections, becoming more like what they want. The collusive process encourages the transfer of past feelings onto Sarah, consistent with their feelings for past authority figures, who provided good enough nurturing and caretaking. This allows most employees to feel good about Sarah and themselves and each other. Similarly, Sarah's transference may well be consistent with parenting and caring for employees who need caretaking. She tries her best to take care of her employees and organization.

In sum, her employees feel safe in their roles, joined with Sarah who has become their wise and caretaking parental figure. Note that this same dynamic can create a leader who is bad or evil and employees who are good and being victimized. And, also to be considered, is that if Sarah ever fails to fulfill expectations, there may occur a collapse in the idealizing projections and positive transference, evoking disillusionment and anger that can become destructive of self, others, and the organization.

We now turn our attention to discussing the other two helpful theoretical perspectives. Each makes a unique contribution to understanding the workplace that inspired the applied poems in this book.

Group Relations Theory and Wilfred Bion

Organizations are composed of individuals who most often work in one or more groups to accomplish the work of the organization.[2] These groups operate along a range from working on task to being diverted to meet the defensive needs of their members. Much the same can be said of inter-group dynamics as well as all the groups that together create the dynamics of the organization as a whole. Wilfred Bion developed in the 1940s concepts that provide insight into what groups are doing or not doing and how to understand these group dynamics.[3] In particular, he suggests that there are three basic assumption groups that are *defensively* oriented and a fourth group, the work group, which is more intentional and able to work effectively on the group's *tasks*.

Basic Assumption Groups

Wilfred Bion observed behavior in group therapy sessions that often avoided the task of therapy. This focus on group dynamics contributed to the group relations movement and in the U.S. the development of the A. K. Rice Institute that sponsors group-relations conferences that use experiential learning to explore and understand unconscious group dynamics driven by stress and regression.

Bion described three group dynamics that arise in response to psychological *regression* that comes from joining a group where anxiety increases relative to losses of self and personal autonomy. Psychological regression involves a retreat to more primitive psychological defenses that were developed early in life. Group members who share the regression and defensive basic assumption group response to anxiety take the group off of its work on its declared primary task. An important feature of this group dynamic is that individuals enter groups with particular defensive tendencies or "valences" to retreat to one basic assumption group. Rioch writes, "In his [Bion's] concept of valency he is saying that everyone has the tendency to enter into group life, in particular into the irrational and unconscious aspects of group life, and that people vary in the amount of tendency they have in this direction."[4]

Also consider that the individuals are along a range more or less vulnerable to psychological regression and that they retreat to one of the basic assumptions groups. The entire group may not join in the regression and the emergent basic assumption group. These individuals and perhaps the leader may then offer some resistance to the development of further regression and greater reliance on one or more defensive basic assumption groups. We now briefly describe the three basic assumption groups: fight/flight, dependency, and pairing.

Fight/Flight

Fight/flight is a deeply familiar bodily response to distressing anxiety that generates intensity, released by mounting an attack or turning away in flight. When fight or flight happens, thinking and reflectivity are often lost. The group requires a leader who shows hate or fear toward the enemy within the group or organization (or outside the organization or nation in international relations). The leader and the group are willing to accept member casualties. Some members may be seen as part of the problem, perhaps leading to termination or being left behind as the group moves on, as might occur during an organizational restructuring. The group is not particularly reflective, preferring to focus on taking action against the threat by moving against it or away from it (see the later section in this chapter on The Tripartite Theory of Karen Horney). Fight and flight are common in the workplace and must be acknowledged in order to redirect this basic assumption group back to working on the organization's mission.

Dependency

The dependency group appears to have attained security by being protected by someone, usually a leader. Group members act as though they are less than competent, inadequate to handle current operating problems, and not able to take care of themselves or deal with threats. When an individual is identified to take care of (lead) the group, he or she may be idealized. Everyone now waits to receive direction from the leader. Splitting and projection of personal competencies, and the leader's identification with these projections, contributes to this outcome, as per the example of Sarah in the previous section.

If a leader if not identified, the group patiently waits, often eventually creating enough anxiety in the group due to not dealing with operating problems that a member decides to try to lead to relieve his or her own anxiety about waiting. This new leader must face the probability that this dependent group can never be fully cared for. Any failure to meet the group's dependency needs arouses their disappointment and hostility, perhaps leading to a fight or flight response, terminating the leader and locating a new and better leader.

Dependency is a familiar workplace dynamic especially where leaders have hierarchical roles that empower them to be in charge. There is then a potentially collusive dynamic that exists in hierarchical organizations, where dependency basic-assumption groups form much of the basis for creating and sustaining the culture of hierarchical command and control that is enabled by subordinates seeking security.

Pairing

This group hopes a leader, new idea, or new strategy will emerge to save them from the problems they have encountered. This group's members are attentive to each other and focused on the hope that the future will be better, but the members do not invest much effort in dealing with operating problems. Paradoxically the rise of a leader who holds expectations for the group to take action is to be avoided as threatening and potentially coercive.

It is important that the leader, the better idea, or new strategy remain unborn and unthought. These may also only be present in fantasy. In particular, it is hoped that the change that contains their anxiety about current problems will almost magically occur. Everyone expects something good will happen to reduce the anxiety and group regression. Hope is abundant which, as noted, includes not having to act to deal with the stressors and reduce the anxiety that promotes regression in this group defense.

An organization that has a constant turnover of leaders that creates a context where there is no clear sustainable direction leaves employees hoping times will get better. However, they also prefer to simply be rescued and not have to assume responsibility for taking actions to improve operations and reduce the stress and anxiety.

Work

This type of group, Rioch asserts, is "very rare and perhaps even non-existent in pure culture."[5] This group possesses maturity and is able to engage in reflection. It is well structured and works on a clearly defined primary task. Rioch also notes, "Each member of the group belongs to it because it is his will and his choice to see that the purpose of the group is fulfilled. He is therefore at one with the task of the group and his own interest is identified with its interest."[6] The group is willing to test its assumptions and conclusions and learn from experience. It strives to acquire knowledge and continually questions whether what it is doing is the best way to accomplish the task.

Clearly this work group is largely free of regression to basic assumptions but not necessarily free of stress and anxiety. The group is able to effectively deal with stressors, minimizing the experience of anxiety. The work group is present in organizations that are able to make accurate assessments of operating problems, threats, and opportunities and can locate action plans and implement the plans that are then monitored for satisfactory outcomes.

Discussion of Basic Assumption Groups

Bion's basic assumption groups as described increase our awareness of irrational and unconscious group dynamics that do not contribute to working on the organization's mission. Basic assumption groups are especially likely to arise during stressful periods. During these times leaders are often expected to provide clear and reassuring direction to deal with the sense of threat, as may be the case for the work group.

Equally important to consider, however, is fight/flight. For example, fighting back against intrusions on one's turf is a common response in organizations. If the incursion is perceived as dangerous, flight into fantasy, intellectualization, denial, and rationalization may develop. To the extent that this happens, there may be greater dependency on a leader who is willing to try to save the organization—or, if currently there is no one, to wait for an omnipotent leader or new idea that will deliver the organization from its distress.

The basic assumption groups inspired many of the applied poems, where organizational dysfunction was the experience of the moment if not the past, present, and future. We now turn to discussing the third theoretical perspective.

The Tripartite Theory of Karen Horney

Understanding human behavior in large or even small organizations can be challenging without a conceptual road map to understand what one observes in the workplace.[7] We have found that Karen Horney offers us a thoughtful, accessible model for understanding the observed workplace behaviors and their underlying psychodynamics that can be understood to be the outcome of various levels of inadequate parental nurturing.[8] In particular, instances where there are serious and persistent caretaking failures in infancy, childhood, and even at work yield well organized and durable defensive reactions (strategies) that introduce workplace dysfunctions and toxicities.

Childhood and Personal Development

These psychodynamics and their accompanying workplace dysfunctions arise when the child is not loved or insufficiently loved (anxious attachment) and must arrive at some way to cope with these intense threats and anxieties. Karen Horney speaks to the problematic nature of these anxious and often painful attachments, and she offers three possible solutions.[9] In one, the child might respond by not giving up on seeking to be loved, hoping for secure and supportive attachment by becoming more loveable, including submission and changing one's self in the service of seeking loving attachment. This is a *movement toward* others and is also described as the appeal to love and the self-effacing solution to anxiety.

A second possibility in the interpersonal world is to fight back and resist unacceptable caretaking of others. This is described as *moving against* others, which is the appeal to mastery and the expansive solution to anxiety. This response represents to some degree an abandonment of hope of being loved. Moving against others can be expected to threaten the quality of attachments to others, creating a self-fulfilling outcome of not being nurtured and loved, and perhaps failing that, feared.

A third possible direction of movement is that the child responds by abandoning hope of being loved and receiving adequate caretaking from others. Loving attachment is just simply too painful to try to acquire by either of the other two appeals—to love or to mastery. One accepts that he or she is not worthy of being loved (moving toward others) and that fighting back against others (moving against others) is too stressful and futile. The choice is then to *move away* from others, becoming the appeal to freedom and the resigned solution to anxiety.

These three directions of movement are psychologically defensive responses to insufficient caretaking by others and stressful interpersonal relationships. They are coping responses that contain within them elements that threaten attachment to others as well as one's self-integrity. They resemble reaction formations that are steadfastly and compulsively pursued to allay anxiety in the interpersonal world. We now discuss these three directions of movement in more detail.

Movement Toward

Movement toward others, Horney's appeal to love and the self-effacing solution to anxiety, is the opposite of moving against others. This individual must not feel superior to others or wish to dominate and control others.[10] Feeling inferior, a failure, and contemptible (including some sense of self-hate) is present. Pride, triumph, and superiority are shunned. In their place is willingness to subordinate oneself to others, including a morbid dependency on others as well as being submissive to make one's self lovable and worthy of secure attachment. This individual is deeply invested in an idealized self-image that has many lovable qualities such as goodness, generosity, and humility. In the workplace, this pursuit of being acceptable and loveable may focus on others who possess power and authority, who are feared and admired much like parental figures.

Denial, splitting, projection, and transference, it should be noted, are present, contributing to this outcome. To curry their favor, this individual may rely on submission to gain attachment to these powerful others, paradoxically reinforcing the dominance and control by the desired object of attachment. As a psychological defense mechanism, every effort may be made to sustain this solution to anxiety, including avoiding thoughts and feelings that the powerful other is abusing and degrading this individual. The balance between depleting one's inner self and maintaining one's personal integrity is a challenge created by one's submission to powerful and controlling others in order to maintain secure attachments.

Observers might see an individual who is willing to do whatever it takes to acquire and keep an attachment, regardless of the personal sacrifices that are embedded in this interpersonal "contract." A common workplace expression, "sucking up," speaks to this defensive movement. There may also develop a perverse sense of loyalty as well as idealization and unquestioning submission to authority—which means death to labor solidarity and unions.

Movement Against

Movement against others is the appeal to mastery and the expansive solution to anxiety. We consider this defensive response to contain manipulative elements in the pursuit of narcissistic supplies, as well as interpersonally aggressive and destructive elements when this individual's expansive sense of pride is harmed by others (narcissistic injury). This individual's idealized and prized self is felt to be able to accomplish just about anything and to solve any problem. This inflated sense of self and arrogant self-pride that the person can accomplish anything makes this individual the right person to be in control. This defensive response, paired with arrogant pride, often promotes interpersonal aggression and violence, where anything may be risked in order to vindicate injured expansive pride. There is often present an enemies list.

Organizational positions that receive a lot of attention and possess considerable status, authority, power, and control resident in the position are especially desirable to have. These positions also fulfill the narcissist's desire to appear charismatic, authoritative, and worthy of fear and admiration, while at the same time providing the means to vindicate and repair injured narcissism and expansive pride. Others observing or experiencing this individual in this role may also appreciate that their narcissistic leader is affectively disconnected from followers. Empathy, interpersonal authenticity, and the ability to connect with others are often lacking. This paradoxically echoes and recreates the underlying caretaking dynamic in childhood attachments, where low empathy and a lack of authentic interpersonal availability and nurturing created punishing and anxiety-ridden attachments. The dynamic is therefore familiar.

This individual tends to manipulate and dominate others, preferably creating dependency and encouraging others to admire and look up to him or her. However, it is also common that individuals and groups create narcissistic injury. The arrogant-vindictive response focuses on using the power that resides in one's hierarchical position to gain and maintain control while simultaneously alienating others. This individual in a leadership role may appear self-righteous and tends to attract, in particular, self-effacing followers willing to submit to the leader to achieve secure attachment. These followers become enabling sycophants commonly found in many large organizations. Others are merely objects to be used.[11] Employees within the organization may describe this leader's behavior as bullying, threatening, and intimidating.

A key element of these dynamics involves appreciating that, since this individual has largely abandoned being loved and admired (although it there is always a preference), he or she has nothing to lose by aggressing others. The possibility of loving and caring attachments is not threatened, since none are thought to be possible. Therefore, getting even with others is a priority—one pursued with enough energy at times to become self-destructive, creating excessive fear and anxiety of this individual in the workplace.

Movement against others, we suggest, offers a lot of explanatory power in terms of understanding some of the more common and prominent workplace dysfunctions. The applied poems are often inspired by toxic workplace dynamics linked to these workplace dynamics of moving against others.

Movement Away

Movement away from others, Horney's appeal to freedom and resigned solution to anxiety, we consider to be a response to the stresses of the interpersonal world by essentially dropping out.[12] This individual gives up trying to cope with others and prefers a solitary life. This response is the result of inner irresolvable conflicts that have made moving toward and against others unsatisfactory. This individual abandons striving for success, which is indirectly expressed in philosophies that renounce nonessentials.

Life becomes streamlined and less complex. Being loved and admired as well as achieving, while perhaps desired, are largely abandoned. There is a feeling of a lack of confidence in one's self that reinforces avoiding trying to achieve much at work or in one's life. Being alone and being left alone are comforting when the interpersonal world is stressful and filled with conflicts. Various other coping strategies have been found to not work, or they are too stressful to rely on.

This defensive positioning in the interpersonal world creates a hyper-sensitivity to influence, pressure, coercion, and change. In a workplace filled with these eventualities, this individual, it is understood, prefers to be left alone to do his or her work and is resentful of supervision, due dates, and performance expectations. The most desirable positions at work limit interpersonal contact. Routine work and work not subject to change are preferred as well as work that avoids demands, account-ability, and deadlines.

Certainly, it is the case that movement away from others and the appeal to freedom are often encountered in the workplace. Paradoxically, some leaders who find their responsibility stressful may appeal to freedom, where they depend on others to make the tough decisions and deal with the tough problems often generated by interpersonal conflict. This allows them to be left alone to perhaps focus on financial analyses in splendid isolation.

Mixed Models

It is always problematic to speak of pure types in a typology. People are complex. They have developed a system of psychological defense mecha-nisms that work for them. These defenses are a necessity for everyone, but for some they become rigidly adhered to, becoming much like a char-acter or personality disorder. It is also the case, given the complexity of human nature, that more than one of these defensive responses may be relied on. A typical mixed model, we have found, in the workplace is vacillation between moving against and toward others.

An example is a leader who prefers to move against others trying to dominate and control most aspects of an organization and make deci-sions at all levels of the organization, which is enabled by modern infor-mation systems. Anyone who gets in the way is disciplined or discharged. At the same time, this individual is easily made to feel anxious and uncer-tain when an out-of-control situation is encountered or a highly visible decision is questioned by someone higher in the organization. This leader may suddenly need secure attachment, reassurance, nurturing, admiration, and even love—the movement toward others. An inner circle of enablers must shore up this fragile sense of self in the moment to permit the leader to once again feel self-assured, admired, and back in control, which in turn restores the leader to an idealized but also dominating and abusive state.

Movement against others may also be paired with movement away during stressful periods where just simply avoiding the stress is in order. The leader might suddenly take a business trip or go golfing to create soothing down time away from the stress. Leaders who most often move toward others may, during times of stress, rather than move against others move away, withdraw, and become unavailable for secure attachment as well as leadership.

In conclusion, the three directions of movement—toward, against, and away—offer an intuitive framework that helps to account for what one often encounters in life and at work. These three defensive directions of movement provide the basis for and insight into many of the applied workplace poems in this book.

Reflections

The three theoretical approaches used in this book do not nearly exhaust all the possible approaches that might be used. We, in fact, do use other theoretical perspectives as appropriate. If anything can be said about using psychoanalytic theory to understand the workplace and the applied poems, it is that the theory provides vitally important ways to organize and interpret the data that one finds when observing human behavior in organizations. The theories are not perfect for interpreting the workplace, and they must be cautiously and intelligently adapted to provide workplace insights.

We hope this book both promotes critical thinking about the workplace and also shows how psychoanalytically informed analyses contribute to (or not) understanding and perhaps changing the workplace, to improve organizational performance and at the same time create a more humane workplace.

In Conclusion

We conclude by humbly submitting the following consideration. Any approach to understanding the immense complexity resident in human nature and groups at work will necessarily come up short. However, we also suggest that not trying to understand these complex workplace dynamics is not a good option either.

We dedicate the remainder of this book to the proposition that many valuable insights can be gained by using psychoanalytically informed perspectives. We also suggest that it is particularly essential to make this effort in order to avoid the many negative aspects that the dark side of human nature and group relations introduces into our lives at work. We all need to be dedicated to trying to understand human nature and the negative effects it has on our lives at work. In sum, we need to be able to learn from our experiences—good and bad. Applied poetry in toxic workplaces can be an instrument of that learning.

Notes

1. Some of the books used to discuss object relations are:

   Grotstein, J. (1985). *Splitting and projective identification.* Northvale, NJ: Jason Aronson. Kohut, H. (1984). *How does analysis cure?* A. Goldberg (Ed.). Chicago: University of Chicago Press. Segal, H. (1973). *Introduction to the work of Melanie Klein.* London: Karnac. Greenberg, J. & Mitchell, S. (1983). *Object relations in psychoanalytic theory.* Cambridge, MA: Harvard University Press. Scharff, J. (1992). *Projective and introjective identification and the use of the therapist's self.* Northvale, NJ: Jason Aronson. Tansey, M. & Burke, W. (1989). *Understanding countertransference.* Hillsdale, NJ: The Analytic Press.

2. Some of the books used to discuss group relations are:

   Allcorn, S. & Diamond, M. (1997). *Managing people during stressful times: The psychologically defensive workplace.* Westport, CT: Quorum Books. Colman, A. & Bexton, H. (Eds.). (1975). *Group relations reader.* Sausalito, CA: Grex. Colman, A. & Geller, M. (Eds.). (1985). *Group relations reader 2.* Washington, DC: A.K. Rice Institute. Czander, W. (1993). *The psychodynamics of work and organizations.* New York: Guilford Press. Diamond, M. & Allcorn, S. (1990). The Freudian factor. *Personnel Journal,* 69(3), 52–65.

3. Bion, W. (1961). *Experience in groups.* London: Tavistock.
4. Rioch, M. (1975). Group relations: Rationale and technique. In A. Colman & W. Bexton (Eds.). *Group relations reader.* Washington, DC: A.K. Rice Institute Series. pp. 11–33.
5. Rioch, M. (1975). Group relations: Rationale and technique. In A. Colman & W. Bexton (Eds.). *Group relations reader.* Washington, DC: A.K. Rice Institute Series. pp. 11–33.
6. Rioch, M. (1975). Group relations: Rationale and technique. In A. Colman & W. Bexton (Eds.). *Group relations reader.* Washington, DC: A.K. Rice Institute Series. pp. 11–33.
7. Some of the books and articles used to discuss Karen Horney are:

   Diamond, M. & Allcorn, S. (1984). Psychological barriers to personal responsibility. *Organizational Dynamics,* 12(4), 66–77. Diamond, M. & Allcorn, S. (1985a). Psychological dimensions of role use in bureaucratic organizations. *Organizational Dynamics,* 14(1), 35–59. Diamond, M. & Allcorn, S. (1985b). Psychological responses to stress in complex organizations. *Administration & Society,* 17(2), 217–239. Diamond, M. & Allcorn, S. (1986). Role formation as defensive activity in bureaucratic organization. *Political Psychology*, 7(4), 709–731. Kets de Vries, M. (2006). *The leader on the couch: A clinical approach to changing people and organizations*. San Francisco, CA: Jossey-Bass.

8. Horney, K. (1950). *Neurosis and human growth*. New York: Norton.
9. Horney, K. (1950). *Neurosis and human growth*. New York: Norton.
10. Horney, K. (1950). *Neurosis and human growth*. New York: Norton.
11. Babiak, P. & Hare, R. (2006). *Snakes in suits: When psychopaths go to work*. New York: Harper; Schouten, R. & Silver, J. (2012). *Almost a psychopath*. Boston, MA: Harvard University Press.
12. Horney, K. (1950). *Neurosis and human growth*. New York: Norton.

4 Leaders and Followers in the Workplace

Leaders and leadership, as well as the nature and quality of followers as individuals and in groups, are by far one of the most dominant features of any workplace. Although they are in one sense separate, distinct roles, they are embedded in an unconsciously fueled relationship. This reality becomes progressively clearer as this chapter unfolds to explore the dark side of organizational life.

The applied poems that follow, together with discussion and analyses of each poem, speak to this often-exceptional amount of suffering that takes place in the workplace. We acknowledge that there is a pervasive sense of darkness to these poems, the chapters, and indeed the book. We both regret this but also embrace it. We cannot sense, understand, and better know the nature of work and toxic organizations by ignoring what is often a pervasive, powerful, and at times deplorable experience of ourselves at work, of others at work, of our jobs and our work, of groups, and of the organization as a whole—by turning our individual and collective heads away in hopes that if we look back, it is not really there. To be truthful, we wish that it were not happening to us and to others.

We now turn to what applied poetry has to offer in learning about the workplace. In triangular fashion, we combine (1) the poems with (2) insights into the origins and inspiration of the poems, followed by (3) a psychologically informed insight into the poems and stories. We further inquire into what social science perspectives can teach us as we explore the links between the poems and the workplace.

We note that Howard's description of the origins of his poems, the stories, is written in the first-person singular to emphasize the lived first-hand experience of the poet. The stories at times contain a biographical quality depending on the nature of the context. This helps to further anchor the reader in the experience of the context and workplace and the origins of the poems. This proviso also applies to all the following chapters.

Transformational Leadership

The new CEO
arrived with a flair,
like a god on a chariot,
this shaman of change.
He followed Nietzsche's dictum,
that "great creators must
be great destroyers,"
Shiva in the flesh.
He drilled down his will
into the soul of the organization,
replacing their thought
with his thought,
until only his thought remained:
one corporation,
one mind,
one will,
lockstep awe,
the culture of a cult,
a divine kingship.
His power glittered as the gold
of productivity,
of profit
of perfection,
a well-oiled machine
submitting to only one machinist.
Besides him
there is
no corporation.
There is only "I."

Discussion

This poem was inspired by the subject of a widely accepted and lauded organizational concept and ideal: *transformational leadership*. It was, and remains, a long-lived and unquestioned dogma of business. It is the topic of countless books and papers. Its subject is the dynamic, driven, charismatic, and sometimes charming leader who "takes charge," "knows exactly what is needed," and "gets things done."

Questioning the assumption that the transformational leader, most often male, is an organizational asset who raises productivity, profitability, shareholder value, and morale is important. Our examination of transformational leaders and the associated cherished myths about exemplary leadership is informed by decades of work experience as members of more than a half dozen health sciences centers. This experience revealed how personally and organizationally destructive many transformational leaders actually are.[1]

Analysis

Any new leader, much less a transformational leader, is burdened by the *baggage* (internal psychodynamics) he or she brings to the task of leading, as well as the vastness of the psychodynamics of close subordinates and the larger organization as a whole.[2] The poem speaks directly to an inner life, where many of these leaders, faced sometimes with sky-high performance expectations to save the organization, have developed or quickly develop a magnified sense of self that is expansive enough to measure up to the perceived task. As perhaps a defensive response to the exceptionally anxiety-ridden context, they must identify with a sense of self grand enough to be able to be a leader. This self-conception of course, along a range, is a psychologically defensive response to the stressful context and the distressing anxiety it evokes.

Also to be considered is others' perception of this grandiosity. As in all groups, some people may identify with this leader and bask in his or her radiant glow. Others may be and forever remain skeptical, seeing some good and some bad in the leader's decisions and how they are enacted. Finally, there will be some who resist the leader's grand presence or flee from it by taking a job elsewhere. These are the inevitable eventualities for this leader that are filled with many individual, group, and organizational psychodynamics.

We will now explore the use of object relations theory in understanding the poem. The new CEO, in order to maintain a sense of self equal to the task, may split off aspects of self that are not thought to be up to the task and perhaps even despised, such as any sense of weakness or fear. These bad aspects of self are projected onto members of the organization, allowing the CEO to understand it is *they* who are deficient and therefore must have a powerful and authoritative leader to take care of them and save the organization from their poor performance. At the same time, many members of the organization may have much the opposite psychodynamics happening. They split off and project their best and most capable attributes and locate them in the new CEO. They experience themselves, then, as deficient as compared with the CEO and in need of being saved and taken care of. Thus, the CEO has projected deficiency and weakness and is left with a sense of self that is overly confident, capable, and able to lead the organization and its members to great success—or disaster. The employees did the opposite, endowing the leader with their own abilities, creating a leader with an expansive sense of self.

To be appreciated is that within this dynamic there is an unconscious collusive win-win strategy where everyone can benefit, including the organization as a whole. This dynamic contributes to understanding

Bion's notion of dependency. The dependency group as discussed in Chapter 2 appears to have attained security by being protected by someone, usually a leader. Group members act as though they are less than competent, inadequate to handle current operating problems, and not able to take care of themselves or deal with threats. The grandiosity projected by the leader magnifies this dynamic. These dynamics in practice can be found to create an exceptional organizational turn around—or a collapse into despair and non-existence in some instances, such as Enron's sudden and catastrophic failure.

Last, we note that this new CEO may also be understood from Karen Horney's perspective of moving against other (the expansive solution to anxiety). This solution complements the object relations perspective by describing the psychodynamics of the leader from a different perspective, one that results in over-determined self-efficacy as a defense against anxiety. The movement toward the leader (self-effacing solution) also contributes insight in that a very real sense of dependency on the leader to care for everyone arises.

Corporate Greed: A Fantasy

The corporation has a body,
a hungry body.
The corporation has a mouth,
a chief executive mouth,
and not far below it
a hungry maw,
incapable of being filled.

The chief executive mouth
is urged on toward
greater consumption
by the many other
parts of the body—
accountants and bankers,
attorneys and consultants,
directors and securities dealers,
regulators and financial analysts,
and shareholders.

The chief executive mouth
feeds the corporation,
until at last the corporation,
wasted away,
still empty,
has consumed itself.

Discussion

A decade ago, the eminent psychoanalytic organizational researcher William Czander was writing a large study of corporate executives' destructive greed, published as *The Death of the American Corporation: The Psychology of Greed and Destructiveness Among CEOs and Bankers.*[3] After reading an early draft of this manuscript I was inspired to write this poem and I shared it with him. He thought the poem nicely captured the essence of his experience and the book. The psychology behind self-serving pursuits of greed as well as narcissistic supplies that very often produce destructive interpersonal, group, and organizational outcomes must be appreciated in order to avoid these types of outcomes.

Analysis

This poem and the context for which it was written is sobering. The title of the book is perhaps more than sobering. It is scary, and so is the poem that so aptly captured the essence of the book. The poem and the book speak to the darker side of leadership and followership, which together can create a context where power and competitiveness run amok and virtually any idea or thought that is more risky and aggressive than the last is potentially embraceable. There can develop a shared group dynamic where anything is possible and there are no limits. We duly note that an experience like this can be exhilarating, exciting, and filled with a sense of limitless potential for one's self, the groups involved, and the organization as a whole.

There is then a shared fantasy about the organization and its members that becomes intoxicating and is not open to inspection in any meaningful way. Everyone on the bus that is running at high speed cheers, all way to the impact of the bus upon the ground after running off the cliff—as was the case at Enron. How very often the headlines of the business pages describe the carnage, leaving all to wonder—what happened?

Psychodynamically, the insatiable hungry mouth of the CEO is fueled by organization members in what becomes a feeding frenzy of sorts. If taking a major risk and succeeding for no good reason was a winner, taking many more risks is even better. This becomes an excuse for unethical and illegal behavior, so long as it feeds the mouth of self-interest, higher pay, and bonuses, and not-to-be-forgotten, the stockholders. This dynamic is sometimes referred to as a slippery slope or "group think" that can result in an ill-considered action such as the Bay of Pigs invasion during the early part of the Kennedy administration.[4]

The excitement, greed, and distorted individual and group dynamics expressed in the poem can in part be appreciated from Horney's movement against others (the expansive solution), where arrogance and narcissism are in abundance, and anyone who happens to call into question what is happening may be vindictively destroyed or banished. There is then resident in this dynamic a process of selecting in and out. There are those who identify with the leader's hunger for success and profit, and those around him or her who enable this behavior (movement toward). There are also those who view it with skepticism and may even reject the dynamics as perhaps a testosterone-driven boys' club that may just as well include women (movement away). These dynamics tend to create a homogeneous group of followers who enable a charismatic leader to feed a deeply felt hunger for admiration, success, and wealth.[5] Also to be considered are common psychological defense mechanisms such as rationalization, denial, and intellectualization that help to create a shared-group altered reality that enables the excitement and feeding frenzy to continue without accurate reality testing, reflective thought, and critical thinking.

Splitting and projection contribute to understanding these dynamics in that they serve to create an aura of being all-knowing, an outstanding group, or perhaps the smartest guys in the room.[6] In this case any personal deficiencies are cast out via projection onto others who are skeptical: competitors, regulators, and even the stock market. This streamlines consciousness and creates a context where the excitement of the frenzy is intoxicating and to be maintained.

Bion's notion of the fight/flight group dynamic also offers insight. The sense of a highly aggressive movement against others and competitors that fuels the pursuit of success and profit is in large part the very nature of this group dynamic. Nothing—including morals, ethics, and laws—may stand in the way of this group's pursuit of triumph.

Stewardship

A large convocation of foxes
gathered to consider how to manage
hundreds of chicken coops
and hen houses. The lead fox proclaimed:
"We need the best hen and chicken
managers we can find to fulfill
our fiduciary responsibility."
After days of rumination,
nomination, speeches, and voting,
the best among the foxes
were elected managers
of chicken and hen houses
throughout the land.
Gradually the hen and chicken
population declined in all precincts,
with fewer and fewer coops and houses

to oversee. In this crisis, an emergency
meeting of the supreme council of foxes
soon discovered that their appointees
were eating those in their charge.
More time passed, and the depleted
houses were now empty of inhabitants.
At the next council meeting,
the wise supreme leader calmed
his fellow foxes with a wink of his eye,
saying, "You know, foxes will be foxes,"
whereupon the council set out to find
other, new, untapped precincts
of hens and chickens
over which to exercise their
sacred stewardship
until the last hen and chicken
had disappeared.

Discussion

This poem began to germinate when Scott Pruitt, Attorney General of Oklahoma, was confirmed by the U.S. Senate as the Director of the Environmental Protection Agency. My heart sank because of Pruitt's consistent record of championing industry over environment in Oklahoma. I felt I saw the future in the past, and further, felt echoes of many noxious organizations with which I had consulted and had read about. Specifically, the leader who was supposed to be the steward of his or her organization sabotaged if not destroyed it instead.

The era in the U.S. since President Ronald Reagan that is marked by the triumph of the ethos of deregulation has yielded disaster for the environment, corporations, savings and loans, banks, and the nation.[7] The presidency of Donald Trump and his choice of cabinet members makes clear that deregulation will continue.

The presumed fiduciary relationship (psychological contract) between corporate leaders and employees, customers, stockholders, and other stakeholders (customers and the public) has long been nullified. There is an Orwellian quality to all this: those leaders brought in to revitalize the organization destroy it instead. As has been noted, for many decades the *official* corporate fiduciary duty to stockholders had at least in part been *mediated* by the psychological contract between employer and workers. However, since the early 1980s, the contract has been annulled, and the only thing that matters now is maximizing stock prices through the relentless quest for profit.

In short, the confirmation of Scott Pruitt unleashed in me a flood of associations and memories of all kinds of unpleasant workplace organizations under leaders who he resembled. The resulting poem turned out to be a parable of corporate and political reality.

Analysis

The year is 2017, and Mr. Pruitt is now in charge of the Environmental Protection Agency that he used to sue all the time. Go figure, or maybe not. Is there not a sense of perverse logic to this? The poem brings to our attention that taking care of others and the environment often runs counter to corporate and industry interests and to maximizing stockholder value. It is reasonable to wonder how the pursuit of profit for the fossil fuel industry, which is supported by targeted campaign financial donations for political supporters that excludes similar support for environmental and social well being, can be done in good conscience. Thus enters psychodynamic consideration of the hen house management.

The foxes are involved in what Chris Argyris refers to as single-loop learning where the tendency is to keep on doing what you are doing sometimes with modifications, never calling into question whether what you are doing is the right thing to do.[8] However, very often we have found dysfunctional organizations that have divisions, and sometimes the entire organization, that operate like this. There is no reflective practice, no critical thinking, and a shutting out of conflicting points of view and information, all of which support a rigid adherence to an ideology.[9]

A context such as this, while filled with rationalization, denial, and intellectualization, is not so much involved in Horney's notion of moving against others (expansive solution) as her appeal to freedom. Everyone just wants to be left alone to do his or her job. The organization appears to embrace a fantasy of timeless existence where little changes and the primary task is to continue to improve on the current methods and processes. This amounts to an institutionalized group and organizational defense.[10] There exists in a dynamic like this a sense of homogenization in at least upper management, where everyone thinks alike and self-differentiation (a new idea) is to be avoided. In contrast, a charismatic disruptor-type leader may arise to fill the leadership void, creating change without insight and feared out-of-control change (movement against).

Denial, splitting, and projection are also at work. Other than denial as a defense against accurate reality testing, also denied are aspects of self that do not conform, such as critical thought and reflective practice. Given the shared social defense aimed at keeping things the same all of the time, these creative and critical thinking attributes must be split off and projected onto others who must then be defended against. In contrast, the loyal and unquestioning team players and group members who support the group and its direction are embraced (movement toward each other). As nearly as possible, everyone needs to be at peace with this solution to operating in what is sometimes a turbulent operating environment, where one hopes to just simply be left alone to do the work (movement away and the appeal to freedom).

Bion's fight/flight dynamic also contributes understanding. Anyone who is not with us is against us and must be contained or "or taken out." Those people become the despised establishment bureaucrats—The Deep State. Resignations are encouraged, open positions are filled with loyalists, and many are shipped off to organizational gulags.

Alone

Dean, provost, CFO, CEO—
they report to few or to no one,
but everyone reports to them.

Feared even when they don't provoke fear,
targets of envy from overworked employees,
expected to solve all the workplace's problems,
they rule from on high but alone,
isolated from the outside world
they so need to know
by those who would protect them
from bad news—who dares tell
the leader that his cherished
plan is a fiasco, making the fiasco
far worse than it might have been?

Isolation breeds suspicion, then
even more strenuous attempts
at protection, now from their own demons.
Sometimes they talk to fellow leaders
of other organizations or branches,
but can they trust them with their secrets?
They fear they will make a slip with competitors,
then become even more withdrawn
in their luxurious solitary confinement.

Consummate power is prison and trap;
walls of invulnerability
make for more vulnerability—
a downward spiral of great peril.
None feel more forsaken
than leaders at the top.

Discussion

This poem is inspired by our workplace and consulting experiences. The many hard-to-believe, toxic stories we became aware of led us to begin to question accepted business school and cultural understanding of the experience of being a CEO. We also began questioning the assumptions behind widely held and cherished truths about leadership. By applying a psychodynamic lens in our work to more closely understand what it is like to be an upper management executive with immense power, we more fully appreciated the sense of isolation at the top of the management pyramid. This poem, "Alone," is my attempt to evoke this inner experience of executives of many kinds of toxic organizations.

Analysis

Being alone at the top is in some ways a terrifying experience, especially for individuals who hunger for approval, attention, and admiration. Another image is the notion that success has many fathers and failure is an orphan, but true failure has only one father—usually the CEO. There are then in this appreciation the many times the awe-inspiring stress and anxiety at the top of the organization must be confronted by less-than-exceptional leaders who, due to their limitations, create more avoidable stress and experience life at the top as out-of-control or nearly so on any given day.

How then does someone who is alone at the top cope with the stress and anxiety and endure this lonely existence? Is high pay, perks, and sometimes a devoted staff the answer? The answer is sometimes yes. You can find leaders who are enamored with all of the accoutrements of high office and the power that resides in their position. They immerse themselves in this, often to the exclusion of taking on the high-stress tough decisions, allowing the organization to drift and its performance to become compromised. They live a bubble, protected by sycophants and see the world through a lens of denial and rationalization.

Individuals who take up the challenge of leading may have adequate self-esteem, good-to-outstanding skills and abilities, and not rely to any great extent on self-, other-, and reality-altering psychological defense mechanism. They are reasonably well integrated and up to the task.

Others, however, along a range, find the position and the challenges stressful and continually work to locate ways to manage the accompanying anxiety or to avoid an awareness of it. Their response to feeling alone at the top and responsible for the organization, its people, and its success is often to defensively split off aspects of themselves that seem to not contribute to coping and to project them onto others, who are then identified as the source of the problems. The splitting and projection allow the leader to feel more competent, in control, and worthy of admiration.

Fight and flight also have something to contribute. For instance, for some leaders there is a tendency to fear making highly visible decisions or confronting and resolving interminable internal conflict (flight). They, in a sense, leave a *power vacuum* sometimes filled by others at risk to themselves and their careers. These leaders when faced with stress may compensate by locating feelings of being tough enough to take all of this on. They are willing to *kick butt* (fight) and move against others as needed (the expansive solution to anxiety).

A third common response to stress is to defend themselves from being held accountable for poor results by resorting to hiring cadres of external consultants who can almost by default end up running the organization. From Bion's perspective, they are in flight from their responsibilities and accompanying anxiety. This externalization of responsibility allays anxiety and is common. If failure arises, the consultants are to blame, which is a fight response and movement against these outsiders leaving them to metaphorically "swing in the wind." What a relief!

Followers in the Workplace

Leaders may have followers who are, along a range, loyal and unquestioning, or at the other end of the range, steadfastly oppositional. There is of course a vast array of other possibilities between these two poles. Also to be considered is that these many forms of emotional attachments to a leader may vary over time depending in large part on how the leader acts and treats followers. There is then a lot of potential variability in what one might observe among followers of any given leader.

Finally, leaders also vary in terms of the length of their tenure. We have encountered large and small organizations that have a continuous turnover in leaders, and similarly, organizations that have the same leader for decades.

When there is a lot of turnover in leaders, followers have a challenge in terms of bonding with and idealizing every new leader. Followers may retreat from these new leaders, preferring to focus on their job and trying to keep the organization running. It is equally true that long-term leaders may gradually change their leadership style and approaches to running the organization. The bonds must then continually adapt to the changes. There is, therefore, to be appreciated that leader and follower dynamics can be ever-changing.

Leaders and followers are then emotionally bound together in a largely unconscious "dance." Although they each occupy distinct roles and statuses, they are connected through the meanings and feelings they project (transfer) onto each other and come to embody.

The following poems raise to awareness some of the more problematic aspects of *followership*.

Who We Are

A matrix of sacred clichés
proclaims to the world,
"This is the way
we do things around here—
don't mess with it."
We don't dream of
thinking outside the box.
We are the box.

Discussion

This brief poem came from,reflection on the common admonition in organizations that, in order to be innovative and competitive, executives, managers, and employees should strive to "think outside the box," that is, to think outside the comfort zone of the familiar.

Boxes are ubiquitous in American organizations, ranging from cardboard boxes of every size to the Dilbert cartoons of life in the modular corporate cubicle. A moment's reflection leads to the realization that strait-jacketed thinking and following, toeing the corporate line, are more the rule, and that "thinking outside the box," while extolled as an ideal, is often forbidden and punished. Many who contemplate offering something new understand that they must assume risk to do so.

As with vertically integrated, hierarchical organizational silos, inhabitants of organizational boxes often identify with the box (silo), carefully guard their box, take it into their inner mental spaces, and become one with the box, that is, inseparably fused with it.[11] Further, they are often highly protective and defensive toward their corporate prison cell. Alien others, who often receive negative projections and who can become larger than life from projection of positive attributes, must be defended against.

Analysis

A box that has a fundamental essence is a prison cell.[12] We often find in meetings, task groups, and daily work that we are locked into following the rules, being a team player, and looking good to the boss by, in particular, avoiding saying and doing things not thought to be approved of. The expression "We don't do that here," is occasionally heard. This is not our way. The implication of this unstated enforced conformity is fear that may take many forms.

Most fundamentally you might lose your job by thinking outside the box. Certainly, you might be publicly humiliated (disciplined), or perhaps your loss of face becomes indirectly known to others by rumor. You may not see the raise you had hoped for or be passed over for a promotion. And certainly, self-differentiation also carries the threat that others will find your getting outside the box to be dangerous to them and their careers. The superstar may well be extinguished to save others from the poor comparison.[13]

In sum, one's job may well function like a prison cell, where freedom to be one's self and be creative and think outside the box, while *seemingly* supported in some instances, might also become a death sentence carried out by management and even one's colleagues. These are powerful others we create in our minds by splitting and projection where we project onto them power and control and we retain a sense of weakness and vulnerability. Having a better idea at an unconscious level becomes filled with existential anxiety. Fear is an omnipresent part of the workplace, as is illuminated by this poem.

Fear might be understood to encourage conformity to achieve dependency. This is the movement toward others that Karen Horney describes as the self-effacing solution to anxiety, an appeal to love. The individual is concerned with receiving approval and maintaining attachment, safety, and security. This individual is willing to voluntarily self-edit thoughts and actions that might conceivably threaten this solution to anxiety.

Bion speaks to a similar dynamic in his discussion of pairing. As discussed in Chapter 2, the pairing solution to group anxiety is one of waiting for a leader or for the spontaneous development of a new idea that saves the group from its vulnerability, implicit in its willingness to patiently wait for this to happen. A better near-term future is hoped for, and this will be achieved without the group thinking outside the box. However, paradoxically, it is usually better for no leadership to arise that involves disrupting the safety of the box-like group culture. Bion also speaks to flight where, in the case of staying inside the box, flight is from one's self efficacy but also the fear of self-differentiation by offering a new idea.

Taking It Personally

> For the longest time
> I have been trying
> not to take it personally.
>
> You tell me your decisions
> are not personal.
> The trouble is, I am.

Discussion

This short poem comes both from a long-standing pattern in my workplace experiences with some supervisors and from consulting with toxic organizations that had abusive supervisors and leaders who denied and rationalized their abuse, saying that their behavior was "nothing personal, just business."[14] Even though officially, business decisions are not supposed to be personal but focused on maximizing profit, in reality they are often deeply personal.

Managers and leaders often mask their psychological brutality with the rationalization that competitive business requires it and that they are not being brutal in the first place. The poem is at once, protest, plea, and a bearing witness to the common frailties and dark side of humanity in the workplace.

Analysis

The poem brings to the foreground the two sides of the metaphoric coin or equation that reside within the intersubjective nature of the interpersonal world. The workplace offers a context that splits apart the nature of relating to each other. In particular, actions taken by authority figures often do harm to others within their organization. Of course, the figures may also be kind, nurturing, and helpful. We applaud those instances. However, the darker side of the workplace often creates outcomes that are hard to live through for those upon whom harm from authority figures is inflicted.

For the victim of the action, it no doubt does feel very personal. You were humiliated in front of others, yelled at, demoted, or even fired. Some of these events happen en masse, such as downsizing and major organizational restructuring. When are outcomes like this *not* personal? However, one's very real sense of this can be challenged by those in management roles who say they were merely carrying out orders and doing their job. To their way of thinking, it was—just business. Psychologically this claim requires jumping through some psychologically defensive hoops.

Defenses such as rationalizing the action as necessary to save the company, denying that what happened is harmful—after all outplacement was provided—and of course management explaining that the financial analysts and external consultants all clearly indicated it was necessary (intellectualization) are abundant. A notion like compartmentalization allows managers and executives to put the bad feelings, guilt, and possibly shame in a box cordoned off from one's conscious awareness and perhaps even soul.[15]

From an object relations perspective, those who are disciplined, fired, or laid off in large numbers might be understood to have deserved it. They were organizational fat that was weighing down organizational performance. They were surplus labor, possibly lazy and unproductive, even working against management and the organization's best interests. And by comparison, management may have split off and projected many of their self- perceptions such as having mismanaged the organization and placed them into the bad workers. This allows them to feel much better about having taken the necessary actions—moving against others. They feel good about themselves. Bion's fight or flight is also a way to understand these dynamics where management must fight against incompetence and laziness. Employees who are aware of these psychodynamics understand that their sense of fear is fully merited. It is then natural for employees to want to flee from management, their responsibilities that might expose them to harm, and sometimes flee their jobs because they are too stressful.

Throughout history others have been turned into evil, hated, inhuman others and then treated accordingly, including the many genocides that have occurred worldwide. The poem may then be appreciated from the perspective that its very few words become a Pandora's Box filled with the necessity to reflect on life at work as well as in our local, national, and international societies.

Lost at Work

Our miasmatic organizations that range from small family enterprises to large international organizations with hundreds of thousands of employees and multiple worksites often unfortunately have cultures and contexts where many members feel alienated from themselves, each other, their work, their skills, and abilities, their leaders, and the organization as a whole. All too often organization members may feel like human assets (as in departments of Human Resources) identified with employee numbers and badges—a person in a position at a desk in a cubicle, his or her existence reduced to an endlessly repetitive set of tasks that are quality assured, monitored, measured, and many times motivated by incentives much like a trained animal.

The fate of the self-at-work is no simple matter to be taken for granted. It can be attacked, besieged, damaged, and shattered. As a result, one's *sense of place* in the workplace is incompletely accounted for if one only looks at the person's official role, status, job description, and place in the organizational chart. Employees can have a fulfilling identity or feel like nothing and nobody at all.

The poems that follow speak to an awareness of being lost at work where one's sense of self is diminished, disappeared, and lost. It is about the experience of being a non-person, reduced to a human resource (an organizational asset, a fuel to run an engine) performing a function.

Anonymous People, Nameless People

These are the shadow people—
mostly faceless, nameless;
they come, do their work,
then disappear into the day or night.

They go by names
of what they do:
janitors, garbage men,
hotel housekeeping,
letter carriers,
parcel deliverers,
restaurant cleanup.

We see only the results of their work:
clean offices, empty dumpsters
ready for another week of trash,
immaculately made beds,
mail in the boxes,
packages on the porch,
tables readied for another meal.

Christmas draws near:
I ran to my mailbox this morning
as the postman drove up—
wanted to thank him
for all he did the past year,
to redeem him from facelessness—
if for only a moment,
to bring him out of the shadows.

Discussion

This poem was inspired by my own moral awakening and remorse (guilt) for past dehumanization of the people who perform these vital services. I wrote this poem after staying in a hotel for a conference. The uniformed people who cleaned up our messes and left the rooms clean, came, worked, and left, mostly when we inhabitants of the rooms were not there. They went by the name of "housekeeping."

We all know and see these nameless, anonymous people. We see and encounter them every day, often at a distance. We seem to not to want to notice them. Sometimes we do not even see them, but know that they have been present by the results of the jobs they leave behind. To many people, they are mere functions, "cogs in wheels," not real, sentient humans. They come silently, perform their jobs, and disappear.

Should we not reconsider their presence among us? I resolved to speak with, briefly visit, and give generous tips to, these crucial anonymous people who keep our hotels, businesses, and streets running and to thank the people who bring mail and take away garbage.

Analysis

The workplace is filled with people who, like the garbage man, are defined at least in part by their job title, profession, or type of work. There are so many—the truckers, the dock workers, the secretaries, the clerks, the IT (information technology) geeks, and of course the managers and executives. Sometimes knowing their names is an inconvenience, with the names lost to time but not perhaps their job titles. There is resident in this appreciation an omnipresent sense of potential anonymity we all live with at work. There are then a few reflections to be considered when it comes to anonymity.

Are there not to some degree feelings of discomfort (guilt and shame) when we acknowledge the presence of these people who contribute to our well-being often from their comparatively lower social status positions? Rather than be confronted ourselves with these feelings, perhaps it is much easier to simply not acknowledge their presence or their humanity. Yet another element is the life gap between their lives and interests and ours. Might we be uncomfortable acknowledging them, briefly speaking to them, or even thanking them for their work? And might they be offended if we did so?

There are many social anxieties that encourage us to locate psychological defenses to be rid of them so that we no longer feel anxious, uncomfortable, and sometimes even fearful. The creation of "them" as an alternate category of human existence is common, enabled by denial, splitting, and projection. We are free to make "them" up in our mind and then treat "them" in a manner consistent with our freely created image of "them" that contains some parts of ourselves we would rather disown. While this is a part of daily life, it is also the substance of genocides and ethnic cleansing.

On the other hand, perhaps "they" do not deserve our respect or attention. They may be disposable "human resources" (objects to be used up, not people) not only for those who are around them but also for the toxic organizations that they work for. And it is not a far step to consider that many others in the workplace are disposable regardless of job titles, educations, training, and job title. Who are the essential workers?[16] Are we not all ultimately disposable human assets for organizations? There is perhaps in this appreciation a sobering linkage from the janitor to the CEO.

Horney's three directions of movement may all apply. The poem and story speak of moving toward these "others." Our anxieties related to encountering them however may lead to moving away from them, avoiding contact. As when viewed as "human resources," moving against them is in a sense authorized. Bion's notion of fight or flight also offers insight. The poem and story are filled with the problem of resolving these two tendencies—to neither avoid (fight) nor confront (fight). This tension is sometimes spoken of as approach/avoidance where the closer you get the more you wish to avoid the other person. Finding a balance in these defensive responses to anxiety is always a challenge.

Car Ride

> In the sanctuary of my motor vehicle,
> he spoke with such diabolical candor
> as to incline me to press toward
> our distant destination:
>
> What is it with you Jews?—
> he began the unexpected trial.
> You act just like the other Jews
> I've known all my life,
> like you're all so special.
> Look at Weimar before Hitler—
> a turn in the road I should have
> expected he would take.
> Jews were overrepresented
> in government, in the arts,
> in science, in medicine,
> in the media, in everything.
> They controlled the whole country.
> Can't you understand why Germans
> wanted to get rid of them
> to get their own country back?
>
> I thought to pull over
> and find a phone
> to obtain for him another ride,
> but I feared he would
> construe it as persecution.
> I drove on, attentively—
>
> You Jews bring persecutions
> on yourselves; you Jews
> push your way into everything.
> I know it's terrible to say—
> and I'll deny that this conversation
> ever took place if you say anything
> about it back at the office.
> What happened to them
> was horrible, but much of it

was of their own doing.
It's the same here in America.
Jews have infiltrated the government,
the arts, the news media, science.
They want to control everything.

And you're just like them.
You act as if everyone is against you,
and it's not true. You get surprised
when we push back. Your future
in the organization depends
on your ability to be less rigid
and to trust me. I'm looking out
for your best interests.

I'll say it again:
If one word about this
gets out to anyone,
I'll completely deny it.
It is our secret, he said
with the slightest quaver.

We rode in silence
to our destination.
I felt endangered,
but must admit
to a minor thrill:
outside the car,
he was as much
a captive as I.

My tormentor, my superior,
your secret has no more power
than mine. O great hunter,
you are now the hunted, too;
you are now a little
of my own kind—a Jew.

Discussion

This narrative poem documents a threatening experience with one of my supervisors in my car on the drive to a remote company site. Until that day, I had long suspected that I was the target of anti-Semitic Jew-baiting and discrimination at work. Nevertheless, I tried to deny it and dismiss it as a product of my imagination and over-sensitivity.

This singular event shattered any doubt that remained because it was so raw, so blatant, and so undisguised. It was an emotionally disorganizing experience, one that I had no idea what to "do" with. Only later did I have the word *traumatic* to label an experience that left me feeling helpless and defenseless. Certainly, at one level I was not helpless and defenseless, since I turned passive victimization into the symbolically assertive act of writing the poem.

It still haunts me that such an event could place in the U.S.—long before the 2015–2016 presidential candidacy of Donald Trump and the overt Jew-baiting expressed by the Alternate Right, white supremacists, and Neo-Nazis in Charlottesville in 2017. Shortly after the car ride I wrote the poem—to put the experience outside of me so that I would not be trapped with it and to bear witness to the reality of what had happened. It was something that I could not make up.

Analysis

The workplace undeniably contains considerable discrimination that takes many forms—religious, ethnic, sex, age, education level, and even discrimination against over-achievers.[17] The poem exposes this sometimes-ghostly presence in a haunting way. Did the event happen or not? Was it said or not? Certainly the many women who have stepped forward to speak of sexual abuse and violence that invariably takes place in private spaces can attest to the fact that what happened may be said to not have happened at all. Are the victims really victims if there is no blood in the halls? Clearly the poem underscores the everyday harm created by biases and discrimination. The pain and harm are very real, but we prefer to turn our gaze away to avoid seeing, hearing, and acknowledging them.

What would we do anyway? There is indeed much that we *can* do. We can refuse to silence ourselves, and thereby become accomplices with our tormentors. We start by simply bearing witness that this really happened, and then letting others know about this piece of reality. The poem accomplishes these: it acknowledges the reality of the experience, puts it into thought, and puts the thought into words in the form of a poem.

The poem speaks directly to the *alien other* in our presence. This presence, in particular, is made all the more present and powerful by splitting, projection, and transference. These psychodynamics and defenses help to explain how we come to experience the others as so threatening, bad, and despised that we are permitted to hate them and label them as despicable and undesirable. We deposit in these others many of our bad self-thoughts and feelings, leaving us feeling much purer (racially or otherwise) and justified in a self-righteous manner to discriminate against the others. This often includes their termination in both a figurative workplace sense (fired or laid off) and literally as in workplace violence and social violence with an end point of socially sanctioned genocide.

There are also other group-oriented defenses such as Bion's fight and flight group dynamic. Both of these groups are mobilized by excessive anxiety accompanied by strong emotions such as fear and rage. Fight and flight are fairly common in the workplace if one takes a good look. Flight often arises when one group or department does not wish to deal with another group or department. Organizational silos are a metaphor that speak to this sense of defensive group boundaries where others outside the silo are not welcome.[18]

Organizational fight takes many forms, such as attacking and undermining intra-organizational competitors who criticize, condemn, and try to remove or displace another group. These sometimes-interminable intergroup dynamics filled with aggression regularly yield organizational dysfunctions that detract from performance, but also often create an endless array of victimized individuals, some of whom are eventually eliminated from the field of combat.

Fight and flight dynamics are of course very often fueled by splitting and projection, and can become highly energized by transference of past traumas onto the present. Occasionally workplace mediation must be considered to permit two groups or their leaders to work through unresolved conflict or to work on a shared problem. Certainly, this is the case in the international area where wars and terrorism underscore the inability to avoid fight and flight.

There are also in the poem and story aspects of moving against others, where members of the "we" not only see the other as bad but themselves as good. Horney makes clear that this defensive response, paired with a sense of arrogance, promotes interpersonal aggression and violence, especially when harm to one's arrogant pride must be vindicated. At an extreme, anything may be risked in order to defend against the threat the partially self-constructed other represents.

The poem is a catalyst for reflecting on the darker side of the workplace, society, and human nature where *not me* and *not us* become an issue of personal, group, and national identity that contains many unconscious dynamics.[19] The alien other is in the poem and also resides in our daily lives.

D.A.W—Dead at Work

We have heard senior level executives say that massive organizational changes like restructuring, downsizing, selling off divisions, closing plants, and mergers had the effect of *cutting the heart out* of the organization. We have heard employees speak of themselves as the *working or walking dead, zombies* in their own work lives. Their leaders have gradually cut their hearts out, reducing them to simply showing up to receive a paycheck. They find they feel like they are rearranging the metaphoric deck chairs on the doomed *Titanic* or playing in the orchestra as the cold north Atlantic water begins to wash over their feet.

There is often much mourning of the many friends and colleagues lost in downsizing and restructuring—people their leaders and managers ordered them to forget. There is the ever-present question—"Will I be next?" A book the authors developed with two other colleagues' years ago on downsizing a hospital was, after being read by the acquisitions editor, tentatively titled *Death and Downsizing*.[20] He understood the real story of downsizing in this hospital. This working title, however, was not ultimately used in order to avoid putting two words together in a title—*death* and *hospital*. We therefore suggest we are not engaging in sensationalism when we title this section *Dead at Work*. Just as one can feel very much alive in a fulfilling workplace, one can also feel emotionally numb and lifeless in an emotionally deadening toxic organization.

The poems that follow help us to understand why feelings of death, dying, dead, walking dead, and even zombies are images that one can get in touch with under frightening and oppressive leadership styles.

Poor Aim

You kill me because
you died so long ago
and cannot bear
to see your living anywhere.

You keep killing me
because you know
you have not died enough
and still have many
deaths to go.

I commit the unbecoming sin
of reminding you
that you once lived.

I am the killed
who refused to die—
I am the living
where you still hide.

Discussion

The voice of the poem is that of the target of scapegoating. I have observed the behavior described in this poem both in the course of consulting with clients and groups, and in my own experience at work.

This poem is about a particular kind of *organizational scapegoat*. This scapegoat is the object of envy, often because he or she is especially creative and productive, out-performs others along a range from fellow employees to leaders, and embodies talents or virtues that others wish they possess as they pursue their own tasks and careers. The workplace superstars are a threat to others in many ways and must often be limited, maligned, and removed from the organization for the sake of all others.[21]

This envy differs from admiration in a fundamental way: admiration is constructive and encourages the other person, while envy tries to sabotage if not destroy the other person, to make it increasingly difficult for the targeted person to perform his or her role. The envious employee or leader says, in essence: "If I can't have what you have, I will do my utmost to take it away from you, to spoil and berate and destroy it." This envy is then fueled by fear and hate and a sense of inadequacy and shame.

Analysis

How very often do we hear a lot of criticism about others who are said to be by comparison to one's self inferior, inadequate, and unworthy of recognition and even employment? We may build ourselves up by tearing others down. We are in our minds better than this other who has been denigrated. This dynamic is all the more important when the other individual or group is noticeably better than I am or we are. There is a real threat to being out-performed and out-shined at work. Others receive raises and promotions we do not receive. Who will be the first to go in a downsizing?

This sense of threat can be unconsciously accentuated by our projecting onto the superstar(s) many of our best attributes, reducing us to an inferior comparative status. While this may seem paradoxical, the presence of a superstar on, say, an athletic team, is also comforting, and may relieve us of some responsibility for achieving high organizational performance ourselves. However, simultaneously we are envious and grow to fear and despise this "other," who is both very real and also inflated in our imagination. This "other," by comparison, possesses the qualities we wish we had but do not, in part because we split them off and projected them on this the superstar.

Karen Horney offers insight by providing us the notion of moving against others. In particular, those among us who possess an expansive sense of self that is often not entirely warranted by actual performance may more readily identify and feel threatened by others who are high-performing. This threatens the hard-to-defend excessive self-pride that is operating and often leads to arrogance. When this expansive solution to anxiety is punctured by the reality of a higher-performing other (or group), a tearing down and getting rid of this source of fantasy-puncturing reality is necessary and expressed in the form of vindictive triumph.

Depending on the individual or group who feels threatened, and the degree that their arrogant pride is injured, almost any measures might be considered, including measures that might ultimately lead to a self-destructive outcome. Vindication of arrogant pride may lead to, as in the contemporary expressions—"doubling down" or "getting even 5 times over."

Bion's notion of fight or flight also contributes insight. The individual who is threatened by the high-performing other is at some level in flight from the awareness that the other offers a threatening performance comparison as well as exposes one's own shortcomings—something to be avoided. At the same time the high-performing other may be targeted to limit and minimize the person's ability to achieve high performance to remove the sense of threat. And to be appreciated much of this may be acted out with conventional workplace behavior such as manipulating budgets and access to resources to undermine performance, making these toxic dynamics not particularly open to discussion.

Office and Theatre

> I watch my bright-lit office
> as I do *Richard III* and *Othello*
> in a darkened hall.
> I hold my breath—
> maybe this death can be averted.
> If only I could leap on stage,
> as with a therapist's flair,
> call "Stop! Do you not see
> where treachery heads?
> Can we not halt history,
> and with forgiveness,
> exit its thrall?"
> But no—where betrayal begets betrayal
> and obligation to avenge,
> no one heeds, or draws a curtain,
> till blood flows.
> "Justice! Innocence! Vengeance!"
> we cry, and cannot restrain ourselves.
> We say we only watch,
> but we also plot what we suffer.
> We sail the Ship Inexorable
> to its triumphant sinking.
> History is what consumes us;
> we applaud the play as we drown
> in the doom we contrive
> as we await.
> In this, our tragedy:

what we suffer,
we first wish;
the fate we curse,
we first rehearse.

Discussion

Although the experience related in this poem comes from a single organization with which I consulted over many years, it could have come from many others. This was the era of powerful, charismatic organizational "turn-around artists" such as Jack Welch, Albert Dunlap, Dennis Kozlowski, and Kenneth Lay. They were the leaders of dramatic restructuring and reengineering, magic-like downsizing, and outsourcing overseas—all promising to revitalize organizations in productivity, profitability, competitiveness, and shareholder value. For the long-term, these cult-like practices were often disastrous for the organization and for the people in them.

Sometimes as consultant I could only bear witness, compassionately listening to managers' and employees' stories, and affirm the simple human dignity of the people speaking. I could validate that what they experienced really happened—"You couldn't make this up." I have seen first-hand how toxic organizations self-destructed while harboring the delusion that all was well and that the company was creating stockholder value. I felt vulnerable and helpless like the members of the organization—counter-transference.

Analysis

This poem and discussion remind us that sometimes the light at the end of the tunnel really is a speeding train. For instance, Michael Hammer and James Champy in their 1993 book, *Reengineering the Corporation: A Manifesto for Business Revolution*, argued for rigorous redesign of business processes and for throwing out that which did not contribute to value. This, combined with downsizing as a strategy to create lean organizations, was a popular, supposedly winning strategy, in the 1990s.[22] This led to endless layoffs, often with the announcements timed to manipulate stock prices.

These common organizational dynamics and their accompanying fad-like fantasies led to an eventual realization that these were poorly conceived and even sadistic, where the missing bodies of the fallen had to be metaphorically stepped over by the greatly overworked survivors. One senior human resources professional who worked for a large organization that had been through multiple downsizing events spoke of the experience as "cutting the heart out of the organization."

There lies in this appreciation the *irrational* power of management fads, blindly followed in many instances to show that the CEO and others were in charge and being effective—looking good for that next bonus.[23] The level of organizational toxicity introduced by the use of these methods was noteworthy in terms of its breadth and depth of despair and degradation of organizational performance.[24] Indeed, it seemed to the survivors that the ship was going down or had gone down. All that was left were the life rafts and floating remnants of the organization—an organization leaned out to skin and bones and engineered to run more efficiently but perhaps not effectively.

The psychodynamics of a context like this are self-evident but are also so broad and complex that they defy ready discussion. Denial, splitting, and projection contribute to turning employees into wasteful organizational fat that has to be surgically removed via reengineering to improve productivity and reduce staffing ratios, and via the internal recombination of departments and operating units to eliminate layers of management and staff. Also to be considered are the psychodynamics of the leaders who adopt these toxic fads in the belief they were doing the right thing, following the recommendations of outside experts and, of course, looking good to their boards and stockholders/stakeholders for adopting the glitzy new fad.

What one comes to appreciate upon closer inspection is that often these organizational leaders are insecure and afraid that their inadequacies will be uncovered (flight from awareness or acceptance). In order to avoid this, defenses are deployed such as hiring outside experts, sometimes in large highly expensive numbers, and adopting management fads so these leaders will be seen as following contemporary management wisdom. In a sense, the CEO and senior management group might also be said to be in flight from being held accountable. These defenses accomplish this by introducing any number of possible scapegoats into the toxic dynamic. There is also present Horney's defense moving against others, who (in this case) may be disposed of out the back door.

In order to make the idea of announcing thousands of layoffs sound effective and boost stock values, organization leaders must steadfastly maintain their psychologically defensive levels of rationalization and denial. For example, one CEO expressed surprise to learn that hundreds of his employees had been rounded up by armed guards on a Friday morning and escorted to large room, carrying their possessions in a box conveniently brought by the guard. Upon their entering the room, the door was locked behind them. They were sent down a line of tables to have their termination processed by human resources staff, and they exited onto the parking lot, never to return.

The poem speaks to the harsh, almost fantasy-like, nature of executives who use management methods like this that create mass casualties and considerable collateral damage in terms of how the organization is able to operate after the event. The poem is bearing witness—yes, these events really happened in the 1990s and continue to happen today.

Songs and Dances of Death*

I will sing for you; I will dance for you—
songs and dances of death,
an ode to downsizing and reengineering.

Watch the black star
suck meaning from every soul.
until only *Muselmänner* are left to work here.
We call them the walking dead,
hired by the company for a wage,
but that is all. The rest is up to them;
no benefits: health, insurance, retirement.
These are of no account
to those who rule from the top floors
of a skyscraper in a city far away.

They are as good as steelworkers
a century ago in the factories,
incinerated by molten iron.
Let their families come
for the bodies and bury them.
Once they can no longer work,
of what use are they to the company?
They can be replaced by others
hungry for work.

Listen well to these hoarse-sung songs,
and watch carefully the dance
of these skeletons with only skin,
for there is no longer joy
in sound or movement,
only the monotonous clatter
of computer keyboards
and the stench of flesh
waiting to die. We are all
now special workers
destined for special handling.**

*a song cycle by Modeste Mussorgsky
**Sonderkommando* (SOKO) and *Sonderbehandlung* (SB) in the Nazi death camps

Discussion

This surreal poem was inspired by my hearing a performance of Modeste Mussorgsky's bleak song cycle, *Songs and Dances of Death*. Its implacably dark mood triggered memory of over three decades of "managed organizational change" that I witnessed and learned about from other people's stories, a social movement more than a mere economic policy, one that continues unabated today.

This relentless social movement haunted me. Its imagery and emotional devastation often intruded into my consciousness. Rather than taking downsizing, restructuring, reengineering, and outsourcing at face value as "normal," "good business sense," I felt them to be strangely irrational. My thoughts repeatedly vacillated between the past and present human destructiveness in toxic organizations and the Holocaust, which many people said it *felt like* to go through downsizing and restructuring. Seth's book title, *Death of the Spirit in the American Workplace*, also captures this soul-stripping destructiveness.[25] The poem echoes and parallels the experience of work and workplace throughout these decades.

Analysis

Applied poetry and music are art forms that offer aesthetic appreciation of the dark side of organizational life. Poetry is an art form in which human language is used for its aesthetic qualities. Music is an art form which uses sound as its medium. Both are evocative in nature, where thoughts and feelings spontaneously arise as described here. In particular, the creativity expressed in the poem arises within a psychological context of reverie and free association. Words arise, linked to remembrances, images, and emotions.

The poem encourages the reader to reflect on the horrific nature of the images and what must surely have been an experience of the workplace that contains traumatic elements—never to be forgotten, but also perhaps preferably suppressed out of awareness as preconscious content that is paradoxically both available and not available for recall. It is equally the case that some toxic workplace events are so hard to live with that their memory is put out of mind (suppressed), both for the person downsized out of a job, and for those who remain who are overwhelmed with the work left behind by the missing, and aware they too may have a target on their back. Anyone aspiring to do good quality work is left to despair, as too much work does not leave enough time to do anything well. We are left to wonder whether it may be the case that those who remain suffer a higher form of pain than those cast out on the street.

The affective landscape of the poem and story once again is a reminder of how easily others can be turned into useless objects to be disposed of. They are blamed, but more profoundly, they become objects created in mind to contain the distressing awareness of performance problems and the accompanying anxieties over what harm management will do next. They become labeled as the source of the problem because they are viewed as incompetent and marginal performers who have created the current problems. "They deserve what they get," one executive was heard to say. These executives may be thought of as being in flight from being held accountable and willing to fight back against any perceptions that they created the current problems by blaming vulnerable others. The idea of these executives as moving against others to defend their arrogant pride is an equal part of this toxic organizational dynamic.

The poem and related music selection are reminders that the workplace always contains the latent potential to harm those who work there. Turning away from this appreciation does not do justice to all those who have fallen before.

Reply to Adorno

> "To write poetry after Auschwitz is barbaric."
> Theodor Adorno, 1949[26]

After Auschwitz, I want to speak,
knowing that whatever I say,
it will not be enough to hold
the horror that threatens to break
every vessel it enters.
Still I try to find the words—
there must be some redeeming value
in trying, even if no word is enough.

The unspeakable must be spoken.
What happened must be given a voice
if only to say "This really happened,"
to allow to have happened,
what could not, should not, happen.
The horror haunts us until it can be uttered.
And sometimes even speech is not enough.

It is the trying that is enough,
that must be enough, because
it is all that we can do.
Words make it real: the poetry of atrocity
bears witness to the erasure
of all meaning and hope.

So many names for the slaughter:

Auschwitz, Cambodia,
Rwanda, Bosnia, Armenia,
can only become past
once we have allowed them
to be fully present.

Barbaric is to be silent,
to visit upon ourselves
a kind of killing once again.

Discussion

The applied poet is compelled to find a "language" or idiom that articulates and contains what traumatic organizational change feels like.
The great scholar and theoretician Theodor Adorno wrote shortly after
World War II that after the Holocaust—the systematic attempt to wipe
Jews from the face of the earth—to write poetry was morally repugnant.
I wondered the same about the linguistic sanitizing called "managed
organizational/social change." Yet I felt compelled, obligated, to write
applied poetry about organizational atrocity *in order to* bear witness to
what happened and was continuing to happen. Thus, for me, the paradox of Adorno's admonition: what *cannot* and *could not* and *must not*
be said in poetry, *must* be said—or at least the attempt made.[27] Poetry is
never a constant, a finished product, but is always striving to give voice
to experience.

"Reply to Adorno" takes off where *Songs and Dances of Death* leaves
off. Employees, managers, and leaders have often made reference to the
Holocaust when trying to convey to me in metaphor what downsizing,
restructuring, reengineering—*feel like*. I could not dismiss their metaphors as exaggerations and overblown. Anyone who has faced for years
the possibility of being terminated knows well this self-experience in
toxic organizations.

Analysis

The poem, while not explicitly about the workplace, is implicitly about
the workplace, where major events like downsizing, major layoffs, the
selling and reorganization of companies, and the internal redesign and
reengineering of departments and processes all create a dreadful sense of
confusion, loss, and fear. The loss of one's friends and working relationships is distressing. The loss of one's job, however, approaches in the
moment an existential threat to one's identity, meaning in life, self-worth,
roles outside of work, and especially family roles. These many threats,
fears, and losses tend to create psychological if not spiritual deadening.[28]

Organization members, when confronted with change like downsizing, often locate the Holocaust as a *metaphoric* representation of what often seems like a vast impersonal top-down set of imposed changes that relegate sometimes many thousands of employees to numbers on a page that is used to decide "this one stays, this one is terminated." We do not suggest equivalence, but rather that resemblance to general knowledge of the Holocaust does spontaneously arise in the hearts and minds of employees subjected to often never-ending rounds of downsizing, reengineering, and ever more drastic leaned-out processes and work groups.

The psychological nature of organizational changes like this is unmistakable. Employees are not viewed as people but rather as objects and human resources on a page that usually depicts their cost and not value to the organization. Denial, splitting, projection, and transference are all powerful elements of these dynamics. Employees are transformed into disposable objects, and those who impose these events are often viewed as unquestionably out of touch, uncaring, and even evil.

Bion's fight and flight group dynamic is clearly present. Top management may be observed to be fighting to save the organization that they perhaps first ran off the tracks, and also in flight from the responsibility of having inflicted so much harm on their employees. The employees may be observed to fight back against the changes in various ways—sometimes referred to as "organizational resistance to change." At the same time, they may be in flight from the unfolding events and unable to acknowledge and cope with the fear, anxiety, and pain involved in all the changes.

Karen Horney's perspective of moving away also contributes to understanding these workplace dynamics. Employees, when confronted by the distressing anxiety-ridden dynamics, may retreat from other people, management, and the organization itself, preferring to be just simply left alone to do their job. They do not want to have to acknowledge or deal with what is happening around them. It is too painful and threatening. Sometimes this is referred to as "taking shelter" in organizational foxholes that allow the incoming fire to pass overhead and to and "stay under the radar" to keep from being noticed. Movement against others, management, and what is happening is also present in the form of resistance to change. The notion of the Deep State is a contemporary example.

Resistance to change may take many forms, some of them ritualized and bureaucratic in nature, and some may be destructive, including crimes against property and others—"going postal." Movement toward would not seem to be available to many since the overall context is punishing and threatening. However, some employees will have this as a response as they try to curry favor with management by being highly conforming and even willing executioners of their policies (identification with the aggressor). To survive, anything may be tolerated.

In sum, dynamics in the workplace that lead organization members to associate them with genocide and war are not uncommon when it comes to downsizing, reengineering, and restructuring, where relationships may be changed or lost and employees disappeared from the workforce. Not acknowledging these events as traumatic, we suggest, is misguided.

Reflections

"O horror, horror, horror! Tongue nor heart/Cannot conceive nor name thee" (William Shakespeare, *Macbeth*, Act 2, Scene 3). *Horror* is hardly a word that comes immediately to mind in conjuring the "business-as-usual" façade of countless American workplaces since the early 1980s. Yet this chapter has offered portraits of organizational life that boil like a volcanic cauldron beneath the deceptively serene grass-and-snow-covered surface of a mountain.

We have explored what underlies the rational crust of much of organizational culture and revealed a psychosocial world ruled by psychological violence and dread. We wonder what stories—or poems—this evokes in the reader, who might well have work experiences similar to those described here and which are reawakened by the worlds of work portrayed here.

In Conclusion

In this chapter, we have evoked through applied poetry various dimensions of leadership and followership in contemporary American toxic workplace organizations. We have written from the perspectives of leaders, followers, and people who feel lost at work. Through immersion in toxic organizations, the poet was able to access the inner experience of leadership and its effects in organizational life. Applied poetry added new dimensions and new data to traditional methods of understanding leadership and its human consequences.

Further, *triangulation* of applied poetry, organizational stories, and psychodynamically informed analysis offers fresh insights into toxic workplaces and their leaders. Each perspective informs and complements the other to access the inner experience of leadership and followership in countless toxic American workplaces. This triangulation helps to illumine the dark side of what takes place in workplaces, where individual and group destructiveness and the structural organizational violence amplify each other in a downward spiral that ultimately degrades those who work.

From a focus on workplace leadership and followership, we turn to a ubiquitous expression of often ruthless leadership since the early 1980s: downsizing and its associated forms of "managed organizational change." Chapter 5 offers a far darker picture of downsizing than the commonly stated one of economic necessity.

Notes

1. Allcorn, S. & Stein, H.F. (2015). *The dysfunctional workplace: Theory, stories, and practice.* Columbia, MO: University of Missouri Press.
2. Allcorn, S. & Diamond, M. (1997). *Managing people during stressful times: The psychologically defensive workplace.* Westport, CT: Quorum Books; Diamond, M. (1993). *The unconscious life of organizations.* Westport, CT: Quorum Books; Diamond, M. (2017). *Discovering organizational identity.* Columbia, MO: University of Missouri Press; Schein, E. (1985). *Organizational culture and leadership.* San Francisco, CA: Jossey-Bass; Schein, E. (2010). *Organizational culture and leadership* (4th ed.). San Francisco, CA: Jossey-Bass; Czander, W. (1993). *The psychodynamics of work and organizations.* New York: Guilford Press.
3. Czander, W. (2012). *The death of the American corporation: The psychology of greed and destructiveness among CEOs and bankers.* Irvington, NY: William Czander.
4. Harvey, J. (1988). *The Abilene paradox.* San Francisco, CA: Jossey-Bass.
5. Diamond, M. & Allcorn, S. (1990). The Freudian factor. *Personnel Journal*, 69(3), 52–65.
6. McClean, B. & Elkind, P. (2003). *The smartest guys in the room: The amazing rise and scandalous fall of Enron.* New York: Portfolio.
7. Allcorn, S. & Stein, H.F. (2012). What me worry: Deregulation and Its discontents. In S. Long & B. Sievers (Eds.). *Towards a socioanalysis of money, finance and capitalism: Beneath the surface of the financial industry.* Oxford: Routledge, 2012. pp. 120–134.
8. Argyris, C. (1982). *Reasoning, learning and action: Individual and organizational.* San Francisco, CA: Jossey-Bass.
9. Stein, H.F. & Allcorn, S. (2011). The unreality behind the ideology of deregulation. *Psychology and Education*, 48(1–2), 1–15.
10. Diamond, M., Stein, H.F. & Allcorn, S. (2002). Organizational silos: Horizontal organizational fragmentation. *Journal for the Psychoanalysis of Culture & Society*, 7(2), 280–296.
11. Diamond, M., Stein, H.F. & Allcorn, S. (2002). Organizational silos: Horizontal organizational fragmentation. *Journal for the Psychoanalysis of Culture & Society*, 7(2), 280–296.
12. Allcorn, S. & Stein, H.F. (2015). *The dysfunctional workplace: Theory, stories, and practice.* Columbia, MO: University of Missouri Press.
13. Allcorn, S. (1991). *Workplace superstars in resistant organizations.* Westport, CT: Quorum Books.
14. Stein, H.F. (1998). *Euphemism, spin, and the crisis in organizational life.* Westport, CT: Quorum Books; Stein, H.F. (2001). *Nothing personal, just business: A guided journey into organizational darkness.* Westport, CT: Quorum Books.
15. Allcorn, S. (2002). *Death of the spirit in the American workplace.* Westport, CT: Quorum Books.
16. Stein, H.F. (1997). Death imagery and the experience of organizational downsizing: Or, Is your name on Schindler's list? *Administration and Society*, 29(2), May, 222–247.
17. Allcorn, S. (1991). *Workplace superstars in resistant organizations.* Westport, CT: Quorum Books.

18. Diamond, M., Stein, H.F. & Allcorn, S. (2002). Organizational silos: Horizontal organizational fragmentation. *Journal for the Psychoanalysis of Culture & Society*, 7(2), 280–296.
19. Diamond, M. (1993). *The unconscious life of organizations*. Westport, CT: Quorum Books; Diamond, M. (2017). *Discovering organizational identity*. Columbia, MO: University of Missouri Press; Volkan, V. (1997). *Blood lines: From ethnic pride to ethnic terrorism*. Boulder, CO: Westview Press.
20. Allcorn, S., Baum, H., Diamond, M. & Stein, H.F. (1996). *The human cost of a management failure: Organizational downsizing at general hospital*. Westport, CT: Quorum Books.
21. Allcorn, S. (1991). *Workplace superstars in resistant organizations*. Westport, CT: Quorum Books.
22. Hammer, M. & Champy, J. (1993). *Reengineering the corporation: A manifesto for business revolution*. New York: Harper Business.
23. Micklethwait, J. & Woolridge, A. (1996). *The witch doctors: Making sense of management gurus*. New York: Random House.
24. Allcorn, S., Baum, H., Diamond, M. & Stein, H.F. (1996). *The human cost of a management failure: Organizational downsizing at general hospital*. Westport, CT: Quorum Books.
25. Allcorn, S. (2002). *Death of the spirit in the American workplace*. Westport, CT: Quorum Books.
26. The Theodor Adorno quotation is from his famous 1949 essay. www.marcuse.org/herbert/people/adorno/AdornoPoetryAuschwitzQuote.htm
27. Stokes, P. & Gabriel, Y. (2010). Engaging with genocide: The challenge for organization and management studies. *Organization*, 17(4), 461–480.
28. Allcorn, S. (2002). *Death of the spirit in the American workplace*. Westport, CT: Quorum Books.

5 Downsizing the Workplace

For the past three-and-a-half decades, there have been massive disloca-tions in our public and private organizations that have stripped work-ers of their jobs and incomes that sustain their sense of worth and their families. Much of this change has been essential to remain competitive. We acknowledge that organizational change is essential to adjust an organization's structure, methods, and workforce to respond to internal and external opportunities and threats. Changing regulations, actions by competitors, and economic recessions make this essential. At other times, though, some of these changes direct our attention to CEOs desiring to look powerful and in control, as well as "making the numbers" look good at the end of a corporate quarter to improve value for stockholders. The nature of the timing and manner of announcement, we suggest, is often suspect.

Beyond the necessity and timing of change is the choice of the *methods* used to make these often sweeping if not desperate and drastic changes. Downsizing as a method of choice introduces highly destructive outcomes into the lives of their employees, families, and communities. Announcing a downsizing just before the end of a quarter can make the CEO appear to be in charge and taking control of the bottom line. However, there are other ways to adjust the size and nature of the workforce that are at least as effective—more gradual change that includes retraining and redistributing workers, as well as not making a grand announcement of downsizing that puts a target on everyone's back.

We also suggest that having to suddenly downsize is not an indication that management has been on the ball, making timely adjustments to keep the organization competitive, the workforce trained, and the organ-ization operating at a level consistent with demands for products and services. When downsizing is the *first* resort, it is clear that management is shifting the burden of their own poor performance onto the employees, who then suffer all manner of negative consequences.

There are then a range of reasons for rapidly adjusting staffing lev-els, some of which are reality-based and some of which are unreason-able.[1] The unreasonable ones, and the choice to use downsizing as a management tool, is to say that there are often *irrational* reasons for relying on these tumultuous changes that are presumably rational, reality-based business decisions. Downsizing and its often disastrous worker outcomes, when added to compromised organizational performance and research that often indicates that downsizing is ineffective, direct our attention to asking *why* some CEOs choose to downsize. It is not necessarily a *logical* first choice. Instead, it is one that often tears the organization apart, cutting its heart out, as one executive who survived a number of downsizings said.

Understanding some of the underlying psychodynamics of downsizing is essential to expose the darker side of the selection of downsizing as a management method for creating change, and it is equally important to making sense of how change is implemented—something the following poems attest to in terms of how destructive such implementation can be.

We now turn to exploring how our triangulation approach illuminates organizational downsizing and similar events and the experience of those subjected to them—the employees.

Invisible

> words for the pain
> unacknowledged by those
> who inflict it
> and by those lucky enough
> to have survived
> until the next wave:
> leaden words,
> wooden words,
> magical words
> recited like an incantation
>
> downsize
> rightsize
> RIF
> redundant
> restructure
> reengineer
> outsource
> offshore
> deskill
>
> people disposed of
> like trash for profit,
> not folks but figures,
> hopes and dreams,

livelihoods and worlds,
turned out into the street,
forgotten (Did they ever work here?),
sacrificed on the altar
of the Sacred Shrine
of the Bottom Line.

Discussion

This poem was not inspired by a single event, but from cumulative, converging events. Downsizing and reductions in force were on my mind every day as I contributed to a book on downsizing.[2] I was emotionally as well as intellectually immersed in this world of organizations, management decision-making, and downsizing that had begun thirty years earlier.

In addition, a more recent project brought back the memories and re-lived realities as both consultant and employee (transference).[3] I remembered how protectively steeled executives, managers, and employees were from having guilt, remorse, compassion, and shame over the loss of hundreds and thousands of fellow employees who had vanished. The co-workers were not only physically gone, they were put out of mind. They were *invisible*, the starting point of the poem. They were corporate sacrifices offered to preserve the "body" of the company.

The further questions become: What/who is the body of the company? Or the essence of the company? Or the soul of the company? The company-in-mind, so to speak, *that ultimately matters to decision-makers* is the creation of upper management, stockholders, trustee boards, corporate attorneys, etc. They "own" the corporation, both financially and psychologically.

Analysis

The poem makes clear that the word *downsizing* is not a word taken lightly by employees of any organization. Rumors of downsizing are often distressing if not terrifying largely because many people have already been through one or more downsizings or know someone who lost their job to downsizing. Downsizing also speaks directly to an enforced sense of helplessness and vulnerability on the part of the members of an organization. They know from experience that anyone at any time might be swept up for termination regardless of the value created by that employee. Furthermore, for those who have been through downsizing and survived, they know those who remain will have much more work to do. Everyone loses.

Downsizing is often driven by outside experts who analyze staffing patterns, productivity, and work processes with an eye on locating the least number of employees needed to still get the work done. It is a numbers game, and in the end employees and their futures are determined "by the numbers." Decisions are made top-down, and implementation is usually sudden, during which many and perhaps hundreds or thousands of employees are suddenly laid off.

The experience of these dynamics by management is most often insulated by the use of outside consultants, who specialize in these matters, and by somewhat sterilized reports and analyses that are reviewed and approved. The executives who are involved and make the decisions are in a good position to rationalize and intellectualize their actions, and of course they can claim they were only acting on the recommendations of the consultants. Object relations are also important, in that for some executives the soon- to-be-disposed-of workers ("organizational fat") are mentally transformed from people with their own lives to live into being the source of the organization's problems. They are turned into objects that can be disposed of, and these objects are manipulated in the mind via splitting and projection to become less than human. Sometimes heard is the notion, "They deserved what they got."

The employees on the receiving end of these dynamics readily come to feel like they have a target on their collective back and that they will be treated impersonally by the numbers. Some will be terminated and some will remain to work much harder to keep their jobs, at least temporarily. Words like *stress, trauma, anxiety*, and *depression* describe responses to organizational changes such as downsizing. Employees come to feel like the dehumanized objects that the reports, analyses, consultants, and management basically say they are. Their world of object relations becomes harsh and punishing. They are threatened by the world they have come to know. Their sense of themselves as valued human beings is diminished if not lost.

Feelings of fear, anger, and rage arise, and those in management become the focal point of employees' projection onto them of evil and malevolent attributes as well as perhaps of incompetence—after all weren't they responsible for creating the problem now being remediated at their extreme personal harm?

Bion's notion of fight and flight also helps to explain group dynamics where fear promotes a sense of flight and getting out of any organization that would do this to people.[4] Fear may also promote fight in terms of finding ways to resist the consultants and discredit the reports and analysis, as well as the recommended strategy of downsizing. Karen Horney's moving away from other (the appeal to freedom) and its wish to be just left alone, also contributes to understanding the wish of many employees to not be swept up in the changes.[5] Many just want to be left alone to work.

There are then many psychodynamic features to downsizing both in management and among employees that must be considered as part of downsizing or other major organizational changes. However, executives and consultants are seldom prepared to address these considerations other than providing temporary support and such things as outplacement.

Company Man

Fired ten thousand employees in the US,
hired five thousand people
in Asia, South America, and India,
away from family
three weeks a month.

Trained new workers
to do the job of two
for less pay than one,
taught them about bowing
and shaking hands,
eye contact and language—
and how not to insult each other.

Received promotions and bonuses,
a successful man, a corporate hero,
looked forward to retirement
and time with his family.

Let go without warning
in his thirtieth year
for someone half his age
who could do the job of two
for the price of one.

They told him:
nothing personal, just business,
collateral damage.

No gratitude,
forgotten,
a nobody—
as if he'd never been there.

Discussion

This poem was written when, like the previous poem, I was writing about ongoing traumatic organizational change. It felt like a juggernaut, a relentless monster that consumed and destroyed everything in its path.

I felt the all-pervasive vulnerability of everyone to its force. Ultimately, no one was safe. There was virtually no high ground to run to. Everyone felt imperiled by downsizing, restructuring, and outsourcing. Not only "rank and file" employees and managers were threatened, but also upper management and executives. No one was indispensable in this financial solution.

This poem considers the journey of a company executive from a position of seemingly insuperable power to the status of a discarded, unremembered nobody who "got what he deserved." The supreme leader who had axed thousands eventually fell under the axe of shareholders and the board of trustees for not making recent quarterly reports look better.

My emotions about this turn of fate ranged from glee at his comeuppance to compassion for his sudden fall from grace. Contempt vied with pity. I felt inspired and compelled to tell this story that has been played out countless times in American organizations for over three decades.

Analysis

The last line of the poem is striking—*as if he'd never been there*. Consultants to and employees of organizations that have been downsized know firsthand that this line strikes at the terror in the hearts and minds of management, employees, family members, and the larger community that is often degraded by major layoffs and plant closings creating the image of the "rust belt."

The psychodynamic nature of having *never been there* is in some ways horrifying. For those who remain who remember the friend in the next office or on the company softball team, there is the lingering image in one's mind, especially if contact with the person is entirely lost. How is she doing? Where did he end up? How is her family? How good was outplacement?

Eventually this object in mind gratefully fades. Missing the person changes from merely remembering the person to eventually little recall of the person at all. And to be noted, this process may happen rapidly due to high stress on the job for those who remain and the distress of remembering. What happened is simply not discussed after a week or two. Life goes on. It is also the case in some instances that this object is manipulated in one's mind to justify what happened. The lost employees may have "deserved" their fate for not working hard enough or not producing high quality work or for working in a marginal area that was more of a cost center than a revenue center.

Bion's notion of flight contributes to understanding why the now-missing employees are forgotten to the point that they might as well have *not been there*. It is just simply too distressing to remember, and what happened has left all those remaining with the fear that one day they will also have *never been there*. On a global political scale, this is reminiscent of people who have "disappeared" in Stalin's Soviet Union or the Argentinian "Dirty Wars" of the 1980s.

Those who are in fact *no longer there* have a deep sense of loss and even interrupted existence, accompanied by anxiety and not infrequently depression. They have lost their job, livelihood, job title, and sense of value as a contributing worker. They have lost their status relative to their family and, during the great recession, perhaps even their home. There is also the problem of explaining the infernal employment gap to possible new employers. The word *despair* comes to mind. Despair arises when hope for a better day is lost or hope that, by working, hard workers will be treated fairly—a fantasy linked to the old notion of the psychological contract between worker and employer—now *no longer there*.

All these psychological eventualities and a pervasive sense of loss must be coped with, by most often using psychological defense mechanisms such as denial and rationalization that, in turn, encourage reliance on splitting and projection. The former employing organization may be manipulated in one's mind as an object in ways that make what happened more tolerable. The company was perhaps incompetently led, not reinvesting in plant and equipment, and not supporting its loyal, now also *no-longer-there* employees. Others such as friends and family members may also be subjected to splitting and projection depending on the now *no-longer-there* individual. And certainly, fight and flight as well as dependency may all arise sometimes during the same day. Fighting back against these toxic organizational dynamics when they occur on a broad scale is not often possible. The sense of feeling like fighting back against the dynamics is very real, which is why many times employees are escorted by armed guards out of the building. Flight also contributes insight in that we often look away from harm to others and wish to avoid our self awareness when it is us. Just being left alone (moving away from others—the appeal to freedom) to sit on a park bench is then an appealing metaphoric respite from the stress, anxiety, fear, and threat of being discarded and becoming unemployed. It is equally demoralizing for the employee to come home and tell the family about the abrupt job loss.

Indeed, *as if he'd never been there*, is the last line of the poem but the first line in pondering life beyond nonexistence.

The Wrong Ending

> Rubbish is what he felt like—
> garbage wrapped in newspaper
> and taken out to the metal cans
> near the mail box.
> After thirty years of service
> fired without notice,

a company man his company disowned.
("Where did I go wrong?" he wondered.)
"Dead wood," "trim the fat,"
that's what the paper
said the next morning,
just one of three thousand let go,
all in the same day.
Thrown into the street—
Garbage!

Discussion

A recurrent theme in toxic organizations is the human toll from downsizing. Many terminated employees speak of a moral crisis when they are abruptly terminated. They turned the blame (for management actions) inward, just as executives projected the blame—and their guilt—outward onto employees. "*I* must have done something to bring this on myself," collides with "Those employees were never an asset to the company. *They* deserved to be fired for all the things they did to hurt the company."

The image of employees being tossed out onto the street is a haunting image that emerged in the late 1980s. People were treated literally as "human *resources*" to be used and used up, giving up their life energy. The storyline of what happened differed distressingly from the expected story of their lives. Now, it was the story of unimaginable, devastating, non-reciprocity, and betrayal. Loyalty and commitment mean nothing.

Analysis

What is it like to be escorted to a conference room or auditorium with your box of possessions and terminated all within an hour? What is it like to suddenly find yourself standing next to your car looking back on your former place of work? And what can conceivably be said to a spouse and children or one's parents and friends? Being laid off contains traumas of many kinds that affect the employee and everyone else, including those not laid off who must work harder, fear they are next, and experience survivors' guilt. All of this is hard to imagine but also readily imagined, given our twenty-first-century organizations. The intensity of the experience is palpable in the poem.

Objectification of those targeted for layoff seems almost essential for those making the decision to lay them off, sometimes by the thousands. Objectification also seems important for those who become the termination force who must handle all of the details. Throughout history there are endless examples of turning others into objects and other subhuman representations, opening the door to ruthless elimination. Layoffs may be thought of as leaving the body alive but killing the human spirit.[6] We have all become potential organizational fat that, once trimmed, is wrapped up in the paperwork of termination and placed at the curb for garbage pickup.

Group dynamics must also be considered, since often large numbers of employees are swept up for disposal, and groups of employees must handle the disposal process while everyone else is left to clean up after the departures. This requires doing more work, where doing it may magically lead to keeping one's job. Certainly, fight and flight are deeply embedded in these dynamics, where groups are essentially pitted against each other for survival. Consistent with fight and flight, Karen Horney's notion of moving against others is played out both in terms of the terminations and also in efforts to resist being terminated by doing more work. Fighting back actively (unionization) or passively (sick outs) can also be an option. What are they going to do? Fire you?

For many, movement away is also a valuable coping mechanism, from the perspective of avoiding eye contact with those being rounded up for termination or perhaps when meeting them at the nearby grocery store. What does one say to the dearly departed? Movement away may also help avoid one's being called on by management to make the ultimate sacrifice for the managers to keep their bonuses. There are many interpersonal, group, and organizational dynamics to consider when management orders the downsizing.

Downsizing

> People I worked with yesterday,
> Today are whisked away;
> No one asks where they go—
> Or even wants to know.
>
> There is no blood to show
> For their disappearance;
> They just are
> Not around anymore.
>
> The signs all
> Read the same—
> On the highways, in the stores,
> On the elevators, in the halls:
>
> What is happening
> Has not happened,
> And if it has,
> We do not want to know.

Discussion

This poem arose from my serving as consultant to help "humanize" an organizational downsizing of a workplace that employed thousands of people. This emotionally wrenching work and the experience of the downsizing influenced my writing two books on downsizing: *Euphemism, Spin, and the Crisis in Organizational Life* and *Nothing Personal, Just Business: A Guided Journey into Organizational Darkness.*[7]

This poem is a metered and rhyming poem. Its relentlessness parallels the human devastation I witnessed, and tried to soften, even if only slightly. Much of what I "did" as a consultant was to listen and bear witness to people's stories—those who were terminated, and those who survived, at least for a time—to try to help them process their overwhelming and crumbling reality. My lived experience was their disbelief and numbness. You could not make it up. For example, in one organization, the director of Human Resources asked upper management if pizza could be purchased so as to offer lunch to the people waiting in the long queues for final termination processing. The request was denied.

This experience of the harsh realities of downsizing, restructuring, and reengineering made vividly real the scope and depth of denial. Many people did not want to know what happened, all the while fearing that they had a target on their back and could be next to go. The brief poem evokes and affirms the fact that "this really happened."

Analysis

The poem and discussion yet again surface for inspection and "knowing" the devastating nature of downsizing and similar management actions. In this case, we are reminded that some things are too painful to see, witness, or remember. We must manipulate what happened in our mind to make it more bearable and more easily suppressed from consciousness. We must either not perceive what we see or look away (flight from awareness). In either case we are spared the distress of knowing a colleague has been abruptly and without warning laid off as well as many others. Perhaps it is important to do this to spare ourselves the realization that they first came for my friend and they may next come for me.

There is in this poem the appreciation that some of these abrupt and powerfully imposed organizational changes are so fantastic in nature that those who survive may not believe that what they experienced actually happened. The World War I notion of "shell shocked" comes to mind. Those who are left perhaps have a distant empty gaze in their eyes as they proceed to do ever more work, relying on the fantastic hope they will survive as an essential worker. These "essential" workers are left to cope by denying, rationalizing, and moving away from the leaders, their organization, and each other (alienation). They understand they are potentially disposable and no more important than a despised object in the minds of those in charge. Safety is perhaps available in flight from this toxic organizational life or at least from what happened.

We are aware of instances after events like these of what scholars call "revisionist history." Accordingly, what happened really did not happen. The revision is usually gradual, with some elements changed and recast to eventually arrive at perhaps the realization that what happened was actually good for those who were terminated as well as for those left with the work overloads. Denial and rationalization fuel outcomes like this as well as manipulate events and others-in-mind, thereby creating objects and events that are less distressing to know of. Those terminated are better off, even though there is no evidence to support believing this.

There is then to be appreciated how powerful mental manipulations can be in terms of altering others and events as remembered or recorded. The flight from distressing awareness is a powerful motivation.

Where Is the Blood?

> Night at corporate headquarters—
> The four of us who studied the company's downsizing
> Walk silently through a long, dim-lit,
> Blank, cream-painted corridor,
> A place where phantoms dwell and wait,
> A place where walls seem to close in on us.
> We all look around,
> As if we are looking for something.
> After about twenty paces into this antiseptic cave,
> I ask aloud, "Where is the blood?"—
> My three friends say they were thinking
> The same thing.
>
> A consultant team, all in black suits,
> Had recently studied the financial books
> And recommended to the CEO
> That they could save lots of money
> And make the company look good to shareholders
> By firing a thousand employees immediately—for starters.
> "Mandatory downsizing to keep the company alive,"
> "A necessary sacrifice for the sake of the company,"
> The leader said to those gathered
> In a locked auditorium before they were ordered to stand
> In long queues to people-process
> Impersonally, efficiently, in a well-oiled machine,
> And finally escorted to the parking lot, never to return.

The four of us knew the story,
See it unfold before us again
In that cavern, as we walk and relive it.
The walls and carpet bleed,
Cover our shoes and clothes
In still-warm, thick, crimson blood,
Like in a horror movie.
The story hovers in the air;
Its ghost will not leave.
It speaks to us with great sadness;
Even the ghost could not rid itself of the memory,
Could not abandon the prison of knowing too much.
The four of us look at each other,
The story alive in all of us.

Bathed in fresh blood, we leave the building
And re-enter the night,
Carrying the hall's darkness with us.
We had been through the mass firing
Even before it happened.
We knew too much—
The blood will not wash off,
Not now, maybe never.

Discussion

This narrative poem tells the story of a downsizing that was extensively documented in the writing of a book on downsizing.[8] This book is a "case book" that spans a year in the lives of one major urban hospital's employees during a consultant-driven downsizing. The study consisted of interviews with more than 20 managers and staff every four months for a year. The work on the book was distressing, emotionally taxing, and confusing. It was stressful. The research on the book concluded with a meeting in the city where the hospital was located. The four co-authors visited the hospital. As we walked through the hospital's halls, I could feel myself walking back into—reliving—the stories of trauma within the book manuscript. The poem is both testimony and memorial. Far more than I realized, it captures my experience of a reawakening in me of the horror documented in the longitudinal case book.

Analysis

This poem reminds us that researchers, authors, and outsiders are not immune to feeling as though there might be blood on their hands even though they are merely bearing witness and documenting events. Turning others into disposable organizational fat and then moving against them leaves inescapable history. When the reality of these types of organizational change are fully embraced—the magnitude of the suffering imposed by downsizing, often facilitated by consultants who specialize in downsizing—we are left to feel invaded by our awareness and left to track the blood on our shoes through our consciousness. Identification, compassion, and empathy go a long way to account for what happens to the inner life of organizational researchers when they encounter the full implications of downsizing.

For the researchers in the poem, much had to be imagined as they walked in the dark hallways, although they also knew much of what happened from their work on the case book. Also to be appreciated is that as the years pass, the employees in their memories retain a sense of the vulnerability and harm created by institutionalized organizational violence. It remains available in memory to be transferred onto the present when the present resembles the past. Unconscious transference changes experience of the present that in turn stands in the dark shadow of the past. Splitting and projection also arise when executives speak of downsizing or massive organizational change. The reactions can be extreme at times. The carnage of the past is readily located as a possibility in the present. All the accompanying memories, pain, and suffering arrive in the moment largely intact, powerfully changing one's reality.

We wish to add that friends and families of those who are downsized out of jobs, sometimes more than once, also have in mind the "blood" that forever stains their soul.[9] The presence of the threat and pain of downsizing a friend or loved one may have readily evokes in one's mind the possibility of it happening again. And much the same can be said for communities where events like this create massive dislocations in the social fabric and economy.

The harm we suggest is enduring, never entirely forgotten, sometimes reimagined to reduce its distressing nature, but always readily recoverable in the form of transference that can fuel splitting and projection, creating a past reality in the present. There is then no ready exit strategy from this experience. Flight from the experience is not entirely possible if at all possible. Denial and rationalization, revisionist memory and history, and moving away from the events and memory may not be adequate—there may be no easy psychologically defensive response to cope with what happens in a major downsizing.

Downsizing the Company, or, the Perfect Bureaucrat

how
on so emerald
a planet,
to make the perfect hell?

heed the words
of a perfect bureaucrat
to awaiting
clientele.

"your papers are in
order, but
not valid anymore.
I am the final
recourse—
no options to
explore."

he pauses,
then says with studied
precision,
without so much
as a hint of
derision:

"as rules go,
there is but one
thing more:
have your papers
stamped just outside
my office
door.

"you have long
served us well;
your ultimate distinction
is to preserve us now
with your immediate
extinction."

Discussion

This poem is a surreal fantasy about widespread organizational life. It is about my observation of managers and leaders hiding their sadistic pleasure at disposing of people behind bureaucratic and business protocol—nothing personal, just business. It is about the summary cancellation of the "psychological contract" between employers and employees, which had assured job security and a comfortable future retirement in exchange for hard work and company loyalty.

In the poem, the "perfect bureaucrat" symbolically tears up the contract in front of the employee as he fires him (or her). The terminated employee becomes the organizational sacrifice, a kind of business-style burnt offering on the altar of the sacred shrine of the bottom line, which supposedly preserves the company. No matter how well one had his or her papers in order (Jews in Nazi Germany and immigrants throughout the world), the paperwork might suddenly mean nothing to the employer, who no longer feels morally bound to abide by them. Is our validity as a human being dependent on our papers? The poem was inspired by the echo chamber in which dwelled my organizational experiences as consultant and employee, and my personal cultural history—and it resonates with recent events at the southern border of the United States.

Analysis

The notion of having to have the right papers or documents is of course a recurrent theme in the early twenty-first century when it comes to "undocumented workers" who are "illegally" here in the U.S. They are not infrequently swept up at work by federal immigration enforcement authorities, temporarily creating a shortfall in employees to do their work in slaughterhouses, orchards, and fields. They join all the other potentially disposable human resources in their acute personal and often familial vulnerability.

The commonly accepted sense of a psychological contract that secured employees their jobs if they worked hard and made their employer successful and profitable fell by the wayside as downsizing, restructuring, mergers, and similar events tore up the contract. Workers were relegated to disposability no matter how much they contributed to the well-being of their organization. Object relations theory helps us to understand how once-valuable workers are turned into disposable human resources to reduce costs, improve profits, and increase stockholder value.

The stamping of employees' paperwork literally or figuratively has been around for as long as stamps, often royal, have existed—thousands of years. The stamp is a symbol of power over others, often wielded by petty bureaucrats on behalf of powerful authority figures. We were told a short story by a woman with a stamp (signature power) about layoffs. She said, "I will be the last one out the door because I have to approve all the termination forms." This is a painful but true insight. It also highlights the impersonality that is created in order to do this work of laying-off people who will have their lives interrupted, if not permanently changed.

We understand that stamping of the paper is by extension a stamping down of one's life at work and outside of work. Those who are laid off are relegated to numbers, paperwork, and a problem to be managed by processing. For the many involved it is truly the case, "this is not personal, it is just business as usual." People are turned into objects that are disposable, and the people who wield the stamps are sometimes turned into hateful others in the minds of those who are being terminated. Everyone loses by becoming objects. Splitting and projection can fuel these dynamics. Transference from previous negative experiences of being depersonalized and treated like a sheet of paper arises to make the moment one filled with powerful emotions and accompanying psychological defenses.

The imagery in the poem also reminds us how in many ways threatening and disgusting routine business processes can become, depending on their purpose. It is not unreasonable to understand that for many, flight from these impersonal dimensions is a way to cope with their presence. Fighting back often seems impossible and even inappropriate because the impersonal system of paperwork and stamping is simply a manifestation of conducting business as usual. It is also the case that downsizing strips away any notion of movement toward others (dependency and the appeal to love) that Karen Horney describes. To be considered, then, is the dynamic of moving away from others and the appeal to freedom. Once the employee is out the door, he or she is freed from the oppressive, threatening dark forces of the organization.

The Box

> without warning the security guard
> appeared in his office
> handed him an empty *box*
> ordered him to put
> all his personal belongs in it
> and accompany the guard
> to an auditorium for special processing
> he was dazed but followed the command
> after all the guard carried a gun
> he quickly gathered his things in the *box*
> and followed the guard
> into the auditorium with many others
> the guard locked the door behind him
> the CEO entered and announced
> that the company had a financial crisis
> and had to downsize five thousand
> employees immediately
> the guard returned and ordered him
> to bring his *box* to the long queue with everyone else
> turn in his keys and badge and parking card
> and everything else that belonged to the company

he brought his *box* clung to it
the guard escorted him to the parking lot
and to his car told him that he would
receive his final paycheck in the mail
in a couple of weeks and that he was
to leave and not return to the company
he held his *box* all the more tightly
sat in his car with his *box* on his lap
for several minutes before
starting the engine
drove all over town
with his *box* all that remained
of his twenty-five years with the company
once he arrived home he sat in his
car with his *box* in his hands
he did not get out of his car
for a very long time unsure
whether he was alive or dead
he felt unreal alone with his *box*
the only thing in his life
that felt real now
a coffin of sorts
what would his wife and children say
what would they think of the *box*
what would they think of *him*

Discussion

This poem was inspired in part by an informal consultation with a client. She told me the story of her workplace downsizing, in which employees to be terminated were handed a box by a security officer, who instructed the employee to put all his or her personal belongings in the box and to proceed without explanation to an auditorium.

The poem gives an account of a mass termination, an event repeated thousands of times since the 1980s. The focus and protagonist of the poem is the box itself and the box-as-metaphor. For me the anthropomorphized, personified box became an almost living character. I imagined this entire, surreal process as seen through the "eyes" of the box. What was rationalized as a business decision was to me *unreal*.

In the poem, I share my sense of the bizarre, the ghoulish, the irrationality of a process that was supposed to be rational, objective, and necessary. The poem is about ritualized death and death of the spirit—the eerie feeling that something horrible is taking place, masked by a façade of business-as-usual.[10]

Analysis

The poem provides us a very real sense of the dread and finality of how many layoffs are handled. Once-valued and productive executives, managers, and staff are suddenly turned into useless human waste. The organization disposes of them as easily as possible and often without much thought, and certainly without acknowledging feelings associated with years of devoted work being suddenly devalued. Employees discover they can indeed get their entire life at work inside of a file or copy machine paper box. This is of course a stunning revelation. Sometimes it is all they are allowed to have.

The box in the poem takes on a life of its own, becoming a container for one's life at work—a *coffin*. The coffin speaks to what Thomas Ogden refers to as "autistic-contiguous" experience, in that the sides of the box, because they are simply there to touch, become a life- reaffirming surface.[11] I still exist because it exists. It is in a sense held for comfort and reassurance that I am still here, and there is the sense it contains now my former life at work.

The existence of the box is magnified by our projecting all manner of experience onto and into the box. Feelings may also freely flow. The box may be thought as a container for life experience. We place our life at work into it, along with perhaps our fear, anxiety, anger, and rage. It must be strong enough to contain all this work of the mind. We hope it will hold together—and hold us together—in the face of psychic fragmentation.

The box as an object in mind becomes the container of many thoughts and feelings and one's life history at work. Clearly to also be appreciated is the very real sense of flight from what is happening and the inability to resist or fight against what is happening. Dependency on the organization, one's job, and compensation is entirely lost. There is a loss of hope as the organization's leaders move against these vulnerable employees and their boxes. Movement away from this experience and the organization follows termination. The experience is likely too hard to adequately process anytime soon. Moving toward family and community is the only comfort left.

Reflections

What more can be said of the poems and downsizing and plant closures that has not already been said? Ultimately the use of downsizing and other management methods that intentionally create the devastation described in the poems remains in the twenty-first century an omnipresent feature of how CEOs and consulting firms approach their notion of business as usual. The lasting harm that is done often exceeds any temporary gains. These events are never lost to organizational memory, although they may become changed and mythologized. The poems encourage the reader to recover memories of similar events imposed on oneself or others. Finally, we have emphasized that downsizing is not merely a bureaucratic exercise of processing an individual employee's termination, but rather it is also an organizational event that traumatically affects families and communities.

In Conclusion

It is little wonder that downsizing—and its cognate manifestations such as reduction-in-force, restructuring, reengineering, deskilling, outsourcing, and off-shoring—has generated so many poems and has merited a chapter of its own. The magnitude of its human destruction is incalculable. For over three-and-a-half decades downsizing has dominated American workplace life, and its cultural tidal waves have left virtually no corner of society untouched. It has left in its wake constant, relentless, and traumatic organizational change that has devastated millions of individual lives, families, workplaces, communities, and has even left its mark on politics. The poetry has served as an instrument for getting to the heart of darkness of downsizing.

In this chapter, we have explored the experience of downsizing through poetry, workplace experiences that found expression in poems, and psychodynamic interpretation that helps us to understand the "why" of downsizing's toll. This chapter's journey has confirmed that unconsciously based irrationality often drives organizational leaders, managers, and employees alike. Poetry's "findings" (data) give the lie to the official cultural doctrine that workplaces are governed by reason, reality, objectivity, productivity, and profit. Paradoxically, we have shown that psychological terror and terrorism have long characterized workplaces by Americans from within our own boundaries.

In Chapter 6 we turn our attention to an equally dark side of organizational life—that of alienation from self, others, and one's work, created by hierarchical bureaucratic structures. Through poetry we evoke the experience of disappearance of self. The poems offer a stark contrast to the official ideology of bureaucratic rationality.

Notes

1. Allcorn, S., Baum, H., Diamond, M. & Stein, H.F. (1996). *The human cost of a management failure: Organizational downsizing at general hospital.* Westport, CT: Quorum Books.
2. Allcorn, S., Baum, H., Diamond, M. & Stein, H.F. (1996). *The human cost of a management failure: Organizational downsizing at general hospital.* Westport, CT: Quorum Books.
3. Allcorn, S. (2002). *Death of the spirit in the American workplace.* Westport, CT: Quorum Books.

4. Bion, W. (1961). *Experiences in groups.* London: Tavistock.
5. Horney, K. (1950). *Neurosis and human growth.* New York: Norton.
6. Allcorn, S., Baum, H., Diamond, M. & Stein, H.F. (1996). *The human cost of a management failure: Organizational downsizing at general hospital.* Westport, CT: Quorum Books.
7. Allcorn, S., Baum, H., Diamond, M. & Stein, H.F. (1996). *The human cost of a management failure: Organizational downsizing at general hospital.* Westport, CT: Quorum Books; Stein, H.F. (1998). *Euphemism, spin, and the crisis in organizational life.* Westport, CT: Quorum Books.
8. Allcorn, S., Baum, H., Diamond, M. & Stein, H.F. (1996). *The human cost of a management failure: Organizational downsizing at general hospital.* Westport, CT: Quorum Books.
9. Stein, H.F. (2001). *Nothing personal, just business.* Westport, CT: Quorum Books.
10. Allcorn, S. (2002). *Death of the spirit in the American workplace.* Westport, CT: Quorum Books.
11. Ogden, T. (1989). *The primitive edge of experience.* Northvale, NJ: Jason Aronson.

6 Alienation and Bureaucracy at Work

We, our lives, our work and labor, and our workplaces provide us meaning, sustenance, and purpose, but often not without exacting great cost from our lives and our experience of the workplace and the organization we work for. It is this fact of life that we wish to focus on in this chapter. We as authors, employees, and organizational consultants know this reality deeply, painfully, and speak of it with considerable trepidation. We have not escaped the oppressive, demanding, irrational, and soul-stripping nature of working in twenty-first century large hierarchical and inevitably bureaucratic organizations. Bureaucracies are social structures, and by being human social constructs, our organizations contain unconscious and intersubjective building blocks.

The poems that follow are based on actual organizational events that happened often to the authors in various workplaces. They are described of course with a tincture of poetic license. One of the most difficult facets of the poems for the writer is how bizarre they sound, based on stories that you could not make up, yet how "normal" and ordinary they were for the workplace. Our task is to *make the bizarre familiar and recognize that much of the familiar is indeed bizarre.*

The poems and the events they describe become metaphors for much larger, mostly inexpressible, stories. They belie organizational secrets that everyone knows but cannot, must not, speak about. They speak not only to alienation in the bureaucratic workplace, but also alienation from oneself. It is terrible enough to be treated as a stranger by others in the workplace and anywhere else; it is far worse to have taken that stranger into oneself, becoming estranged from oneself. The poems offer insight into becoming lost to others, the workplace, and ourselves. They are the proverbial canary in the coal mine.

The Routing Slip: How Things Work Around Here

Dear Mr. Stein,
This is the Department of
How Things Work Around Here.

Although your poem was accepted
for publication by our journal,
and you signed the contract,
you still must fill out
our routing form, then
walk it through the many offices
of people who must
also sign it in order for it
to be institutionally validated.
You will note on the routing slip
all the places you must trudge
in sequence, and have
all the officers sign it
by tomorrow. This will not
be an easy task, but
think of it as following
William Stafford's "golden thread"
to an outcome that can never
be known at the outset
of the journey. Still,
you must try if you want
to have your poem published
in our fine journal.
Good luck!

Discussion

The events described in the humorous and ironic poem really happened—
amplified with poetic license. The poem is about an encounter with a
bureaucracy about a poem that had been accepted for publication in a
journal. By the end of my phone conversation with a very polite woman
permissions officer, I was at once frustrated, amazed, astounded, alienated, and incredulous that this conversation even took place. The experience was at once humorous and exasperating. Given the phantasmagoric
machination of bureaucracies that Franz Kafka and Max Weber made
famous, I should not have been surprised.

It seems that there is nothing too small for a bureaucracy to not try to
control. The accepted poem is precisely 131 words long. Not exactly a
shipment of rolled steel or pipe. "Bureaucratic overkill" is a phrase that
applies here. Nothing, apparently, is beyond the red tape's stranglehold
on getting things done. It is as if the bureaucracy lives for its own red
tape—which, like a machine out of control, takes on a life of its own.

"You could not make this up" is a thought that comes to mind. I was
afraid to ask the obvious question, "Why?" for fear of being given the
standard reply: "That's the way we do things around here." Or "We've

always done it that way," or "We don't ask that question." When a thirsty Primo Levi, a newly arrived inmate of the Auschwitz concentration camp, pulled off an icicle from above a window, a guard snatched it from his hand. When Levi asked him the question, "*Warum?*" ("Why?"), the guard replied, "*Heir is kein Warum.*" ("Here there is no why.")

In organizations, perhaps the answer to "Why?" is buried in some unremembered historical trauma, such as a costly lawsuit, a disastrous executive decision, or a downturn in profit. No one knows, or even seems to care about why we are doing it this way. The rule simply must be enforced, and unquestionably so. Obsessive-compulsive routine is equal to or surpasses achieving actual work in urgency. Rigid compliance takes on mythic, totemic, even sacred proportions. No one dares question it. The consequences—from being reprimanded, to being considered crazy, even to being fired—are too unthinkable.

Still, there are a few noble exceptions: courageous contrarians who call the whole matter into question and live to tell the story and maybe even change "the way we do things around here." At the same time, however, they sometimes pay a terrible price for their audacity, madness, and termination being chief among them.

Let me offer a brief story about encountering bureaucracy and creating change. A family medicine resident (trainee) in a large city's training program sometimes consulted with me about patients with whom he was having difficulties. One day he approached me about his indigent patients for whom he had tried in vain to link with services at the local Department of Human Services (DHS).

He said that when he phoned DHS, or when one of his patients did so, they ended up being shunted from one office to another or put on terminal hold. Rarely were they connected with the service the doctor recommended. What could I do? How could I help? I said that perhaps if he went to DHS and spent some time with them, he would learn more about the organization and meet the people on the other the end of a phone line. During his days of "fieldwork" there, he spoke with many people, some of whom referred him to speak with yet other people. He asked questions about how things worked. What was it like to work at DHS? How should physicians go about getting services for patients?

He was finally told about "the little man who had the Blue Book." *He* knew the rules-behind-the-rules and knew how to make things work. Virtually no one on the outside of DHS knew of his existence. DHS people between him and the outside world protected him by serving as a barrier to keep people from getting to him. The doctor was able to visit with this administrator in his small office. He learned that the famous Blue Book referred to a policies and procedures manual which the administrator knew a lot about, including how to get around official rules.

The doctor explained that he was there to learn how DHS worked and to figure out a way that he could better help his patients get the services they needed. Could he help him? Surprisingly the administrator was friendly and brainstormed with him a way to solve access problems. He also acknowledged that the system was cumbersome and that many physicians encountered problems helping their patients. The physician left with a new approach that would lead to better outcomes for his patients. His visit to learn about how things worked also generated an unintended outcome. It opened up a number of possibilities for improved future communications between the agency staff and community's physicians. The doctor had become an agent of culture change. He learned that by getting to know organizations from the inside out positive change was possible for everyone. Although my vignette has a "happy ending" (the achievement of greater organizational functionality and improved patient care), most of the time such success is elusive, and bureaucracies remain bogged down with their sacred rituals of red tape. Organizational change to improve performance often seems unfortunately optional.

Analysis

Who among us welcomes the opportunity to deal with a large bureaucratic organization? Since this is a rhetorical question, we will answer it—only those who must, and they must then grin and bear it. The Department of Motor Vehicles comes to mind, but then again, your local utilities providers or cable TV guy also comes to mind. The poem speaks to institutional validation from the perspective that, if you are not under "their" control, you may not exist at all.

The intensity of the complexity and layers of carefully organized (or not) screenings, form completions, and approvals described in the poem and the story are likely familiar to our readers. We are turned into small children all too often hoping we have brought the right papers and forms and progressed through the system in the right sequence. "Do as you are told." There is in this appreciation of the enforced dependency Karen Horney describes. We are all helpless and infantilized when confronted with a system that treats everyone like a number. We are turned into objects that preferably do not think too much or feel too much. We must simply "do or die." The dehumanizing system requires dehumanized others who are dependent on it. Our sense of our own competence (or personal agency) is split off from us, leaving us feeling less than capable relative to what we hope is a competent system.

The clerk behind the counter is also turned into a thing in our minds, a bureaucrat, who receives many of our worst projections and the accompanying transference. We may hate the person immediately, even before we approach the issue of our dependency on institutional validation. We may really want to fight back but, unless we are willing to persist, we may never find the person who holds the knowledge of the little blue book of policies and procedures. The indifferent or possibly malevolent gate keeper who holds the keys to successfully navigating the bureaucracy, whose image we have created by splitting and projection, may, upon our getting to know the person, not be so evil after all.

Progressively

> For the longest time,
> they only told me
> my computer was incompatible
> with the network,
> later with the printer,
> then with e-mail,
> soon with my own
> floppy disk drive
> so I could not
> save even to myself
>
> which was why
> I felt isolated but was told
> I wasn't, I shouldn't, how dare I,
> weren't they trying?
> Until they gave me notice,
> without explanation,
> a dash of regret hand-written
> On their pink-slipped "*Juden raus!*" ["Jews, get out!"],
> saying only that "You are
> in violation of the law."
>
> It was pointless for me
> to inquire into particulars,
> since they were the law.
> When I pointed out
> their negligence and flaw,
> they would only repeat
> their refrain: "You are
> In violation of the law."
>
> When, for the last time,
> I walked out the door,
> I knew their equipment
> had finally been fixed.

Discussion

This poem comes from an inhospitable workplace. The equipment (computers, monitors, printers) that was provided to do my work—the organization's work—consisted of the discarded office equipment that others had had before they were upgraded. Although I was good at my job, obstacles were thrown in my path, making it difficult to complete tasks. Even though the equipment clearly had operating problems, no efforts were made to repair it. Nor was it ever agreed that it should be replaced.

When I inquired as to why I did not have state-of-the-art technology, I was usually given doleful replies such as that the organization lacked sufficient funds for upgrades or that I had to wait my turn, even if it took years. It was obvious to me that money was not the issue. The organization leaders and managers put their money into what they valued, and that was not me or my work. I had to rely on informal channels to get help—such as a sympathetic informational technology person to assist with software problems or an offer by a manager outside my unit who had a secretary who would help prepare a manuscript.

Eventually I realized that there was a pattern to this exclusion. Technology became for me a *metaphor* of my outsiderness. I did not feel treated as if I was an accepted member of the organization. What law or rule had I violated? What had I done? I felt excluded, punished, and unwanted. My antiquated technology made me feel that my work and my contributions were not valued.

The workplace came to feel like a Kafka-esque bureaucratic world in which I was trapped. Finding another similar job was not likely. I rationalized that I had at least carved out a niche for myself even though I felt isolated, unwanted, and emotionally dead. I wrote the poem to give form to my experience of this alienation, allowing me to place it safely outside me. I felt a little less poisoned by the organizational toxicity. Alienation was my constant companion, and it is not yet finished with me.

Analysis

The nearly inoperable computer speaks to disposability. The computer and other equipment were hand-me-down equipment that might otherwise have been disposed of for missing parts and software. Why is a high performing colleague marginalized to the point of not being able to be productive? One possible way to understand this is envy.[1] Employees who might be described as superstars often evoke not only envy but also a very real sense of threat, in that by comparison, others are less worthy, intelligent, knowledgeable, capable, and valued. The paradox is that these individuals who make substantial contributions to organizational performance ("rate busters" in old union parlance) are limited and maligned, often seemingly being pointed to the door to leave. They may find themselves subjected to all manner of discomfort, seemingly without much thought or conscience on the part of others. They become disposable and cast metaphorically upon the same junk pile as old equipment.

Outcomes like this are enabled by splitting and projection that turn this threatening and even alien other into an object worthy of being neglected and even scheduled for disposal. The poem also speaks to the "object" created in the mind of the poet of others who were withholding and malevolent. There is then an unconscious contract between the victim and victimizers that becomes standard operating procedure. How very often the only reasonable response is to become an emigrant, leaving the organization in a conceptual exodus. Flight and the appeal to freedom are very real, strongly felt options and psychological defenses.

Departure speaks to Bion's notion of fight and flight. Having failed to effectively resist and overcome this offensive and limiting personal dynamic, one's flight from others, one's job and work, and the organization often seems to be a viable response, especially if the disposable other wishes to maintain personal integrity. Much the same can be said of Karen Horney's notions of moving against and away from others. In particular, this relatively punishing interpersonal world at work (movement against) encourages moving away from others and seeking to be just left alone to do one's work. Fighting back and moving against others vindictively is most often not a good option for someone who is being marginalized by the group, and where resistance becomes a self-fulfilling prophecy of rejection.

Alienation from others, self, one's work, and the organization are words that explain the underlying essence of the poem. They are words that we suggest may well resonate with many workers in our modern society and workplaces.

New Regulation and a Worker's Reply

> Company policy has changed:
> as a cost-cutting measure,
> coffee is no longer free—
> a quarter a cup
> is still a good bargain
> to me.
>
> Your coffee is poisoned
> with the indifference
> of this place.
> Why would I want
> to raise its mug
> to my face?

Discussion

During a period of financial downturn, the company for which I worked undertook an austerity program. One of its measures consisted of charging for coffee rather than continuing to offer it for free to employees.

Although the company continued to pay for expensive items and trips for its leaders, many of its cost-cutting measures impacted everyone, such as turning down the thermostat in the winter and charging employees for coffee. The quality of life at work was targeted.

I realized that coffee was not only about a concrete commodity called "coffee," but was also a *symbol* (metaphor) of employer-employee relationships. The cost reduction measures made most employees feel devalued, taken for granted, and more like a human resource cost to be managed. Many responded by not purchasing company coffee. Instead some brought to work their own coffee makers, ground coffee, and condiments. This ironically took up more employee time and used more electricity in the long run! In some subtle ways, it was a rebellion against top down power.

Analysis

Rebellion rings true and so do unintended consequences as well as double standards. Top-down management decisions often suffer from these types of outcomes. Cost cutting to improve the bottom line by reducing expenses is usually the preferred management strategy when it comes to dealing with financial stresses and strains. Ironically these cost-cutting responses are often themselves, at least in part, the result of marginal management. The people responsible for creating the financial distress are the same ones making decisions to charge for coffee, turn down thermostats (more electric personal heaters), crowd more employees into a space, purchase or lease cheap and often unreliable equipment—to list but some of the strategies. What sense does it make to remove satellite coffee stations in a large building, forcing employees to walk a long distance to where the free coffee is located?

Object relations theory sheds some light on organizational dynamics like this. Executives who make a lot of top-down decisions are also often somewhat detached from the workers and the realities "on the ground." They think they simply know more than the workers. In order to maintain this system of beliefs they have to change the workers in their minds; the workers become seen as less capable and informed. In particular, executives often seem to have no particular basis to think of themselves as superior to many on the workforce, but nonetheless do so, which signals the splitting off and projection of any sense of incompetence on their part and projecting it onto their employees.

These dynamics, when examined from a group relations perspective, also contain collusive and unconscious group dynamics that are based on the splitting and projection that separate executives and managers from staff members and employees. These common splits often yield passive and active fight-and-flight group dynamics, where there is either open or concealed warfare going on between the two groups. This open conflict tends to reinforce the splitting and projection as stress and anxiety ebb and flow within the organization. There are also organizational dynamics that tend to create a group of less capable workers that result from the better workers becoming fed up and leaving. This dynamic in some organizations creates a pervasive sense of mediocrity where those who remain are not as qualified as those who leave. They passively accept the mandate to pay for the coffee, where passivity as an employee trait is not always or even desirable. In this regard, the group may contain dependency dynamics and believe that only management can take care of them. In this case, the workers have split off their sense of themselves as competent and capable and have projected this content onto the managers and executives, who in turn may come to be idealized or feared. The managers may accept these projections, feeling even more self-confident and empowered by their followers.

Karen Horney's notion of moving against others also contributes to understanding the willingness to inflict paying for the coffee upon workers. It is an arrogant move, and if resisted, may lead to harsh and vindictive reprisals inflicted by management. Those who leave move away from the organization (the appeal to freedom) and those who remain move toward each other and management out of a sense of dependency and neediness (moving toward others).

In sum, paying for coffee has a lot to say about management, staff, workers, and organizational dynamics. It is all really there. Enjoy your coffee!

Badges

We wear badges at work
so that others will know
who we are and that we belong here—
and that we are of no danger to anyone.

Eventually we come to wear
badges at work to remind ourselves
who we are and that we belong here—
and that we are one of the good people.

We put our badges on before we arrive
and panic when we have forgotten
where we put them at home or in the car.
We feel naked, vulnerable. We might be
mistaken for the enemy—or begin to doubt
how harmless we really are.

Discussion

This poem was written in the long cultural shadow cast in the U.S. by the terrorist attacks on September 11, 2001. Until then my work-place had been rather informal with respect to visual identification. For the most part employees, managers, and leaders came and went in their regular workplace attire without name tags. Shortly after 9/11, identification tags with name, photo, institution, and ID number were made and distributed to all people employed by the company. Wearing them at all times while on the company premises was mandatory. It felt heavily ritualized, a social defense against anxiety as well as a practical measure.

Even with badges visibly displayed, on one occasion a co-worker who had been a longtime friend and colleague said to me with a smile as we passed in the hallway: "I don't know about you, Howard. Are you *sure* you're not one of those Muslim terrorists?" We continued on our way without my making a comment. In such an atmosphere with a heightened sense of boundaries, boundary violation, and vulnerability, it became urgent to know immediately upon recognition, whether someone "belonged" to us or not, whether one was a safe insider or a menacing outsider. Identity and visual identification were fused.

Analysis

The poem speaks to the success of terrorism around the world. Everyone is afraid. Even those who are familiar can become potential enemies. Those among us who are "us" can also become "them" and blow up buildings and gatherings. Psychological splitting accentuates this dynamic. And in a very real sense the poem speaks to our being victimized by our own fear and flight from anxiety, as expressed in institutional imposition of rules and regulations and official identification in the form of a badge. The badge, other than being square, offers identification no one can see or match to the person wearing it.

We all may then become little more than a badge in some settings. Our identity in the moment becomes the badge. Do we officially exist without it? Does it render our personal identity mute? We are deidenti-fied and lost to ourselves. We and others become objects as compared with subjects. For those to whom the badge matters, the person wearing it becomes an object to match with the picture on the badge during an airport screening or entrance to work. Failure to identify can lead to dire consequences. There are moments of fear when one cannot locate one's identity. Homeland Security is watching!

Denial, splitting, and projection offer insight into the dynamics of the poem where we may doubt who we are. In the eyes of others, we are potentially bad, someone to be screened for badness, and may only pass when our goodness is ascertained. Unconscious splitting of people into "good" and "bad" is the essence of how we often divide up objects in our world. We also understand that the badge is a representation of fight and flight. There is a threat that must be defended against (fight) or fled from. The badges signal the threat that others without badges may move against us. And, while we must go to work, we also seek freedom from our badges (flight and the appeal to freedom) and just wish we could leave them at home. But then again who wants to be interrogated in a lonely room?

Boxes Everywhere

Boxes ubiquitous—
little boxes, big boxes,
enormous boxes,
boxes made of cardboard,
shipping and receiving,
sealing and ripping open,
to be carried out of the building
with personal belongings
when you are fired;
cubicles to work in,
if you manage to keep your job;
office rectangular boxes;
"little boxes made of ticky tacky"*
out in the suburbs;
surrounded by boxes,
buried in boxes.
Last night, deep in sleep,
I dreamt I had become a box;
when I awoke, it was true.

*from Malvina Reynolds, "Little Boxes," 1962, 1990[2]

Discussion

This poem was written during a time when cardboard boxes being carried down a hallway signaled downsizing, restructuring, and reengineering. This awareness made me think of how boxes played a ubiquitous role in workplaces. It also reminded me that boxes, in addition to being *practical material objects* for storage and transport, could easily become *symbolically* loaded and emotionally "hot" metaphors. I allowed boxes to take over my imagination—there were boxes everywhere. Was one meant for me?

Analysis

Boxes of different forms and types are benign objects until they are not. After being hired we are assigned to work within a box-like cubicle or small office. And we may be confronted with a box to pack our belongings in before being escorted to termination and then out onto the parking lot. Our lives at work in toxic organizations can be stressful. All too often our work experiences contain harsh and threatening elements that demean and diminish us and those around us. We come to understand that boxes are not always benign objects and that, we as objects, are ultimately disposable.

Employees are all too often treated as though they are objects to be managed and moved around within the organization. Experiences like this that are lived and observed open our minds up to the realization that often we are nothing more than objects to others to be used, moved about, and discarded when no longer needed.

Objectification is a routine element of object relations theory where others are conceived of in mind as objects. For executives, many times hundreds or thousands of employees are rendered into employee ID numbers and badges, line item expenses on spreadsheets, and resources to be used to the advantage of the organization. In their minds people are stripped of their humanity. There are many times too many people to get to know them very well anyway. Employees may also see management as detached and indifferent, even mythological decision makers, who act as though employees do not have their own thoughts, feelings, and lives. At best, we might only be a box on an organization chart. Everyone in a sense may become a box in everyone else's minds. It is no wonder we may feel boxed-in at work and unable to think outside the box.

The boxes also speak to more primitive coping mechanisms such as fight and flight, dependency, and pairing. Certainly, everyone wants to resist being put in a box by others and failing that, flight from the context may be all that is left. A box-like cubicle is, however, also comforting and reassuring. It provides some sense of boundaries around us and our work, boundaries to be defended but also to depend on. If we cannot depend on others to care for us, the boxes in our lives offer some assurances we will be around tomorrow. And we may also be able to wait and hope things will get better, so long as no one takes our boxes away or hands us one to pack our work life into on the way out.

The poem also speaks to a sense of despair, where we are lost to the all-too-often impersonal nature of our organizations. Our sense of pride may well be vanquished, leaving us to seek the caretaking of management (dependency) who does not seem to care or to seek freedom from these anxieties by flight to freedom in a new job elsewhere and another box-like work experience.

Inquiry at the Office

I inquire in person,
by phone, by e-mail,
to you my supervisor:
can you, could you,
would you find someone
to cover my phone messages
and to check my mail
while I am away on this trip?
Not a large demand.

You say, you will check into it.
Weeks pass, the day of departure
approaches: I inquire
again and yet again.
Always the same reply:
we are checking.

Soon you no longer reply
at all; the date of departure
passes and I leave
exposed to the elements.

You act as if
every request is unreasonable,
as if I should go away,
or maybe that I
should have long ago.

Discussion

This poem is about an ordinary request at my office that became a meta-phor about my toxic organization, my place in it, and my relationship with others and my supervisor. At first, I felt the lack of response was from forgetfulness due to his busy schedule. It gradually grew on me that my request and his lack of response were symbolic of my psychological "place" in the organization. It helped confirm my growing impression that different "rules" applied to me as compared with my fellow employ-ees. A simple request for telephone coverage turned out to not be so sim-ple. The lack of responsiveness made me feel increasingly discounted and an outsider. Other employees received the courtesy of telephone coverage when they were away for a few days. Why was I an exception? Silence was the only reply.

Analysis

So take a moment to at least stand in the supervisor's shoes. What was going on in his or her mind? How was it that a simple request that was not responded to led to more requests without a response and ultimately no response at all—as though the person making the request did not exist or at least did not merit being recognized at all? Everyone has had requests made of them—at work and outside of work. We know this interpersonal turf very well. Sometimes we respond to curry favor, to be appreciated, to receive approval and admiration, and sometimes we do not respond, sending a message that we do not like, respect, or admire the requestor, who is to our way of thinking not authorized to make the request and making a nuisance of him- or herself. If we are pushed, there may even arise a sadistic sense of pleasure at leaving the person "swinging in the wind" and hung out to dry, to use some suitable workplace expressions.

Object relations theory makes clear how we turn others into objects in our mind to be manipulated at will. The object does not have to be invested with desirable, likeable, or even human qualities, and by doing so we are naturally not obliged to be helpful or respond to requests. The poem makes clear the feelings evoked by an authority figure who at first rejects first a request, but ultimately rejects the person and his or her validity in terms of meriting a response of any kind—silence.

Unfortunately, behavior like this is fairly common at work, enabled by splitting and projection on the part of many, creating bad bosses and worthless employees. Sometimes it is surprising that any work gets done at all, especially when toxic group dynamics become involved. One group may not respond to another group and vice versa. Open warfare sometimes exists that can become unrelenting, introducing considerable organizational and operational dysfunction. Everyone loses, especially if senior level leaders are involved. There is little interpersonal space left for notions like dependency and pairing.

Similarly, moving against others often seems to be the case, creating endless organizational dysfunction. Arrogant group or team pride that is injured must be harshly vindicated just about every time. A zero-sum struggle for organizational resources and management's attention, approval, and raises may exist. Vindication can reach the level of creating enough dysfunction that even organizational survival is threatened. The poem reminds us that this is possible, and more caretaking approaches to managing (moving toward others) and responding to dependency needs of others are often absent and perhaps may be seen as a sign of weakness. For many, moving away from these toxic organizational dynamics is the only acceptable response. This allows those who regress to moving against others to engage in combat while everyone else ducks and covers.

Metamorphosis in Reverse

Imagine: Franz Kafka alive now,
entombed as a petty *apparatchik*
in some government bureaucracy,
writing his *Metamorphosis* in reverse.

No human Gregor Samsa, he, degenerating
into an insect, a crawling bug—
but Gregor the Roach transforming
himself moment by moment,
ascending the evolutionary ladder
before his very eyes from
exoskeleton to endoskeleton,
from scurrying around on lots of legs
to standing up, bipedal—and yes,
with it the back aches—
sitting at a small desk, signing
and stamping endless papers

while the Ministers of Our Hate
hurl atomic missiles on
the Ministers of Their Hate,
and they return the favor,
ushering in nuclear winter;
and Gregor Samsa, the last human,
wishing he were a lowly roach
so he would at least
have a chance at survival.

Discussion

This bitter, phantasmagoric poem is from a time I was reflecting on my history with the bureaucratic workplace where I felt like an object than a person. As I reflected on this state of affairs I came to appreciate that Franz Kafka's story, *Metamorphosis*, had long been a theme in my work-life.[3] I wondered fantastically, perhaps as an escape to freedom, what it would be like if the sequence of events in Kafka's story were reversed, wherein an insect "evolved" into a human—a petty bureaucrat. The resulting poem is my fantasy. It is filled with bitter irony. My anger is palpable.

Analysis

The poem offers the reader a sense of personal relief if not catharsis from those instances where bureaucratic experience has overwhelmed one's self and senses. Sometimes we really hate how we and others are being treated by what often seems to be an impersonal toxic organization, but even worse, a despised and out-of-touch management making unilateral decisions and defending its policies and procedures and rules and regulations. These lived experiences we all have, together with the accompanying thoughts and feelings, are given permission to become conscious by the poem. Hate and rage are not uncommon in the workplace and often lead to extreme outcomes, the worst being someone who returns to work with a gun to lay waste to others.[4]

It is worth noting that organizational bullies, while inflicting many forms of violence on others enabled by the institutional means, usually are not the ones who become physically violent—it is their victims who strike back. In these cases, lacking the means to defend against administrative violence, the only resort is to fight back physically or perhaps flee the organization. Fight and flight are strong emotions.

The poem also speaks to the many aspects of bureaucratic structure and processes that turn people into numbers and human resources to be managed much like machines. People are subject to being transferred, retrained, demoted, disciplined, and even terminated as surplus human resources. Once again, we appreciate that denial, splitting, and projection are some of the unconscious enablers of creating outcomes like this. And for those subjected to these organizational dynamics, it is natural to split off one's humanity and competence, leaving a much-depleted sense of self to survive in the workplace. Can employees avoid the Roach Motel?

Reflections

The poems say a lot about life in toxic organizations that often lack compassion and caretaking on the part of management, consultants, and even colleagues. Feeling angry and discounted (if not seemingly entirely disregarded) as a human being are commonplace work experiences, we suggest. You are not alone this experience. We hope that the poems, the stories, and the analyses will help you the reader to feel less alone by affirming your experiences. The poems offer a way to return back to life from objectification, depersonalization, and discounting by providing one a way to acknowledge the alienation and mend the soul. Poetry can at once disturb, confirm, validate, and comfort the afflicted at work.

In Conclusion

It is ironic to have a chapter that "humanizes" alienation and bureaucracy in the workplace. In making sense of how persons at work come to treat others and experience themselves as non-persons, as inanimate things, we bear witness and put a face on and give a mental and intersubjective validity to experiences we had come to variously label as "normal" or "evil." On the one hand, the poems, stories, and psychodynamic analyses give voice and image to things that are often too terrible to know. On the other hand, they validate these frightening, enraging, soul-destroying, and surreal experiences.

They say, in essence, "This truly happened, even if you couldn't make it up." They bring secrets into the light of day. They also show, in a kind of absurdity, how seemingly minor things like routing slips, old computers and equipment, ID badges, boxes, coffee service, and requests for telephone coverage can take us to the heart of darkness of a toxic bureaucratic workplace without heart or soul. They are profound metaphors as well as being ordinary artifacts of organizational life.

Chapter 7 is a logical—and psychological—successor to a discussion of bureaucracy and alienation. It focuses on their consequences and outcomes for the experience of oneself in the workplace. In Chapter 7, we turn to another face of organizational dehumanization: the experience of anonymity, disposability, and disappearance. We portray the experience of the disappearance of the sense of having a valued self and finding in its place the horror of becoming an object that is good only for production. We give words, images, and metaphors to what virtually everyone knows, but rarely consciously thinks of—and officially are not supposed to realize.

Notes

1. Allcorn, S. (1991). *Workplace superstars in resistant organizations*. Westport, CT: Quorum Books.
2. *Little Boxes* is a song written and composed by Malvina Reynolds in 1962. The song is a political satire that mocks conformist middle-class values and identical ticky-tacky suburban tract housing made of cheap materials as "little boxes" of different colors. https://en.wikipedia.org/wiki/Little_Boxes
3. Bloom, H. (1988). *Franz Kafka's the metamorphosis*. New York: Chelsea House Publishers.
4. Allcorn, S. (1994). *Anger in the workplace: Understanding the causes of aggression and violence*. Westport, CT: Quorum Books.

7 Loss of Self
Disappeared Into Anonymity

Our workplaces are all too often filled with spiritual harm that reduces us to "human resources" to be managed and manipulated and perhaps used up. We are told what to do, how to do it, when to do it, and how fast to do it. We find we are alienated from ourselves, our skills and abilities, our self-confidence, our self-worth, from our work, each other, as well as the groups we work in, the organization, its leaders, and aspirational mission statements.

Worse yet, escape to a better existence is often unattainable. We restrain ourselves from "jumping ship" in favor of adding one more year to retirement and benefits coverage. And what of being too old to find an equivalent or better position, or the single mother who has worked her way up a hierarchy of positions and would have to start over elsewhere? After all, who is going to pay for the food on the table, the roof over our family's collective head, and those college educations? Although the tasks we perform are essential to keeping the organization running, other people may look through us, if they notice us at all. We are PWA—present without acknowledgement. We know we are here and working hard, but does anyone in management care?

This chapter explores our loss of self and our *disappearance* at work as a worthwhile person and worker. We may labor in anonymity. These profound experiences are revealed in the poetry, discussion, and analyses of this chapter. We invite the reader to join us to explore life experience that resides beneath the calm and controlled surface of toxic organizations.

The Disappeared at Work

There are experiences at work that are more profound than the alienation explored in Chapter 6. It is easy to find one's self looked past or through by others and management. Have you ever been present when a supervisor, manager, or executive (or parent) was talking about you as though you were not there? For all practical purposes, you have simply disappeared. And so it is often the case in many workplaces that changes and decisions are made that affect you and your work, but without consultation or your being informed. Becoming invisible at work, we suggest, is a commonly shared experience. The applied poems in this chapter highlight this experience.

Exit Visa

I keep trying to obtain
an exit visa from this place.
My pension plan does not
grow fast enough.
Work does not pay well,
so I buy stocks
like it's my second job.
I would buy extra health insurance,
but I do not qualify.

I don't know what
I work for any more.
The boss tells us
we should be grateful
just to have a job.
I never thought
I'd work mainly to keep
my premiums paid up.
I'm surrounded by people
who are doing exactly the same—
nothing to look forward to
except to look out for ourselves.

Work in this place is about
little more than dying,
postponing dying,
and slowly dying.
There is no exit visa
from this solitary confinement.
Even if I left,
there is nowhere to go.

Discussion

In an atmosphere of rampant, recurrent downsizing, restructuring, and reengineering, employees often feel trapped in a vicious downward spiral, circling the drain. Employees and managers feel a sense of doom and soul death. Work becomes robotic, automatic, and mechanical. The workplace and self experience feel lifeless. If there are still benefits, they may have been reduced.

Employees hold onto their jobs for dear life out of fear that they could not find anything comparable, let alone better, anywhere else. They "keep their heads down," "stay under the radar," trying not to be noticed. Fear of "downward mobility" from the middle class makes employees cling to jobs that they may no longer like, fearing any more change will only be for the worse. It is an atmosphere of despair from which there is no escape. There are millions of vulnerable people who work in toxic organizations.

Analysis

When there is no way out of a bad situation, hope is lost, despair embraces us, and we can easily feel that there is not much left to live for other than surviving to another paycheck that covers food and benefits. We are left to metaphorically rearrange the deck chairs on our sinking sense of ourselves of not being alive and valued. Certainly, keeping those health insurance premiums paid may be essential to live one's life.

The psychological implications for the disappeared and disappearing workers seems pretty clear. The workplace can become an instrument of torture where many workers are so undervalued and so disposable that supervisors, managers, and executives many times need not acknowledge their presence, value, or their contributions to keeping the organization running and profitable. They have become disposable objects in the minds of those in charge and perhaps each other. Their value has been split off from them leaving a diminished sense of self. Workers subjected to this experience also collude in their own institutionalized demise by splitting off their sense of themselves as valued and able to perform with excellence, locating them in managers who are experienced as having high value. Denial, splitting, and projection are powerful unconscious dynamics that contribute to creating the horror in the poem.

Also to be considered are individual and group dynamics like fight and flight. In the poem, the ability to fight back is nearly absent, and flight seems to be a remote possibility. Employees are seemingly locked in with no way out and nowhere to go. They are in fact in some ways pathetically dependent on their organization and its life-giving paycheck. This sense of dependency is shared in a larger sense among members of groups that compose the workforce. These individuals are obliged to seek attachment (movement toward) to toxic organizations. Moving against or away from them toward freedom may be foreclosed, leaving a sense of despair.

Getting Lost

They told me
to "Get lost,"
kept telling me
until I finally did,
complied, and left
for where I was
supposed to go—
I can't say where,
but for sure
it wasn't there.

Discussion

This poem is close kin to "The Wrong Ending" from Chapter 5. It draws on our workplace experience and on hearing clients' stories. To be sure, no one was told directly to "Get lost," but the feeling of being unwanted and expendable was overwhelming and pervasive.

The rejection showed up in the "silent treatment" from leaders and managers, in not being invited to meetings, in selectively targeted budget cuts, in a lack of promotions and raises, in being ignored, and in the feeling that others were looking through us. One did not feel welcomed or safe, but rather "disappeared." Long before one was actually fired, one began to feel abandoned, lost, and dispirited.

Analysis

Getting rid of people can be tough in large bureaucracies that have rules and regulations and sometimes have to comply with federal and state laws regarding employment actions. And of course, some people are hard to fire due to their network of connections and supporters or because they clearly add value to the organization, but not without irritating powerful people who are out to get them. Given all of these limitations, many times the angle used is to make their lives so miserable they voluntarily leave. At other times reorganizing is used, as if to say, "You are out of here because your job was eliminated." In the poem and the accompanying rest of the story, the former was seemingly clearly selected.

The victim and victimizer know each other well and both understand their interpersonal contract. There is perpetration and resistance. Who will give up first? Sometimes these things go on for months and years. Everyone knows eventually. No one seems to win. No one seems to lose. The interpersonal and accompanying organizational dysfunction become institutionalized.

These interpersonal and organizational dynamics are easily fueled by splitting and projection. Each side splits off their bad characteristics and locates them in the other. You sometimes see wild assertions made where the assertion does not ring true for the individual against whom it is hurled. But then again, it had to come from somewhere—one's representation of the other in mind. Of course, if the "bad stuff" has been split off and projected, that only leaves a good self who is either just doing his or her job to rid the organization of a bad employee, or there may develop a stand-your-ground mentality to resist and fend off the bad manager or supervisor and preserve the good self as victim.

A context such as this is informed by examining group dynamics that may arise where supporters of each individual are willing to attack the other side and fight back. Flight is not a good option, and moving away and the appeal to freedom are also not consistent with resisting or taking out the other person. Notions like dependency and pairing basic assumptions and moving toward each other are, due to the very nature of the situation, ruled out. Resistance may ultimately be futile, but it is not felt to be.

There is then resident in toxic dynamics like this significant unconscious and underappreciated interpersonal and intergroup relations that can create a stable and enduring conflict, one that becomes familiar and possibly even a welcome distraction to the drudgery of work. These wars of attrition are waged all too often at work, creating a wasteful and dysfunctional organizational landscape.

Thought's Geography

> Before I have a thought,
> you know what mine should be.
>
> You can't seem
> to occupy yourself
> without first
> occupying me.

Discussion

This brief poem highlights that employees often feel that their *boundaries* are constantly being invaded by abusive managers and leaders, as if a kind of "spirit possession" is occurring.[1] One cannot seem to rid oneself of the hostile presence that is not only external but also inside oneself. There is the frightening feeling that "you" are in "me," that you have taken me over, that I no longer exist as a separate, worthwhile person. It is as if there is no escape from the autocratic, micro-managing, abusive boss.

Analysis

The poem and discussion speak to an internalized presence of a set of standards and values, many times acquired from others and sometimes referred to as the superego, from Sigmund Freud's tripartite model of our psyches (ego, superego, id).[2] The superego refers to our sense of moral conscience that reflects social standards learned from others who may come to be forever linked to these standards, sometimes in a punishing way. We take in (integrate) these others and the standards they represent, and may well feel conflicted and anxious for not measuring up to these standards.

Our places of work are filled with powerful authority figures who wield power over our future careers and employment. They are to be respected and feared or perhaps admired, idealized, and even loved. They are seldom known by others in the workplace for who they really are because of splitting, projection, and transference, where the powerful authority figures are created as self object-representations (often resembling one's parents) that become our unconscious way of knowing "them." Stated differently, we must conform to what is expected of us at work in order to survive. We become "auto-controlled." We achieve self-imposed conformity to escape the oppressive and repressive evil, omnipresent, and judgmental eye (panopticon) of our own minds. We integrate the standards and rules of others that become a part of who *we* are.

Groups at work can also take in these standards and values, creating a relatively homogenous group "mind" where little is critically examined, and following the rules and orders becomes a standard operating procedure (an institutionalized group) that is self-regulating.[3] Not only do individual group members, having integrated the standards, feel compelled to conform, but the members of a group may also monitor everyone else in the group for any deviance from the rules, regulations, standards, and group norms. Conformity promises the hope of group survival where little effort is required to maintain the group, consistent with Bion's pairing basic assumption group. The hope is that conformity will yield safety and security that are threatened by self-differentiation.

This level of self- and group-enforced submission also contains elements of Karen Horney's movement toward others (dependency) as a solution to anxiety. Members of the organization are strongly focused on conformity, due to their excessive dependence on the powerful authority figures, who in turn are partially constructed by projection of employees' own competencies onto these figures that dominate and control their lives at work. Staying attached is sometimes all that matters, creating unquestioning submission to authority to achieve caretaking dependency.

Impaired Vision

Just because you do not see
what I see
does not mean it is not there—
unless you presume the power
to declare what is
and what is not,
and then to call that power
"Vision."

I am sorry you cannot see
what I behold;
the problem, though,
is your vision, not me—
though perhaps you can
muster only derision
to mask over so limited
a vision as yours.

Your problem with me
is that you just cannot see.

Discussion

This poem has much in common with "Thought's Geography." It is about the experience of being told what to think and how to see. It is about being discounted. It is about the enforced denial of employees' perception of reality. It is as if to say, "Reality is what I tell you it is." Protest is pointless and futile—and usually punished. Some employees are able to hold onto their own experience of the workplace, even as theirs is discounted. They must remain silent and pretend to accept others' imposed reality.

The poem is about the power to define reality, about whose vision counts, and the desperate attempt to hold onto one's own perceptions as valid, when one is told that his or her vision is flawed and does not count. Many of the poems in this chapter share common themes. It is as though a *single* poem is insufficient to purge oneself of overwhelming experiences and feelings. Many of our clients have told us horrific stories that, when heard, remind us of similar life experiences (what is often called "secondary traumatization").[4] A single poetic catharsis is not enough to place the experience outside oneself. It continues to be haunting. Are these commonly shared experiences of toxic organizations ever completely worked through?

Analysis

The poem raises the question of what it is like to walk in another person's shoes, which is a way of speaking of *empathy*. I see what you see. I hear what you hear. And more important, I hear what you are saying. We are by our nature often lost in our own inner world of self-involvement, to the exclusion of being aware of others and their thoughts and feelings. In many moments, there is perhaps only us, excluding everyone else—and they sense and know this to be the case. The self-absorption and narcissism that are part of Karen Horney's expansive solution to anxiety create in many ways poems where impaired empathy is the theme. We also suggest that in hierarchical organizations where powerful positions are few in number and aggregated at the top of the hierarchy, there is an accentuation of this dynamic of loss of interpersonal connectedness, relatedness, and empathy.

People in powerful organizational positions often think they know what to do, how, and when, although many might say they are disconnected from the realities on the ground. This "knowing" is enabled in part by denial, splitting, and projection where not knowing, not being adequate, not being effective, and perhaps even simply being wrong are denied and split off from self and located in others and employees, who are then thought to have created the problems in the first place. They are not only thought to be the problem in mind but also treated as though they are the problems (projective identification), where they in turn come to believe *they* are creating the problems, not senior management.

Organizational dynamics like this are all too common and lead to interminable infighting and finger pointing (fight and flight or moving against others) that can become a way of life, an organizational culture in flight from accurate reality testing, and in a struggle to maintain control over the fantastic system of beliefs driving the alternate reality. Concurrently there is also a struggle to maintain enough control of the organization to receive another paycheck.

There is then an accurate reality-tested view of the world that is lost to impaired vision of self, others, groups, and the organization. And as described in the discussion, these dynamics are ongoing and ultimately never completely purged from experience.

We now explore yet another soul-stripping, self-limiting, and life-altering reality of the workplace—assumed and enforced anonymity.

Anonymity in the Workplace

Members of organizations occupy a vast range of positions, usually in a hierarchical pyramid that has ever-fewer positions nearing the top of the pyramid that culminates in the great leader–CEO, president, director, or owner. Nearing the broad base of the pyramid one finds many more people in similar roles that are of lower power, importance, and status. We, as customers or clients of these organizations, including the public sector, are often surrounded by them—the janitors, housekeepers, clerks, cashiers, and customer service representatives. These people are in a sense the public face of organizations, those with whom we are in contact. Yet our contact is minimal, if at all, and is limited to seeing them as a narrow function.

This appreciation leads directly to a second realization—how often these people are anonymous *both* to the upper reaches of the pyramid of power and control and to those of us who rely on them every day to patch the holes in our roads and pick up our trash. They do their work and are unseen even if they are visible. Who, then, are the stakeholders? And who has the power to define them, to include or exclude them from their vision?

The poems that follow direct our attention to and deepen our appreciation of these virtually invisible people. The poems map the experience of emotional nonexistence and nothingness. They paint canvases of everyday numbness and silent horror at not being treated as alive. They are living zombies with a salary.

In these poems, the poet's hope is to make visible those who are made invisible in their workplaces and bring the dead back to life. Perhaps the wound of anonymity can, at least in part, be healed by bearing witness and by acknowledging that those relegated to anonymity may be recognized and validated.

Bartender

> He stood there, tuxedoed,
> dispensing drinks to those of us
> crowding the bar. He stood motionless
> through the short speech
> our host gave. What few words
> the bartender spoke suggested an accent—
> though who among us doesn't have one?—
> Russia, Ukraine, Belarus.
>
> I wondered about his life
> when he wasn't standing there,
> tuxedoed, serving us liquor.
> He had one, I hoped
> as much as surmised.
>
> A man in his sixties, maybe
> he had grand kids.
> Maybe, sometimes,

someone served him.
He practiced his anonymous trade
with dignity, with class.
I just hoped that he had
more to his life than us.

Discussion

The scenario depicted in this poem really happened. It was like countless events I have attended. It is about the experience of being seen but
unseen and of being unnoticed and invisible. It is about the feeling of
being treated as if one did not exist as a real person, but only as a function, the performer of a task, a kind of animate automaton.

I have often felt anonymous at work, and countless employees and
managers have told me stories of how they experienced themselves as
anonymous *and* how they experienced the others who treated them this
way. It is a surreal world of existence and nonexistence. When I see someone in that kind of role, I go out of my way to offer at least a moment of
human contact and gratitude—to the man who brings the mail and to the
men who pick up my refuse by the side of the road.

Analysis

Having a drink when faced with this reality helps us to ignore, deny, and
rationalize our experience. We are in fact often numb to this experience
of others and perhaps even more so within ourselves. The idea of being
unseen, unnoticed, and invisible seems to ring true, together with how
distressing this truly is. We must defend against the sense of loss of self,
the annihilation of self and others, and the larger social sense and setting
where we are all potentially not really there. Is the person being served
anything more than a grasping hand?

Objectification in some ways does not account for this social dynamic.
We do not have to turn the other into an invisible presence without a
soul. This is in fact where they start out. It is their job. It is their role.
It is their profession—that of serviceable invisibility. Object relations
theory encourages us to ponder how we can reanimate these individuals
who, in their anonymity, animate our lives with their service. The poem
and discussion speak to this need to de-objectify others, in our minds
re-instilling in them some measure of humanity and individual identity.

There is then perhaps a moment, after having created a whole person in mind by projecting some of ourselves onto these individuals, that
we can make meaningful eye contact, speak to them as possibly having
children or grandchildren, and acknowledge their service. And we may
then also appreciate the dignity that they possess in fulfilling their role,
and even the dignity of their anonymity. At the same time, we also must

appreciate that the person in front of us who we now *think* we know we do not really know, because we have created them as a mental representation within ourselves. Presumption of knowing another can be a horrible thing.

Bion's notion of flight, from what at some level is a distressing awareness of these anonymous others, has relevance in that as a shared basic assumption, everyone in the room must also deal with the presence of the anonymous others who circulate effortlessly, but often invisibly, among us. It is as though both the anonymous others and those who are not have colluded to create a context where group life is permitted to go on within the flight basic assumption, allowing for the contract to be honored between the anonymous and those they serve. Acknowledging this and ending the flight would seem to create a catastrophe of anxiety. If they are there, what should "I" or "We" do to lift their veil of anonymity? Contemplating taking some form of action is anxiety provoking in and of itself. What if we had to acknowledge this intergroup dynamic? What could be possibly said or done?

There is also the opportunity to consider Karen Horney's movement away from others as a way of understanding all this interpersonal collusion. It is often too distressing for individuals and groups to acknowledge the roles of others and other groups, when those roles create others who must assume invisible and anonymous roles. This occurs usually in the service to those who have not been turned into invisible objects by the roles that are created by an organization.

Karen Horney also encourages us to consider the role of excessive narcissism as a defense against anxiety. A portion of this encounter with the anonymous other reinforces our sense of self-worth and importance. The flight to freedom on both sides of this equation also seems to promote some understanding. For the invisible others, they perhaps prefer to just be left alone to do their work, often without having to deal with the awkward acknowledgements of their presence by others. And for those who receive their support, there may be a sense of freedom from anxiety by not having to acknowledge the invisible other which may be extended to not acknowledging the role at all and the organization that creates it. What can be done anyway?

Those Who Clean Up After Us

Silently, wordlessly, flawlessly,
they clean up our tables
after we have finished eating, our office
after we have left work for the day.
They are nameless to us, known
only by their uniform—if we notice
them at all. Today they are

Mexican and Guatemalan.
Thirty years ago they were Black.
Eighty years ago they were
Polish, Slovak, Hungarian, Jewish.
They perform their service in waves
of geography and accent.
We scarcely see them, but they
are paid low wages to tend
closely to us, lest in the morning
a single wastebasket still be full.
In the hotel, they are called
"Housekeeping." I leave the room
a mess in the morning, and return
to perfect order in the afternoon.
What a splendid vanishing show.
(We do not see the bending
and the lifting, though.)
To us, their work of disappearance
and reappearance hints at magic;
to them it is no magic at all.

Discussion

This poem is similar in tone and plea to the previous poem, "Bartender."
If it is about the experience of being depersonalized, it is also about one's
experience of oneself as a non-person. Countless clients have told me
their workplace stories of the feeling of horror at their sense of nothingness. The concept of "alienation" barely scratches the surface of vanishing while still performing their jobs. I have disappeared to myself.

Some people, myself included, took some comfort in the fact that they/
we performed their job well, even though they received no recognition or
gratitude for their dedication, competence, and loyalty. Still, it remained
a constant struggle to feel alive and worthwhile.

Analysis

There are many people who work much of their lives noticed only occasionally as people, but most often for the products of their work, the
quality of which is taken for granted. If the work performed is not silent,
wordless, and flawless, everyone hears about it, and discipline and job
loss are a threat. The poem opens the imagination to wondering beyond
the custodians and housekeepers to what are often large numbers of
employees employed at the minimum wage or some percentage greater,
who also labor in anonymity as potentially disposable (nonessential)
workers. Clerks of many kinds from mail to filing, typists and secretaries,

cooks and mechanics, hairstylists, and buildings and grounds maintainers—they are all often in the same way seen but not seen; but if their work is not done or not done well, this is entirely unacceptable. They may then find themselves publically shamed.

We are suggesting then that we as individuals are often surrounded by others upon whom we depend, but without fully appreciating this dependency. And in our busy lives as we experience them, we may entirely miss the person and his or her work, or minimally acknowledge it. They are doing their jobs, and others are doing their jobs—often for more pay and higher status in our hierarchical organizations.

The psychological dynamics are abundant and underappreciated. We often seem to not invest the time and energy to create these others in our minds and endow them with some of our fantasies and personal attributes. These are not only invisible but absent from awareness and in many ways nonexistent. These psychodynamics often include basic assumptions to defend against anxieties evoked within and among groups at work. Fight and flight dynamics may arise between union employees and management and possibly all other nonunion employees. A large, cohesive group of facilities and grounds staff may confront senior management over poor working conditions, dangerous chemicals, unrealistic performance expectations, improper and malfunctioning equipment, and a cultural attitude toward them that is dismissive and uncaring. Sometimes it is painfully clear that higher-paid professionals are dependent on the underappreciated and anonymous others who surround them, although the presence of a dependency basic assumption group is denied. Everyone knows that if the anonymous others don't like it they can leave. They are replaceable. Indeed, this is what gives management so much power relative to labor.

Finally, Karen Horney's ideas of moving toward, away, and against are all operationalized in these hierarchical social societies in the workplace. Certainly, conflict often arises as mentioned where many employees move against others with considerable emotional and irrational energy. There may also be a coming together of groups to solve a major operating problem that spans many disciplines and other roles all the way down to housekeeping, dock workers, and union laborers. And it is also not uncommon to see many employees moving away from the organization, management, and supervisors, where the relationship is thought to be unrewarding if not even threatening in terms of physical and emotional well-being.

Speak Your Mind

I have for too long
spoken in your idiom—
and yours, and yours—

languages in which
I yearned to make myself understood.

You pressed yourself into me
by way of words and obligations
so much that you have replaced me
with yourself; you insisted
that I could not imagine myself
apart from the words you stuffed
upon my tongue; you said
I was not clear;
you never said you would not hear,
Nor could I recognize what you would not say.

I no longer remember what once
I wished to say—
only that I wished to be understood
in a voice I might have recognized
as my own.
How could I have known you never intended
that I be welcomed
to your community of understanding;
that you asked only that I go away
or stay and disappear
in your likeness?

And who can bear
to hear murder
in so mere a substance
as words?

Discussion

This poem is about the frightening experience of the dissolution of the self, not as in an ecstatic mystical vision, but rather as a violent violation. Even though the poem is ostensibly about *language*, language here serves as a symbol of the attempt to please, if not become, the other as a desperate act to validate one's own existence. Still, all effort is doomed to failure, since the other person—co-worker, manager, executive—has no intention to accept the other person as a fellow human being, sharing in common the human condition.

One can never belong, can never become accepted and included as one of "us," but is condemned to be treated as an outsider, a bizarre alien. The further tragedy is that one still strives to enter a door that is forever locked. Likewise, one also feels invaded, taken over, overwhelmed, if not destroyed. One no longer recognizes one's own voice. Ultimately, the poem describes the experience of soul murder and soul death. One is annihilated while still alive. It is the stuff of horror movies.

Analysis

There is existential suffering and pain in being aggressively seen in some specific way by another person, or others, or a group, or an entire organization, that is not who you know yourself to be. In the twenty-first century, this can even lead to attacks and sudden death inflicted by terrorists on an anonymous crowd, or a rejected loner in a theatre massacre or grade school or high school shoot-out. And more often now, there are others who are mistaken to be outsiders, such as people standing near a Jewish Community Center—the alien others who are not the alien in mind, but who are nonetheless shot.

There are other forms of extreme violence that are underappreciated. In particular, the notion of *unconscious* projective identification, which is considered by some to take a form of *interpersonal* violence, is represented in the poem. The alien other is created as an unconscious process in mind by denial, splitting, and projection. Often, these manipulations of others as mental representations, as mentioned in Chapter 3, leak out to influence interpersonal relationships in subtle ways. However, this dynamic can become much more forceful where the intent is to cause the other person or group to become like the internal and sometimes shared representations. One group may continually coax, coach, and even coerce another group to act in ways consistent with the internal representations. This taking over of others as expressed in the poem is a powerful and insidious process and often occurs out of everyone's awareness. The "other" person or group must simply become the way they are conceived to be. The notion of soul murder echoes in the final lines of the poem.

Bion's basic assumption groups also share some of the qualities expressed in the poem. Basic assumption groups as a shared but also unconscious group defense against anxiety often act as though what is going on is not in fact what is going on, including who and how others outside the group are conceived to be. In order to create and maintain a group that is engrossed in fighting an enemy or fleeing a great threat, the "other" must be conceived of as meriting fight and flight—that is, as evil and threatening. And the basic assumptions of dependency and pairing also require a significant manipulation of the reality in the moment in order for those who use them to wait for rescue from their anxieties.

Karen Horney speaks to solutions to anxiety where the anxiety in part or a large part is the product of imagination, fantasy, and creations of others in mind. Movement against others, who are bad, whether it is with a weapon or projective identification, constitutes interpersonal violence.

Movement toward others can also be fueled by seeing and "knowing" another or others to be willing to provide secure attachment and care-taking, even if this is not felt by the others. And movement away from others can become forceful where the other is simply known beyond any doubt and does at times act in ways that require interpersonal distancing and flight.

On Forgetting Your Place

Have you forgotten
your breed and rank?
How dare you aspire
beyond your place?

Even in America,
we must say, "Your Grace,"
for sure to his back,
if not to his face.

Discussion

This poem is about what sociologists describe as the dichotomy between "ascribed" versus "achieved" status. Ascribed status is fixed, often inherited, while achieved status is attained by working hard, by personal effort. The American ideal is supposedly one of there being no "ceiling," but instead, "the sky's the limit" to be achieved by dedicated effort. Reality, however, is quite different. Employees are urged to believe that they/we can advance through single-minded industriousness, and not recognize that, in many instances, it is both a lie and illusion that *one is nonetheless supposed to believe*. It is about denial of reality. I keep trying and am told to try even harder when I fail to reach my imagined, ever-elusive goal.

Managers and employees strive but are constantly "put in their place." Everyone internalizes the espoused ideal thinking there is something wrong with "us" when "we" fail to advance in "our" workplace and "climb the social ladder" of the American Dream. Blame and self-blame are an echo chamber, and they often lead to despair and possibly self-medication, suicide, and workplace violence. This story is endlessly repeated in toxic organizations.

Analysis

Sometimes getting ahead at work is like walking up the proverbial hill of sand. You think you should be able to get to the top if you try hard enough. But of course, much like the mythic Sisyphus pushing his stone up a hill, only for it to roll down, you find it gets a lot harder the closer you get to the top. And of course, everyone wants to avoid Icarus' fate who, in trying to escape Cyprus, flew too close to the sun with his wings of wax that melted and caused him to fall tragically into the sea. So the notion of try, try again is not lost on workers who often fall short of the wish and fantasy of obtaining achievable high position and have to settle for less—what they can actually achieve. The poem, discussion, and the hill of sand speak to what is an exceptionally common experience at work. One cannot necessarily claw one's way to the top.

Object relations theory offers insights as to how to keep sand out of one's shoes. If an individual has a tendency to split off and project his or her better qualities on others as mental representations, it is not surprising that the person will never measure up to this self-created idealized figure, whether the person merits it or not. "Why try?" it may be thought. Aspiring to high positions with corner offices may be unimaginable. There is then the possibility that we sabotage ourselves when we become anxious and create fantastic others in our minds, idealized others who are too good to match. Those who come to feel they are held in high regard may well project their more marginal personal attributes onto others who idealize them. The integration by others of these inferior attributes may be actively pursued (projective identification) by the idealized other. It is no wonder you then have to say, "Your Grace" to his or her back.

Group dynamics can also mirror the poem, since it speaks to ascribed social if not organizational rank. Entire groups may not feel they merit just and fair treatment, reasonable compensation, and a pathway to the top. Might managers be expected to include a small group of representatives from lower level positions in their organizations as a part of a strategic planning process? Raising this as a possibility by a consultant may seem naïve in many organizations, where those in lower-level positions are relegated to anonymity and non-participation in running the organization. There is also to be considered fight and flight basic assumption groups where one group seeks to dominate another, inflicting upon that group's members inferior status. Fighting back may only yield more damage and denigration.

Karen Horney's typology also sheds light on what may be said to be a dissonance gap between the best envisioned self (our ego ideal that is aspired to) and the reality one lives. Moving against others to achieve high position is a common strategy subsumed in the notion of clawing one's way to the top. This strategy may well be pursued with considerable neurotic energy leading to unethical, dishonest, and even toxic behavior. Sometimes executives are said to leave a string of bodies behind them. Also to be considered is moving away from others, where after a number of defeated efforts on the part of organization members, they give up and accept their position in life. Life is less stressful that way. It is something the appeal to freedom seems to invariably promise, but also in reality does not deliver on either.

We conclude that the psychology of not only falling short of aspirations, but also being actively inhibited in achieving the aspirations, is a common reality in the workplace. It is essential to find ways to cope with this painful and demoralizing appreciation, and psychological defense mechanisms often do the job.

Reflections

What more can be said of this state of toxic organizational affairs? Becoming disappeared and anonymous often seems to be written right into the script—job descriptions and implicit expectations. Everyone has had this experience, even the super wealthy and powerful, if only as children.

The poems underscore this painful realization that takes many forms. We suggest that equally important is the appreciation that the poems remind us that we, as anxious observers of these organizational and interpersonal dynamics, are left to struggle with our own sense of guilt and shame in accepting these organizational outcomes. The poems represent an effort to somehow deal with the anxiety and cope with shame and guilt. Acknowledging the humanity of these anonymous others is an important challenge to meet.

In Conclusion

Existential philosophers have long wrestled with the idea and dread of nothingness and the accompanying experiences of separateness, void, annihilation, and death. The fear of dissolution and falling forever is one of the most developmentally primitive and early catastrophes, and it is compounded through projective identification when another person, say, an executive, invades and poisons an already endangered space.

This chapter on the experience of loss of self and disappearance into anonymity in toxic organizations underscores the presence of recurrent relationships at work that include psychological violation. While disappearance and anonymity in roles may sometimes be a matter of choice, they are most often the result of how someone is treated: as if their *tasks* were performed, but *no one existed* to perform the task. In the poems, the stories behind the poems, and the psychodynamic analysis, we have explored what it is like to have "disappeared," and why, especially in bureaucracy, this is so widespread. We hope that in the course of reading this chapter, you the reader feel validated if your own workplace experiences resemble these.

In Chapter 8, we turn from loss of self through psychological disappearance, to both overt and subtle conflict at work, often driven by projective identification. The picture of unconsciously driven aggression differs markedly from the official ideology of the rationally and objectively organized workplace where there is "nothing personal, just business."

Notes

1. Allcorn, S. (2002). *Death of the spirit in the American workplace.* Westport, CT: Quorum Books.
2. Freud, S. (1923/1961). The ego and the id. In *The standard edition of the complete psychological works of Sigmund Freud.* Volume 19. London: Hogarth Press. pp. 12–66.
3. Allcorn, S. & Diamond, M. (1997). *Managing people during stressful times: The psychologically defensive workplace.* Westport, CT: Quorum Books.
4. Schwartz, H. (1990). *Narcissistic process and corporate decay: The theory of the organizational ideal.* New York: New York University Press.

8 Conflict at Work

The workplace is an interpersonal world articulated by the logic of hierarchical organization structure, professions and specialization, plans and direction, and of course the fruits of everyone's labor that yields our sustenance—money for our family, food, and shelter. The workplace without people is an inanimate collection of artifacts that, while containing symbolic significance, is non-operative and in the final analysis, meaningless. It is the people who come to work every day who create the organization, give it life and meaning, and in the end, give each other meaning and value. The workplace may be rewarding and fulfilling, but it also can become an interpersonal minefield where small and large conflicts are waged every day and sometimes without end.

It is also the case that the outside world crosses the conceptual boundary of the workplace. There are expectations that cross this boundary about fulfilling one's life and potential. Everyone also brings "baggage" from a lifetime of experiencing moments of reflection and empathy for what others have lived through to get to this moment at work.

There is a social and psychodynamic complexity to the workplace that often goes unacknowledged and unappreciated, and sometimes is systematically ignored. How can one help another deal with a past or present injury generated by a toxic organization? It may be said, "It is not my job." This chapter examines some of this historical, world-oriented, distressing, and hard-to-cope-with-and-manage aspects of the workplace. We suggest that in order to hope to cope and to help others, we must first have the courage to embrace what is really there.

Conflict at Work

This section reminds us all that there can be violence of many kinds just under the surface of the "rational" workplace, violence that we know is there and that we have seen and often experienced firsthand. It is a natural human tendency to look away from the distressing and distasteful, and in particular, violent, hostile, degrading, humiliating acts often perpetrated by individuals in powerful positions, but also inflicted laterally among friends and colleagues of similar organizational rank.

It is natural to look away, trying to ignore and shut out the awareness of interpersonal violence. This however only serves to perpetuate it, enabling those who perpetrate it invariably to win out. Who among us wants to confront the playground bully and supporters? Bullying at work has become an acceptable topic to address, just as it has for children at school and on the Internet. Because it is distressing, stressful, and anxiety-ridden to acknowledge, it is often ignored, rationalized, intellectualized, and redefined or reinterpreted away.

The language of the workplace is rife with *military metaphors*. Competition between organizations is often framed in the language of "Kill or be killed," "Where do you want to be in the food chain, eat or be eaten?", "It's us versus them, and only one of us will survive," and "It's a dangerous world out there, and zero-sum." Executive presentations to shareholders, corporate management, and boards often resemble military briefings (war rooms) made within dark, cavernous, auditoriums and conference rooms using PowerPoint lectures. The speakers use laser pointers to identify threats, saying in essence, "You're either with us or against us."

The following poems help to bring into awareness the interpersonal violence that is common in the workplace. At times it can seem like a war of all against all.

Bullring at the Office

In this bullring, little ceremony,
just business. No parades,
no fanfares, no picadors,
no toreadors—
just men and women
in their business suits,
standing around the coffee machine,
seated at the conference table,
riveted upon the PowerPoint presentation.

A bull among us is found,
at first like most of us
standing or sitting around.
We tease. We taunt. We flirt.
We goad. We provoke.
We soon get what we want
from our prodding.
He charges. We move from his path.
He pulls away. We turn from him
and ignore him for a while.

We pick at him from afar,
with glances over our shoulders,
and with words in barbed whispers.
We flash our outrage in his direction.
He charges. After all, he is a bull.
What else can he do?

Still, we are chagrined
that he would attack us.
We are hurt by the thought.
What, we ask, have we
done to him?

He pulls away. He snorts. He thrashes.
He charges at us again.
This time we draw our swords,
plunge them into his flank,
into his face, into his soft gut.
Blood arches in glorious fountains
all over the room, all over us.
It is warm and sticky on our suits.
We are pleased with our distressed carcass.

The ring is quiet. The ring will be quiet—
at least for a time, till another bull shows.

The bull—we tell ourselves—
was a troublemaker, a loner,
never got along, never accepted authority,
never was really like one of us.
We are better off without him.
We turn away to go home,
to take these soiled clothes
to the laundry or the cleaners
before the blood completely dries.

We turn back for one last look.
shaking our heads,
We can only say,
"Bulls will be bulls."

Discussion

This grim poem imagines a workplace office to be enacting a metaphorical bullfight. You often do not have to examine too many toxic organizations before you find instances where individual people or groups (such as divisions) have been singled out and relentlessly provoked until they explode with indignation or perhaps "go postal." Employees, managers, and even executives keep getting "jabbed" with verbal spears, as if the goal were to provoke someone into an angry outburst and then get branded and punished or fired for "acting out."

The focus of attention is on the culprit whose supposed failings and wrongdoings everyone notices—in order not to recognize their own role in the emotional abuse. Meanwhile, the actual work—the tasks for which they are paid—usually suffers as the workplace drama is enacted.

Analysis

The bull as a metaphor surfaces for appreciation that violence may be displaced by a group into an individual (becoming a container) who acts out their violence for them. At the same time the group waves a red flag provoking rage within the bull who charges, feeling justified in striking back. This circularity seems to feel and think in familiar ways. We have seen it. We recognize it. We know it. We have waved the flag. We have fought back, sometimes at great personal risk. Expressions like "the bull in the china shop" and "getting loaded up" (by others) resonate with these harsh, if not cruel, individual and group dynamics.

The creation of the bull in mind readily occurs by evacuating our own anger and fear, then locating it in another person who is known intuitively to be vulnerable to taking in these projections. We first see the bull as a mental representation, and then the bull must *become* the bull if only via considerable urging and manipulation (projective identification). Once the bull is created, we, as individuals and as members of a group, become invested in keeping the bull around. After all we feel much better having projected our anger and fear onto and into the bull. It is also the case we know the bull is "bad" and dangerous and deserves what he gets—abused, disciplined, or even terminated perhaps with one quick plunge of the administrative sword by human resources.

We also see in the poem group dynamics that are similar to Bion's basic assumption groups. Fight and flight are perhaps the essence of the poem. If is almost as though there is what Thomas Hobbes speaks to in his notion of a "war of all against all."[1] Flight from the group's fears, anger, and rage leads to depositing all of these experiences in what is sometimes referred to as a "projective vessel" that is selected not randomly, but rather is based on an individual's known or intuited tendencies to accept the projections and act on them. Fight is then of course what this is all about. These primitive psychologically defensive and interpersonally aggressive dynamics stand a good chance of getting many injured either directly or indirectly, including feelings of guilt and shame. Everyone loses. "Lose-lose" is a familiar expression in the workplace.

Karen Horney offers another perspective on when we consider moving against others. The poem speaks to interpersonal and institutionalized organizational violence.[2] Movement against others in the form of vindicating wounded arrogant pride, exacting vengeful triumph, is a powerful perspective and one that speaks directly to the imagery of the applied poem. The poem provides no emotional space for moving toward others to receive caretaking and nurturance. Moving away from others is perhaps an option. Who wants to witness the bull rampaging through the organization injuring others, while being slowly slaughtered?

Case Report: Caged

A physician from Vietnam,
caged for five years during the war,
given an egg after four
to supplement his daily dole of rice,
came to the United States,
started all over,
his training, his life—
an exemplary doctor now.
We tolerate his accent;
he bows to ours.

We did not want to know
about his past.
We did not ask;
he did not tell
of his not-so-private hell.

Cage of wood,
cage of gold;
We give him room
to silence himself here.
No telling the cages
we've been in—
or occupy still;
Whose war was it,
anyway?

With this foreigner
we strike a bargain:
not to remember,
not to feel;
"Freedom" is the name
we call this deal.

We are each other's
guardian of the scream.
He is quiet;
he is tamed;
he is familiar now.

Discussion

The story behind this poem actually occurred. I worked for several years with this courageous man, now a physician, but once a prisoner in a cage in North Vietnam. Once he came to the U.S., very few people wanted to know the story of what he had endured before coming to work at the hospital. They only wanted to talk medicine and urge him to adopt their upper-class lifestyle. They sought to bury his past in him so that he would be just like them.

I watched the seduction of cars, home, living in the "right part of town," the medical doctor-talk and avoidance of anything personal. He was abandoned to the forced secrecy of his torture, his courage, his history. His colleagues did not want to have their comfort and complacency disturbed.

I admired this man, encouraging him to listen to his patients' stories while letting him know I was interested in *his* story. He was for the most part quiet, reserved, polite, and deferential to authority; he kept to professional discourse and smiled at others. I think that over time, he felt emotionally safe enough to tell his story, although always in measured increments.

He is South Vietnamese. Early in the Vietnam War he was in North Vietnam and captured, tortured, and put in a cage. Like so many other "Others," he was in the wrong place at the wrong time and was treated as a traitor and enemy suspect. He came to despise his communist North Vietnamese captors. When the war was over, he emigrated to the U.S. and sought to pursue a medical career which had been interrupted by the war and imprisonment. His determination and sacrifice were admirable. For a couple of years, when he lacked the income to live in an apartment or shared rental home, he lived out of his car. Despite many obstacles in the U.S.—from racism to a heavy accent—he prevailed, completed his residency, and has been a practitioner for decades.

Analysis

We might reasonably wonder who is actually in the cage that the poem creates—the doctor, the poet, or the reader. Everyone is individually trapped in different ways but also together. Sometimes facing reality is too painful to bear. So is allowing the nightmare memory to become conscious—often the goal of psychotherapy. There is an essence in the poem of no escape, no avoiding, and no resolution. The only hope is maintaining the tacit interpersonal contract—you don't mention it and I don't inquire. It is a standoff where conflicts past and present are tastefully avoided in favor of the new cage of the denial and a house in the right suburbs.

Object relations perspectives suggest that some things are too painful to be aware of. They are denied, suppressed, and split off from awareness but always there nonetheless to influence us. The poem speaks to toxic collusion in workplace dynamics where victims are created and sometimes disposed of. If awareness becomes too distressing, how very natural it is to feel it is the "other" who is at fault for our anxieties.

Group dynamics are also at work creating the context of the poem. In order for the interpersonal collusion contract to work, everyone has to tacitly agree, and those that do not must be pressed to conform. "We do not talk about his past." The doctor had to fight to live, but all those around him are in flight from his fight. The reality must be banished or changed, and knowing must be limited. Flight is a powerful group dynamic that, when mobilized, no one should call into question. It is after all a group defensive dynamic.

The ostensible freedom mentioned earlier speaks to moving away from this long-suffering physician. There is, it seems, hope in the pursuit of freedom from knowing, discussing, or even acknowledging this individual's past life and suffering. "Freedom" is indeed the name we call a deal like this. Freedom from anxiety is what makes him and his past disappear.

Thaw in the Ice

> Imagine—
> age-old foes
> sit down with each other
> in a safe space, tell stories
> of how the other is a monster
> who inflicted grievous wounds
> that can never be forgotten—
> only to hear the enemy's own story
> of vulnerability, of suffering, and of fear.
>
> Each begins to listen more
> by having been listened to deeply
> by listeners who arranged the meeting.
> No miracle, but minute breakthroughs
> of compassion and concern,
> a tiny thaw in the ice,
> a small breach in the wall—

Could the enemy be more human than monster?
Might tomorrow not be condemned
to be the same as yesterday and today?

Discussion

Psychoanalyst Vamik Volkan's path-breaking psychopolitical work in international diplomacy inspired this poem.[3] His work facilitating meetings between historic enemies with their traumas, fears, hates, and grievances–Greeks and Turks, Palestinians and Israelis, Estonians and Russians—provides many insights that apply to toxic organizational life—inter-group animosities, ruthless leaders, groups that were favored over others.

Stories of managers and employees in different and conflicting organizational "silos" or geographically separate divisions are common.[4] Positive change requires everyone to feel safe enough to confront each other with their stereotypes and grievances, and sometimes to find commonality despite enormous differences in role and function and status. In turn, they become more human and less wooden to each other as an outcome. They can imagine a future that simply did not compulsively repeat the injuries and hate of the past. Collaboration is always a possibility even when there is a history of conflict that spans centuries.

Analysis

Organizations can be filled with foes and monsters and terrible swift swords of destruction and termination. At times it seems as though many organizations like it this way. Does it provide an adrenaline rush or provide an outlet for aggression? Does it make a convenient tabloid topic to speak about over coffee, lunch, and at the metaphoric water fountain?

Or—is it the case that some of our fellow workers really are monsters that need slaying? These monsters that are bullies and backstabbers are filled with aggression they often have trouble controlling.[5] They create a riveting but dysfunctional and toxic workplace that harms others, disrupts collaboration, and impairs the ability to work together effectively.

Monsters and evil doers are, in part, created in mind via denial, splitting, and projection. The other ends up possessing our worst qualities, providing us a false sense of knowing the evil nature of the other. And we, by evacuating our bad sense of self, become much better by comparison. We may be so invested in knowing the other person, group, or even nation as "bad" that we encourage them to act accordingly, making projective identification a reality.

Group dynamics are prone to splitting and projection that encourage the emergence of Bion's basic assumption groups to defend against anxiety created by our self-created monster. Fight and flight basic assumption groups appear, creating endless inter-group and intra-group rivalries and conflict. Also to be considered are dependency and pairing basic assumptions where magical rescue from the situation is worth waiting for, especially by an idealized leader who must ultimately and paradoxically fail to care for the group.

Karen Horney offers insights from the perspective of the three directions of interpersonal movement. Certainly, once the monster is located, moving against this individual or group is merited. Defending against and attacking the monster are merited especially in those cases where the harm created by the monster is narcissistic injury to an expansive sense of self. Monsters are also frightening if not injurious, so that moving away from them can become a priority—a flight to freedom. And movement toward others usually within a group (the herd) that has confronted a collectively created monster can be comforting and reassuring. It may also be a retreat into fantasy. The monster will not come for me next.

In the Cross Hairs

"*O mia patria, sì bella e perduta,*" Giuseppe Verdi, *Nabucco*.

O, my country, to what good end
do you put your people
in the cross hairs of a rifle sight?
What do you so fear that you
spew hate to fend it off?
Were we not all somewhere unwanted,
kept on the other side
of a fiercely guarded wall?
Do we not all fear that which
we so long toiled to attain
will be taken away?
We are all haunted
by the same dark night.
I can see my own reflection
in the face of the foe I would kill.

Come! Let us sit at the same table
and dip our ladle in the same pot.
The vineyards are plentiful;
no one need thirst here.
Let us lower our shields
and put to our lips
a draught of reconciliation.

Discussion

This applied poem was written amid the invective and hatreds spewing forth in American culture and its politics. It was and is a time of polarization, when countless political cartoons depicted people with the *cross hairs of rifle sights* on them. Political correctness had given way to open hatred of vulnerable groups in the United States. Compassion was absent and was seen as a sign of weakness. Rage and violent racism prevailed. The topic of "violence in the workplace" and fears that some disgruntled employees might "go postal" were widespread.

The poem is a protest and lament about the national—as well as the organizational—mood. Would it be possible to bridge the rampant splits into irreconcilable "us" and "them" and come to realize that we all shared the same dark night? American politics have become worse. They have culminated in the emotionally savage political atmosphere that characterized the 2016 presidential election—and long after. Reconciliation and compromise are a distant dream—repudiated by many. Splits and chasms occur equally in toxic organizations—such as between shipping and receiving, human resources, production, research and development, finance, and administration, and between leaders.

Analysis

Sometimes reality is a stern task master. To kill or be killed is a painful-to-acknowledge zero sum reality. I win. You lose. Wish is merged with fantasy, and it is merged with a mythical idealized past filled with nostalgia.[6] If only we could sit down over lunch and have a meeting where we make amends, come together in a united cause, and agree there is a higher organizational or international good other than pursuing vindictive triumph. This of course may not happen, leaving organization members locked in a win-lose interpersonal and intergroup dynamic filled with toxicity and organizational dysfunction.[7] It is often the case that it is better to try to ignore these dysfunctions and their hard-to-manage underlying animosities. No one dare to tread in "no man's land."

Object relations theory offers insights into the creation of others who should be in our conceptual cross hairs. We often load others and groups up with all manner of negative thoughts, assigning evil intent with a pathological sense of certainty. They are bad and we are good. We see our reflection in the other, because we are really there to behold. Change in these circumstances is maximally challenging, ideally requiring that we create a safe enough space to surface these many projections of good and bad for reflection and discussion. Sitting at the same table is more than a metaphor. It is essential if the projections are to be observed to exist and perhaps taken back, creating better self- and group-integration, and in this process, allowing for more thoughtful, reflective, and intentional bridging of long-standing and magnified interpersonal and intergroup harm.

Group relations theory also provides insights into the poem and its discussion. Groups fairly readily develop standard ways of knowing and acting, sometimes referred to as a "group culture" or "organizational identity."[8] What one observes may also fit with Bion's three basic assumption groups. The fight and flight group may readily create interminable intergroup and international conflict. Calling the basic assumption groups into question can create enough stress for all concerned; not doing so (flight from this task) can itself become defensive response that cannot be overcome.

The group's investment in these defensive responses can be nearly absolute. As a result, the defensiveness is readily sustainable since it has worked as response to anxiety. And when there is a sense of threat, it is natural for group members to move toward each other to provide nurturance and reassurance in numbers. And there may arise a wish for a great leader to emerge that is thought to be worth waiting for interminably. The basic assumption groups create a context where making peace is at best problematic.

We also see in Karen Horney's three-part model elements that contribute to the dynamics in the poem. In particular, movement against others by putting the enemy in one's cross hairs is a powerful defensive response to any sense of harm inflicted historically or in the present. Getting even and vindication, it seems, are sometimes essential, and the only way forward, is to create an enemy that must be vanquished.

Conflict Avoidance

> Was it her words
> or sunken eyes,
> that led me to think
> of words' disguise?
>
> "I don't want to rock the boat,"
> she said, not once but twice,
> as we spoke of disagreement
> among her fellow doctors on the ward.
>
> "I prefer to let things ride,"
> she pressed the group in a shy aside,
> which led me to wonder more
> about choice of metaphor.
>
> Years before, she fled her country,
> traded war for open sea,
> a raft, a log, a boat, a dare,
> a hope for safety anywhere.
>
> Here, for once, no cliché,
> no mere *façon de parler*,
> but today, on a hospital ward,
> the old terror came ashore.

Discussion

This poem comes from a group discussion with resident physicians. They were discussing the issue of when or whether to speak up when their medical opinion differed from that of their superiors. One physician, a woman from South Vietnam, spoke of her reluctance to disagree. Instead she was especially emphatic and urgent, twice using the image of not wanting "to rock the boat" but to "let things ride." I wondered about her choice of words and the ardor in her voice. Was there more to her story, something more personal? Was her hyper vigilance something developed from her past? Was transference part of her current dread and urgency?

I felt it inappropriate and intrusive to press her while in the group. Later, in a private conversation she confided that she had been one of the "Boat People" who fled South Vietnam during the collapse of the regime. Her keen memory of fear for her life while escaping as a refugee left her forever alert. Not rocking the boat was a potent metaphor for a life-threatening experience that was once literal and real. Her recent encounters on the hospital ward with senior physicians brought it all back. The past became fused with the present. She was vigilant for a reason. Many elements of the present linked to personal survival as a physician in training accounted for her choice of words in the discussion group. Was it not the case all residents were in the same boat together?

Analysis

Can the workplace have poignant moments? Yes, it can but only if we can find the time, place, and will to listen to what is said, what is not said, and the body language as to how it is said or not. We must also possess the courage to listen to the words and the meaning behind the words—the metaphors of life and death. Can we at all place ourselves in a small boat beside her in a rolling sea with a long distance to elsewhere? Her fusion of the past with the present and the wonderment about her choice of words point the way to a higher plain of understanding and interpersonal relatedness.

Object relations theory suggests that we do put ourselves into others both in mind and in practice. Sometimes it is a good thing, opening the way for empathy, self, and other insights, and a more profound level of awareness. Projection, however, brings with it a cautionary note in that try as we may, we can never know her life as she lived it. But we can also try, which is perhaps all she or anyone can hope for. Interpersonal trust and respect can create functional working relationships where there are opportunities to change our mental creations by testing them with the other person in a safe enough interpersonal space, where trying and being wrong are a good thing.

Much the same can be said of many in groups who have had unique experiences at work that should be appreciated and respected, rather than envied or despised. Organizations need not so readily descend into fight and flight basic assumption groups or dependency and pairing. There is always the possibility within a safe enough "space" that defensive group dynamics can be inspected and diminished. Greater individual and group intentionality should be striven for to improve organizational performance.

Karen Horney's psychologically defensive movements of against, toward, and away may also be safely called into question sometimes by members of the organizations or with the help of a consultant, as in the poem and discussion. Dealing with dysfunctional workplace dynamics always remains a possibility, even though at any given moment it may seem impossible, and the boat everyone is in runs aground.

Music Director

He came to the orchestra
five years ago with great anticipation.
He would be the one to lift us
out of our doldrums.
His concerts were all sold out;
his Brahms and Bruckner were sublime.
Come to think of it, his baton
wielded magic with every piece he conducted.
Even the music critics raved.
he looked so young and spry.

How could this be the same man
whose concerts have lately
grown so stale? We begin to wonder:
was he ever any good?
His programs are so tedious to sit through;
he's looking strangely old,
and still has two more years
left to his contract. We are
secretly looking for a music director
to succeed him, someone
who will restore the vitality
he has lost.

This one—
we tell ourselves now
as we have told ourselves before—
will be for keeps.

Discussion

This poem bears witness to the journey of an organizational leader from a triumphant beginning to fall from grace. He had been heralded as a charismatic savior who would turn around the failing orchestra and organization. After several years, he came to be seen in a much less favorable light. He was seen as weak and ineffective, a big disappointment, a cost center. They wondered, "What were we thinking when we hired him?"

Whether the leader actually changed and declined is almost immaterial compared to the fantasized leader who would achieve the greatest of successes—"set up to fail" is an expression that speaks to this dynamic. His fall from grace was more a property of the organization's people and their fantasies than of his own behavior.

The conductor's precipitous decline in the eyes of musicians, audiences, and critics was remarkable and similar to other organizational leaders who fail in a highly visible way. Toxic organizations and outcomes are common. Their story becomes my metaphor for this poem about the fate of some leaders who happened to be conductors. Their story reminds us that "the fall" is rarely an exclusive property of the leader, but rather of a fantasy-driven *relationship* that is played out where everyone loses.

Analysis

How very common it is to find groups of people who seem to instantly idealize their new leader, who it is thought and hoped, will deliver them from evil and raise them to new heights. This leader is great, and we are not. The leader will save us; we not only think this but know. We give ourselves over to the leader to worship, to depend upon, and many times unquestioningly to submit to him or her. But then again, the height of the pedestal we have placed the leader on foretells of a steep fall to come as feet turn to clay and the idealization gradually collapses. Even "I" could do better than him, it may be thought by many.

Object relations offers insight for understanding how we create these shiny new objects in our mind, often based more on fantasy, wishes, and desires than anything else. The creation of an idealized other that diminishes us by comparison, by our projecting our better selves onto the leader's representation in mind, must also have with time the proverbial feet of clay made visible by accurate reality testing. The collapse of the idealization is the essence of the poem and the discussion. That which we create in our minds may also be destroyed. Who will be the next leader to idealize?

Group dynamics are also often at work where a group or organization comes to share a socially defensive a basic assumption such as dependency or pairing. Being taken care of by a powerful other is sought, but ultimately the wish is filled with enough ambivalence that anyone who rises to the occasion will inevitably not meet expectations. Only the hope for a new leader is what remains. The poem and its hope for a great successor speaks to unconscious group dynamics of being magically cared for by the fantasized idealized leader.

The poem also contains elements of first moving toward the idealized leader, and then, when the person ultimately fails to take care of these needy others which is an inevitability, the movement is against (the end of the contract) and once again toward a new leader. It is also to be appreciated that while individuals do act out these movements, so do groups who come to share the same solution to their anxieties.

No Place to Go–No Place to Hide

We are often confronted with an interpersonal world at work that is less than welcoming and perhaps so distressing and toxic at times so as to be entirely avoided, while at the same time unavoidable. It manifests itself in countless ways: the stern voice, rude interruptions, unreturned phone calls and e-mails, and "accidental" exclusion from meetings. These and many other workplace aggressions all speak the language of anger, hostility, rage, violation, exclusion, attack, lies, and betrayal. The feeling of being unwelcome may not be limited to a person or a group of people, but it comes to pervade the atmosphere of the workplace, what Yiannis Gabriel calls a "miasma" and we call the "toxic workplace."[9] What it is like to be here is sometimes foreboding.

Rush Hour Definition

I rush to the place
I don't want to be:

Rush hour is where
you speed to get
where you don't
want to go.

Discussion

This poem is about common experiences we all have. Rushing to work in rush-hour traffic is a norm, but one that becomes somewhat dreaded in the case of toxic organizations that can leave you feeling lifeless and emotionally abused. When we cross the organizational boundary in the parking lot, we metaphorically may become little more than an object manipulated by management. At a more "gut level" we may dread many of the people we have to work with but also: the halls, the walls, the bright lights, the offices, the rows of cubicles, and the more deeply Kafkaesque bureaucratic control and regimentation. The sense of "place" may instill dread and despair.

As for "me," I am productive, but my work may seem meaningless. Leaving my job feels too threatening, promoting a palpable sense of being trapped. Don't get me wrong: I'm not lazy, although I could do more if I felt that it was meaningful to me. I seem to leave myself out in the parking lot to which I am eager to return to drive home at the end of my day at work.

Analysis

Accomplishing good work can and should be a fulfilling experience—a win-win outcome for all concerned. Sometimes it is. Many times, this ideal is not met, and sometimes the anti-ideal is realized, creating an undesirable if not horrific and toxic work environment and self-experience. Much has been written about toxic leaders and toxic and dysfunctional workplaces. These common experiences are long remembered because of the harm they create that alienates employees from themselves and their work, each other, and the organizations. Much of this book speaks to this sad fact of work life. How much more extreme can an image become of leaving one's self in the parking lot before passing through the threshold of a punishing and unrewarding place of work?

Object relations theory offers some insight into the creation of the bad employees who must be controlled and dominated, and the bad organization that contains elements and experience to be despised. The creation of a subpar and deficient workforce in the minds of executives is enabled by splitting and projection as well as by projective identification, where the employees must fulfill the executives' bad and despised images of them created as mental representations in the collective mind of management.

Similarly, can one's work, working relationships, and workplace culture be all bad all the time? This is only possible by creating a despised workplace in mind by placing many forms of negative self-awareness into the workplace that is then familiar in its pervasive sense of "badness." At the same time, we feel better about ourselves, who have become the good person working in a corrupt environment or society. Good and bad splitting and projection create places and work where no one wants to go and where healing the splits is not likely.

Group relations theory also suggests that one result of splitting and projection can be the creation of a hostile workplace. Here, executives, managers, supervisors, and employees become locked into a fight and flight basic assumption group. Life can become a Hobbesian battle of all against all, creating profound and enduring organizational dysfunctions and stresses that feed anxiety and lead to ever greater reliance on a socially defensive system like fight and flight. These patterns of behavior become dependable and familiar, making changing them difficult, since much of the work of change must deal with confronting the splitting and projection that creates the evil other to fight or defend against.

The poem and its discussion also suggest that Karen Horney's three directions of movement offer some assistance in understanding the leaving oneself outside to be protected from the horrors of work life. Movement against others may be understood to include motivations of getting even with others who have harmed one's narcissism and expansive sense of self. The poem offers the specter that many times the harm is omnidirectional—everyone is getting hammered at work, and no one is happy or feels good about their work. And it is also the case that many others throughout the organization are the cause of this toxicity and must be defended against or attacked in return.

It is easy to find organizations filled with interpersonal and intra-organizational aggression and competition that consume time and resources and sub-optimize organizational performance. Sometimes these battles can become all-consuming, e.g. lists of enemies are created and vendettas conducted. In a hostile environment like this, moving away from others for self-protection and even leaving one's self metaphorically in the parking lot may well be felt to be a viable life-saving option. Freedom from institutionalized harm is a good thing, isn't it?

Caulking the Wall

> I speak with you—
> I attempt to speak—
> you say you are listening;
> you say you are speaking.
>
> But all I see
> is a wall of brick.
> You spend the time caulking
> as we continue talking.
>
> I keep walking
> into a wall;
> you insist there is
> no obstacle at all.

Discussion

This poem is inspired by Robert Frost's gentle protest poem, "The Mending Wall," with its wistful refrain, "Good fences make good neighbors." This poem is about *stonewalling* at work, where walls are built and maintained between us.

My companion, the "other," never acknowledges the wall, so I am left wondering if I am imagining it. Still, whatever the subject we are discussing, I experience the other as unapproachable behind a wall and emotionally as well as physically unavailable.

Analysis

The poem first calls to our attention to the symbolic wall that is always present in the form of interpersonal boundaries, and that it is a challenge to manage from both sides. On either side the self is protected from losses of personal integrity, and the other becomes a managed interpersonal or inter-group relationship. Walls (Frost's "good fences") are paradoxical in terms of their life sustaining self-containment while also being barriers precluding communication and interpersonal relatedness.[10] Those who may need the walls and interpersonal boundaries the most may well deny they are there, since to acknowledge not seeing and listening to others might be felt to be a sign of weakness or self-centeredness and being antisocial.

It is also the case trying to tear the wall down only reinforces the perceived need for the wall (the "caulking" in the poem) as protective, at times creating an ever-bigger attack on the interpersonal boundary and a corresponding ever-greater defense of the boundary. No wonder some relationships do not work at all.

Object relations perspectives provide some insights into the creation and maintenance of these interpersonal boundaries that seem to divide up the world into myself (or group) and everyone else. Occasionally a few others may be allowed to cross the boundary, allowing for interpersonal intimacy. Splitting and projection cast aspects of self and other awareness out beyond these boundaries, both as mental representations and in life. The alien other beyond the boundary is too different and threatening, filled with one's fantasies of badness and even horror. The self that remains inside the boundary is magically purer and more innocent and worthy of protection. Good-and-bad splitting and projection implicitly include boundaries in mind and in life.

Groups are notorious for creating group boundaries around one's tribe and land, and one's professional group and specialized work. Organizational silos that are often alluded to as inhibiting communications and cooperation at work are examples of protective intergroup boundaries. They serve many functions, but most fundamentally demark who is in our group and who is not. Intra-organizational conflict is often abundant and often boils down to proverbial "turf battles"—fight or flight basic assumption groups.

The poem also reminds us that the workplace is filled with movement that is sometimes against others but also toward and away from others. The walls inhibit these directions of movement when movement is threatening. On one side of the wall we may understand there is movement away from others. No one is allowed to enter my space. However, the presence of this interpersonal barrier for those who want to move toward the other behind it rules this out, leading to movement against the barrier. Interpersonal or group dynamics like this should be familiar to everyone.

Storytelling, or Flawed Narrative

> I tell the wrong story;
> I tell the wrong ending,
> the wrong beginning,
> the wrong middle,
> the wrong moral,
> the wrong point.
>
> I tell the story in
> the wrong rhythm,
> the wrong cadence,
> the wrong meter,
> the wrong rhyme.
>
> I give the story
> the wrong hero,
> the wrong villain,
> the wrong fool,
> the wrong substance,
> the wrong form.
>
> Whatever story I tell,
> I keep getting it wrong.
> Maybe there's no way
> of getting it right—
> or maybe all along,
> it's supposed to be wrong.

Discussion

This poem is about stories and storytelling and story listening in organizations. All workplaces have stories—official stories, informal stories, secret stories, and gossip-stories/rumors that spread rapidly. There are stories that hold the organization together and some that tear it apart. We are immersed in stories at work and elsewhere.

Organization members who are found to have told the wrong story may find themselves reprimanded for having the wrong ideas. They remember the sting of a rebuke from a supervisor when they spoke what seemed to be an ordinary thought. "That idea won't work here," or "How could you possibly think that?" or "That doesn't fit our organization's mission." With time, these employees share less and less, keeping their thoughts and ideas to themselves. "I" would think that not only were most of my *thoughts and ideas* wrong, but that *I myself* was wrong.

Analysis

The poem and discussion surface for inspection how often individuals in the workplace are "deauthorized" to speak and offer thoughtful, reflective, critical thoughts. If you want to keep your job, towing the line becomes essential, otherwise the stinging pain of rebuke is long remembered. Fitting in can become itself the primary task. Self-differentiation can leave one out on a limb that may be cut off. We are talking here about self-editing and self-regulation in the service of the safety of conformity. Behavior modification with its rewards and punishments works to deauthorize our voices and thoughts and ourselves and our authenticity. "We don't do that here." "We don't think that way here." This gets expressed in many ways to shape who we become at work.

Object relations theory provides the perspective of how individuals and groups become defined and experienced as good or bad in organizations. The investment in denial, splitting, and projection can be hard to overcome. Once you make it onto the "bad" list you may never get off of it. And of course those on the list also engage in splitting and projection, creating others with a much greater sense of malevolent intent and leaving one's self innocent and victimized. This splitting into opposing good and bad representations in mind can lead to projective identification and the shaping of others to become like the in-mind projections. Our experience as consultants and employees is that once this occurs, it is hazardous to call it into question, revisiting the nature of the poem.

Group relations can create similar outcomes where the voice of an entire group of people is disregarded, suppressed, and discounted. They are trying to be heard, but the harder they try the more they are ignored. Might it be the case that sometimes the emperor actually is not wearing clothes? Must the messenger of contrary news and ideas always be scapegoated? Is it ever wise to ignore employees who surface embezzlement or a workplace hazard? Fight and flight are group movements that are implicit in the poem. What is said must be defended against. Must the messenger be limited, maligned, or eliminated? Individuals and groups that are disregarded may simply give up and withdraw from contributing (flight). Should the train run off the track, there is the painful moment of "I told you so."

Karen Horney's three directions of interpersonal and intergroup movement surface for reflection the creation of others who "tell the wrong story" and must be ignored, rejected, or disposed of. Those who harm our grand vision and ideas are sometimes too painful to have around. And of course, if one gets one's hand slapped for saying something not acceptable, withdrawing it from participation is a reasonable response. Flight to freedom and movement away from others who are punishing is entirely reasonable.

Telephone Salutation

I can hear it in your sigh,
in your pause,
as you hear my voice,
then my name.

Your perky greeting
cast to all callers
falls an octave
to tolerant dismay
the way C major
slips down a third
to *a* minor,
or even more dejectedly
into *c* minor,
a mere half-step away.

If you must contend with me
it will be in a minor key—
as if the burden
of my voice and name
were worthy of Schubertian calamity.

My flaw is to sing at all:
not the note,
but the singing
is out of place.

Discussion

This poem is from a time when I had frequent conflicts over ideas and priorities with many superiors and colleagues alike. The sentiment was identical with that expressed in the previous poem. Here, the reprimand and disgust were not expressed in words, but in *voice*. It was easy to feel wrong, different, out of place—an embarrassment not only by words but also by the tone of voice, the silences, the raised or lowered volume of the person on the other end of the telephone.

How often do we not look forward to the telephone ringing because the sound of the voice on the other end may have a condescending tone, signaling there is something wrong with "me"? Feeling punished, paralyzed, a disappointment, an embarrassment sometimes may ring in one's ears.

Analysis

There is sometimes something more profound in the *quality* of one's voice than what is said or not said. The poem provides a point of inspection of how readily we spot the quality of the voice of the person on the other end of the line. Rising intonation or volume sends a signal, as do pauses and speaking softly or lower in pitch. Our voices are magnificent instruments of communication. The poem and discussion draw our attention not so much to whom and what is said by others, but to the effect on the listener.

There is an unstated rejection of the caller in the poem and discussion. Feeling rejected, discounted, and punished—all with a slight change in how words are vocalized—encourages us to enter the world of the listener who hears the sigh and pause. How can we put ourselves into the poem? Perhaps everyone has encountered these experiences and one need not wonder.

Object relations theory contributes to understanding how this undesirable other who is on the phone is to be dismissed as bad. Splitting and projection create and maintain these personas of others as mental representations. When the call is received, others are treated in a way consistent with the projected content, encouraging the person on the other end to accept the projections.

Group relations perspectives serve to magnify the effects of the sigh and pause, in that once the other is identified as bad, the group members, by embracing an undiscussable socially shared defense, are authorized to discriminate against the undesirable other. Dynamics like this contribute to understanding how those who are cast out of groups can choose, as an option, to fight back. It is often those who are bullied who do so, as perhaps in the 1999 massacre at Columbine High School or any number of workplace massacres. The social magnification of the shared defense and basic assumption group becomes a powerful social dynamic that is seldom addressed for fear of also being targeted and cast out.

Karen Horney's directions of movement for individuals and group dynamics also inform understanding the toxic nature of the sigh and pause. The movement against the object on the other end of the line is subtle but clearly communicated. You are, whether you are called or the caller, not welcome. What can one say or do? Moving away from these punishing experiences may be all that is left to do—not call or pick up.

The sense of being free of this yoke of rejection can be refreshing and self-preserving.

The End of the World

I have seen
the end of the world—
it is not a place.

It is when
a wave of killing scorn
rolls across your face.

Discussion

This poem comes from frequent encounters with colleagues and supervisors. Being constantly wrong, having alien ideas, hearing rejection and abandonment in tones of voice and facial expression, being in constant conflict and in turn constantly wary can culminate in a sense of "the end of the world." It is not a cosmic, world-destroying Armageddon, but an interpersonal perdition that can also feel as though all is lost. The much-written-about schizophrenic "internal catastrophe" is in a way being enacted both in my mind and in the interpersonal world. Feeling banished and evicted from sharing a common humanity in toxic organizations is sometimes a reality. In these moments, we must remind ourselves that this is ostensibly an *organization with tasks to fulfill*, one that at times turns into a toxic life experience. Personal or group survival in the movement can be lost.

Analysis

A moment of silence after reading the poem and discussion seems important. . . . . A notion like existential anxiety somehow seems to come up short in terms of appreciating the message and life experience that contain qualities one sees in post-apocalyptic movies. This chapter ends with perhaps the darkest of notes and an appreciation of how soul-deadening the toxic organizations can become when individuals are turned into numbers, fodder, human resources, or assets possibly earmarked for the junk pile. The poem accesses the intensity of the experience of rejection that leads to isolation and despair.

Object relations theory suggests that projective identification is an act of aggression, where the other person or even group is in part taken over by the "attacking" other. When this happens the object of the aggression loses parts of self, but also acquires alien parts of self, that in the poem translate into a dying—if not physically at least spiritually. The object is subjected to destruction. The scorn is an experience of loss of self and self-worth. Interpersonal boundaries have been violated.

Group relations theory offers insights into how groups destroy other individuals and even their own members who deviate from group norms. Other groups may similarly become objects of ridicule and scorn, sometimes allowing for an entire group to be subjected to endless disparagement and punishment, and in world affairs, genocide. Fight and flight basic assumption groups are abundant in some toxic organizations where there is uncontained conflict and competition among groups, leaving little hope that a leader will make life better.

Karen Horney offers insights as well. The contempt held for others that is so clearly expressed is the harshest of movements against others, who, having been turned into objects, may be disposed of. Movement toward others and an appeal for love and attachment in these settings would seem to be futile and self-destructive to pursue. Movement away from those who scorn may yield some peace of mind, but in the workplace, ultimately no personal safety. The rejection can become a fully immersive and soul deadening experience.

Reflections

This chapter has inspected the often-brutal nature of our toxic organizations that introduce dysfunctions that compromise performance. Sometimes attack and counterattack are merged with personal survival and one's paycheck to create an unpalatable stew that becomes the unbearable nature of our lives at work. Who wants to come to work when combat is often waged between those in powerful positions and where many employees can become collateral damage, perhaps to be laid off when performance lags enough? As authors with lived experiences—we are left to wonder.

In Conclusion

This chapter has been a poetic exploration into the heart of darkness of workplace conflict. Our organizations contain much that is good for their members and those they serve. Regrettably and unaccountably, they also contain institutionalized and interpersonal aggressions and assaults that can become soul-stripping, leaving everyone lost in the darkness. It is, then, essential if positive change is to be created, that this toxic, dark side of organizational life must be acknowledged. We hope that the poems, discussions, and analyses have provided a modest step in the direction of promoting reflective insight in the service of change.

Chapter 9 explores an important aspect of all our lives, our health, and the healthcare systems that play a role in keeping us alive and healthy. The poems approach healthcare as one specific type of organization. Medical groups, hospitals, clinical laboratories, skilled nursing facilities, and many more healthcare delivery organizations all contain work experience that may be fulfilling or not. And not to be forgotten is the nature of the patient's encounter with the system and its healthcare professionals. The poems help to peel back the confusing, frightening, and mundane nature of our healthcare institutions as toxic organizations.

Notes

1. Hobbes, T. (1982/1651). *Leviathan*. New York: Penguin Classics.
2. Diamond, M. & Allcorn, S. (2004). Moral violence in organizations: Hierarchic dominance and the absence of potential space. *Organisational and Social Dynamics*, 4(1), 22–45.
3. Volkan, V. (1997). *Blood lines: From ethnic pride to ethnic terrorism*. Boulder, CO: Westview Press.
4. Diamond, M., Stein, H. & Allcorn, S. (2002). Organizational silos: Horizontal organizational fragmentation. *Journal for the Psychoanalysis of Culture & Society*, 7(2), 280–296.
5. Babiak, P. & Hare, R. (2006). *Snakes in suits: When psychopaths go to work*. New York: Harper.
6. Gabriel, Y. (1999). *Organizations in depth*. London: Sage.
7. Allcorn, S. & Stein, H. (2015). *The dysfunctional workplace: Theory, stories, and practice*. Columbia, MO: University of Missouri Press.
8. Diamond, M. (2017). *Discovering organizational identity*. Columbia, MO: University of Missouri Press; Schein, E. (1985). *Organizational culture and leadership*. San Francisco, CA: Jossey-Bass; Schein, E. (2010). *Organizational culture and leadership* (4th ed.). San Francisco, CA: Jossey-Bass.
9. Gabriel, Y. (2012). Organizations in a state of darkness: Towards a theory of organizational miasma. *Organization Studies*, 33(9), 1137–1152.
10. Ogden, T. (1989). *The primitive edge of experience*. Northvale, NJ: Jason Aronson; Ogden, T. (1999). 'The music of what happens' in poetry and psychoanalysis. *The International Journal of Psychoanalysis*, 80, 979–994.

9 Life at Work in Hospitals and Clinics
Modern Medicine and Us

Our many decades of experience in health care and academic health sciences centers allows us to inspect the contribution poetry can make to understanding these organizations where life and death and healing reside. Academic medical centers with their schools of medicine, nursing, and allied health, many research facilities, and linkages to often huge medical centers with massive hospitals and a network of clinics are, some consider, among the most complex organizations on earth. They often have 5,000 to 10,000+ employees and budgets of $500 million to approaching a billion dollars or more. In sum, they are big, complex, hard-to-know-and-manage organizations composed of many professions and subspecialties.

Modern medicine provides its healthcare workers, researchers, patients, and research subjects many different faces and experiences that influence how one knows oneself at work or as a patient, who with one word, can be transformed into an inanimate object. Patients are also often turned into a disease: "the gallbladder in room 758" and "the senior with multiple systems failing." Medical professionals and staff often find themselves pinned in by incomprehensible policies and procedures, laws and regulations, and administrative and financial restrictions that impinge upon the care they wish to provide to their patients. So complex has health care become that it takes "teams" of practitioners to collaborate on the care of many patients. Patients confronted with this may come to feel vulnerable as multiple confusing "inputs" are heard.

The poems here peel back for reflection some of this complexity to reveal the feelings and meanings that reside in the *experience* of working in a health sciences center. "What it's like to work here" is far from limited to caring for patients. It also involves relationships between countless types of professionals and employees. As if this were not complicated enough, everyone who works in these organizations has feelings, fantasies, and defenses relative to the organization, their colleagues, and patients who are dependent and may succumb to their illnesses. Knowing and making sense of this is a worthy challenge for a poet or an organizational researcher or consultant.

Baggage

"I regret to inform you that your papers are not in order."

(Anon)

He enters my tiny office
And stops dead after barely
Crossing the threshold—
Forty years of a teacher's
Books, boxes, and files
Confront him.
He gazes bug-eyed
With a mixture of awe
And terror, then pronounces:
"This is *OCD**
If there ever was."
His slack-jaw closes;
He quickly turns around,
And leaves, speechless.

He could not fathom
That you never know
What old, useless
Piece of paper, buried
In some file or pile,
Might one day save your life,
Get you into another country
Just in the nick of time.
Every piece of paper
Is a potential ticket
That might pull you back
From death's door.

I have a friend, now deceased,
Whose father got his family
Out of Germany that way
Back in 1938, when
It was perilous to be a Jew.

I have no doubt that
People suffer from
Obsessive thought and
Compulsive deeds,
Cannot stop themselves
From their endless rituals

Of counting and checking.
But don't be so quick
To judge and diagnose
My hedge against
A loud thump on the door
At midnight, or a summons
To a railroad yard,
One suitcase per person.

Tell me there is nowhere
In this place a piece of paper
That might redeem my life,
And I will tell you of a dread
So vast that no tidy diagnosis
Can fathom its reach.
There is a ticket to life
Somewhere in this office—
I just don't need it yet.

*OCD is an acronym for the American psychiatric diagnosis,
"Obsessive-Compulsive Disorder."

Discussion

The family medicine resident in this poem had just left a nearby class-room in which he, fellow family physicians, and I had completed our hour of discussing difficult relationships in their work, including, but not limited to, patients. He had never visited me in my crowded office filled with paper in stacks or files and books everywhere. He took one look and was aghast. Speaking aloud, he gave me an instant diagnosis of Obsessive-Compulsive Disorder (OCD) and left in a hurry. His impression was nothing he was willing to discuss with me. In his mind, I and my world were bizarre, abnormal, alien, and so frightening as to make him flee the scene.

The world of physicians relies on meticulous, highly structured and ritualized, controlled processes—at least in ideal. In some ways we are all not that different. Despite appearances there was order in my office, but it did not conform to his expectations, and it was easy to feel my office was an alien world when compared with *his* world. Certainly, he could not stay around to hear from me how I used my office space and the things in it.

Analysis

Labels are powerful tools in the hands of anyone, and especially in the hands of someone who presumably knows how to hand them out. What can be said of the "C" word—*cancer?* Does it not strike terror into one's heart and point to annihilation from out-of-control cells growing at a frantic pace? What can be said of the many labels we are immersed in every day—fat, old, tall or short, unemployed, uneducated, attractive, and wealthy? The food may be too hot or cold, too salty or not, too spicy or not. And we might be crazy, neurotic, narcissistic, or even obsessive-compulsive. We in fact might find ourselves in the eyes of others to be little more than a pile of labels crammed into a space in their mind, where our existence depends on them but is also circumscribed by them. Imprisonment by label gives us the sense there is no way out and no escape—unless of course you can return the label to the rightful owner, reversing the projections.

Labeling others, while seemingly an innocuous, objective exercise (overweight or old), is never just that. The labeling work is first done in one's mind, consisting of a search for the "right" self-created representation of the "other(s)," leading to the location of one label, perhaps among many possible selections. Why does that particular label seem to stick to one's representation of the other in mind? The answer is that there are many unconscious dynamics involved that arrive at the fabrication of the mindful representation of the object and the location of the suitable accompanying label. We may split off a distressing sense of self or fantasized self and place it onto the representation. I am perhaps overweight, but compared with you, I am not at all overweight. Splitting this self-awareness off and projecting it onto the other provides relief in the moment from the distress of my own self-awareness, but at the expense of the other(s) when the label is hung around their neck.

Group dynamics also often contain the creation of labels such as evil empires and despicable or threatening ethnic groups and others who then "need" to be controlled or eliminated. Group dynamics driven by unconscious and socially shared defenses can become a powerful force, leading a group to act in ways most members would not act if left to their own devices. Fight and flight group dynamics, in particular, are not only fueled by unconscious and shared defensive measures but also by the labels assumed and assigned. We know we are right and good. The handing out of labels helps to identify all the other players and ourselves relative to them, much like uniforms and colored arm bands. The labels make clear who is with us and who is against us. It is they who are wrong and bad. We are good. Dynamics like this can lead to fight and flight and entrenched polarization based on good and bad splitting and possibly to destructive social outcomes such as war.

Labeling others is a form of interpersonal aggression as evidenced in the poem and may be thought of as moving against others according to Karen Horney. After all, what more can be said of expressions such as name calling and "Sticks and stones may break my bones, but words will never hurt me." Bullying others through the use of labels is common. However, also to be considered is labeling that draws people together, a movement toward others. The labels may encourage adoration, idealization, and willing submission, creating excessive dependence. And many conflicting labels placed on another, others, or one's self, may lead to a feeling of just wanting to be left alone and movement away from others. "Keep under the radar and try to not be noticed." "Just leave me alone!" There is, many times, a real sense of freedom in the splendid isolation of one's office stuffed with familiar papers.

Importance

The doctor entered the dark hospital room,
Looked down at the baby, woke him
To check his pulse and eyes,
Check the electronic gauges,
Wrote new orders in the chart,
Walked back into night's long corridor.

The nurse followed him by a few minutes,
Adjusted some IV's,
Gave the baby an injection
From the doctor's orders.
She gently patted his bottom
As he cried. She left
For the next room, another baby,
Another chart, another doctor's orders.

Dawn. Housekeeping—clockwork.
The housekeeper came in with her bucket and rag mop
To cleanse the floor of germs.
The baby was still crying, squirming, flailing.
An immense, black-skinned woman, she bent down
And sang to the baby before she mopped—
A Gospel hymn, pianissimo,
As if this room were the manger at Christmas time.
The baby, now asleep, never knew
How far off key she had been.
When she finished, she swung
The wet mop-head with same lilt
As she had sung. She left,
But only after she had lingered.

Discussion

The story that inspired this poem took place and continues to take place countless times in medical clinics, hospitals, nursing homes, rehabilitation centers, and much more. Many physicians see their role as circumscribed to deal only with strictly medical, "hard science" matters. Doctors and nurses awaken sleeping patients to take vital signs or to perform tests or to give medication—including sleeping medicine.

One might say that a crying baby is merely "collateral damage" that is a necessary part of a physician or nurse performing good, competent medicine, on or to the patient's body. "Real medicine" is largely impersonal if not depersonalized. There are, of course, many exceptions to this rule. Still, it is often housekeepers, volunteers, and visitors, who treat the patient as a *feeling person*. Over the course of this book thus far, we have acknowledged many times the impersonal treatment of subordinates by supervisors.

In the world of American medicine, patients are often near the bottom of the status hierarchy. They are gazed upon, poked, percussed, measured, stuck with needles, and often spoken to as if they are inferiors, even non-persons, objects to do things to. They do not question these experts or their treatment. The fact that they are sentient human beings is often experienced by physicians and nurses as obstacles to the assertion of their control and authority that are a part of the performance of routine medical rituals. Often, only the housekeeping personnel take the time to redeem their humanity.

Analysis

We all want to receive compassionate care in the arms of a loved one or from the song of an unknown other. Even a baby will recognize and understand this at an affective level. Is it perhaps the lowly status of the housekeeper, uneducated and trained, that makes her so authentic, accessible, and available for nurturance in the space between her and the infant? The poem suggests this must be appreciated in an otherwise efficient and sterile clinical world of notes and procedures.

Object relations provide the theoretical basis to understand how infants and all patients become in part dehumanized, stripped of their humanity and their modesty during the encounter with healthcare providers, who are themselves often stripped of their sense of values in favor of seeing ever more patients in ever less time. Healthcare economics is a stern task master. Patients enter a context where there is no time to get to know them, and they are almost of necessity turned into objects in the minds of caregivers in order to deliver what is most often impersonal health care. These objects in mind become objects in fact. The objectification is, in its essence, a social defense against realizing how the patients must be treated in order to provide cost-effective medicine. Patients' hopes and fears, anxieties and distresses, must be ignored, referred, or medicated away.

Group relations theorizing also sheds light on hospitals and their organizational dynamics that include defensive value systems and cultures, as

Isabel Menzies discovered.[1] Healthcare staff, ranging from physicians and nurses to technicians and housekeepers, must all cope with the limitations of providing health care to patients seen in clinics as well as in hospitals and other types of inpatient facilities. Medical educators have trained them as to how to think and feel. They learn how to defend against anxieties associated with illness and death as well as neediness and dependency on the part of the patients they serve.

As a result, the healthcare delivery milieu often seems to be filled with deeply embedded and unacknowledged fight and flight basic assumption groups. The workers embrace a system of beliefs that helps them to manage and limit self-awareness. The threat of encountering distressing anxiety requires a shared socially defensive response to fight back against it, and failing that, flight from the context that creates it.

Karen Horney's three directions of movement also offer insights into the poem and the delivery of modern cost-efficient health care. Patients may be understood to move toward healthcare providers in a role of dependency. It is their hope to be healed. However, we also see in the poem that patients may be objectified and turned into abstract "cases" requiring treatment. This may be understood as moving against the patients who become problems to solve, and faster is better, so that more appointments can be crammed into the clinical hour or rotated through hospital beds. Also, to be appreciated is the unmentionable desire on the part of everyone to move away from this economically based and over-engineered context that limits caregivers' time and turns patients into objects. Is it possible that everyone loses?

Appointment at the Doctor's

> She tries to hold her life together
> With baling wire and duct tape.
> Sometimes it stays, other times
> It unravels and breaks apart.
> She and her mother—a grocery store
> Cashier and housekeeper—
> Are the sole providers.
> They can't afford a car,
> And get around town by asking
> Relatives for rides and taking the city bus.
>
> It is a blustery winter day;
> Her youngest of three kids
> Is sick with high fever, cough,
> Aches, kept her up all night.
> She called the doctor's office

In early morning and was worked in
Their schedule today. Her mom
Stayed home and watched
The two other kids. She bundled
Up her little son and walked
To the first bus stop. They waited.
The bus was late—like it was sometimes
Early, you could never count
On the schedule. Then there was
The transfer, and waiting for
The second bus. At last they walked
From the bus stop to the doctor's
Office, more than an hour late
For their appointment. The receptionist
Scolded her for being late; so did
The nurse after her. They called her
Difficult, unreliable, inconsiderate.
Didn't she understand what a schedule is for?
A doctor, a nurse?—
Overheard the clamor, and said,
"Let them stay. We'll work them in.
You never know what some people
Have to go through to get here."

Discussion

This scenario has been repeated in many forms many times. Sometimes it does not have so favorable an outcome, and the late-patient-with-sick-child is turned away. Medical clinics and hospitals are supposed to run like a clock, so that a 2 p.m. appointment means precisely 2 p.m.—nevermind wait times.

Physicians, after all, are busy professionals, and their schedules are usually filled—driven by their institutions to see more patients in less time to generate profit. "Time is money." Physicians, nurses, and administrative staff have little time to "work in" late patients out of fear of "getting behind schedule" and compromising patient service for those on time.

Patients, however, have equally demanding lives that interfere with being "on time." For economically and socially disadvantaged patients who struggle with poverty, an unpredictable world at home, and unreliable transportation systems, confrontation with the rigid schedules of the healthcare system can be challenging. As in the poem, an occasional physician or nurse will have compassion for what these patients must go through and make room for them in the schedule.

Analysis

Access to care are words often waved about by politicians, obfuscating the realities of poverty in the United States and its many times drastic, negative effects on the health of those who live a grinding life in poverty. The poem makes this palpable and painfully available for thoughts, feelings, and reflection. Access is only access when access is possible, or available or provided in this case out of a sense of compassion on the part of the person who intervened.

Object relations theory is part of the essence of the poem and the scene it portrays. The mother and child are late and are transformed from human beings into problems that may or may not be accommodated in the clinic's busy schedule. They are objectified and dehumanized, which is understood by appreciating the role that denial, splitting, projection, and transference play in turning human beings into disposable objects. The staff and nurses see in the mother those aspects of themselves that they despise, such as contempt for others, processes, and systems, as well as feelings of entitlement that are also disowned. In their minds, the mother is turned into that which she is not, and then treated as though she is like the internal representation, as the projections leak out into interpersonal space. Transference fuels the negative emotional energy by the transfer of what may be many past experiences similar to this instance onto the present. "Don't you just hate people like that?"

Group relations theory provides an equally applicable perspective. The mother is confronted with a large organization staffed by different people doing different kinds of work. We all must cope with large, bureaucratic, hierarchical organizations divided up into specialized divisions and departments. We can all locate this experience and the transference that comes with it, the confrontation with this toxic organization in mind, and too often in reality. This subdivision of work generates subcultures, each with its own goals, values, and methods that include unconscious shared defenses against its customers or clients as well as against other subdivisions in the organization sometimes referred to as "silos."[2]

Many toxic organizational dynamics include unconscious fight and flight rituals that impact the quality of the products and services offered. The poem highlights this in terms of the willingness of the staff to aggress and denigrate the mother in life and in their minds as a shared psychologically defensive response. They are fighting back against the mother as "part object" (pieces and fragments and not as whole person or subject)—late, a problem, and a human with feelings and needs that must be ignored. It takes someone outside this defensive system to call their actions into question, returning the group to the reality that a patient as an experiencing individual needs their help.

Also accessible in the poem are Karen Horney's directions of movement. The mother and child have with considerable difficulty come for care—moving toward the healing providers. The providers, however, when confronted with a poor mother with a sick child who have arrived late, are, it seems, authorized in their minds to turn the mother into an object that may be aggressed—movement against the mother. And the reader of the poem would likely also empathically understand that the mother, after being treated as unworthy of respect and compassion, might very well want to get away from this horrific experience—movement away. The reader of the poem should also be considered here. Is there not a movement toward the mother on your part and perhaps away from the staff and their objectionable behavior?

Receptionists at the Clinic

It seems as if receptionists at the clinic
Can hardly do anything right.
They're constantly being reprimanded
For scheduling too many patients,
Or too few; for not giving enough time
For patients to see their doctor;
For working in too many "walk-ins"
Without appointments; for sending
Patients back to the exam rooms
With incomplete paperwork;
For not scheduling follow-up appointments
Or referrals to other specialists
The way the doctor wants;
For putting through too many phone calls
To the nurses and doctors in the back.

Receptionists are called "the front line"—
Sometimes as if the patient were the enemy;
They are the guardians of the boundary
Between the public and the clinical worlds.
So many confusing and contradictory
Rules: when you please one doctor or
Nurse, you offend another.
Then there are the patients—
Showing up late for appointments,
Calling in at all hours, demanding
To be seen *today.*

A frontier is a dangerous place to work:
Herd patients like cattle,
And treat them with respect
As individuals.

Heed the physicians' needs
For "high production" rates
Of "patient flow" and "volume,"
And be courteous and a "good listener"
To assure "patient satisfaction."

If receptionists cannot be
Highly paid, perhaps they
Could be awarded a Medal of Valor
For valor under fire.

Discussion

This poem looks at American medicine from the vantage point of receptionists in medical clinics—people who are often called "front line," as if patients were in some sense the foe. When I first wrote this poem, I shared it with the medical director of a family medicine clinic. He cracked a smile and said, half-humorously, "Don't share this poem with the girls [women] at the front," the receptionists.

For the most part, receptionists are "damned if you do, damned if you don't." They are caught in the middle and in the cross fire between patients, doctors, nurses, and the business office. The first to greet sick, anxious, demanding patients, parents, and families, they often feel that they can do nothing right. And they are among the lowest paid employees of clinics. They are not considered to be "professionals." This poem gives voiceless people a voice, bearing witness to their work and its importance in the "system."

In the corporate or health sciences center's structure—although "patient care comes first," "patient satisfaction," and "clinical excellence" are organizational mottoes—the reality is that they are a poor second to income generation. Operationally this translates into physicians seeing as many patients as possible during each clinic session. As already mentioned, "Time is money." The more time a physician spends with a patient, the fewer patients are seen, and the less clinic income is generated.

Receptionists are responsible for maintaining an expeditious flow of patients to maximize revenue, while also being a cost center, which is also true for physicians and nurses. Spending more time with patients is a cost. If more physicians, nurses, and staff are hired or their salaries increased, there must be a corresponding increase in revenue from seeing more patients faster. There is then to be appreciated a toxic relationship between service and revenue, a zero sum for healthcare organizations and their patients.

Analysis

Many places of work are conceptually (if not in practice) cut off from the rest of the world in order to maintain order, control, and productivity.

When employees come to work they assume the mantle of their job title and job description and preferably leave their private lives outside. The boundary between well-controlled workflows and the chaos that exists outside this boundary is often underappreciated.[3] The poem speaks to the notion of *boundary management* in that the "front line" figuratively and literally exists to mediate between the chaos on one side of the boundary (the patients and larger society) and the regulated and engineered clinic interior that contributes to keeping healthcare delivery humming along. Words like "service delivery design" and "patient volume" underscore that there is not much difference between an assembly line producing cars and a clinic's operations that produce patient outcomes, units of service, and revenue.

Stated in terms of object relations' good/bad splitting, if receptionists, who manage the boundary between inside/outside—the good versus the bad—do not keep the "patient flow" at a steady and rapid rate, they stand the chance of being seen as doing a "bad" job and may be *lumped together with patients* as impeding clinic efficiency. They risk being fired. Likewise, *physicians* who spend too much time with patients are also potentially as "bad," and as "them" rather than as "us." If they fail to shape up on revenue generation, they may also risk being terminated.

Object relations theory also provides insight into tendencies to objectify others. Sometimes heard in clinic management discussions is the phrase "cattle call" that refers to large numbers of patients, historically often poor, indigent, low-paying people on Medicaid, being scheduled for visits at the same time. The patients and their family members fill the waiting areas and sometimes the hallways. This defensive turning of human beings into a metaphoric herd of domesticated animals is enabled by splitting and projection, where a bad "other" is created that in turn may be treated accordingly.

In sum, good/bad splitting is resident in the boundaries of the poem. The lowly paid receptionists are subjected to merciless stresses and strains from both sides of the boundary they manage. Maintaining the boundary between good and bad in this type of toxic organizational experience is a challenge that deserves a battle ribbon for valor. This takes courage but also defensive psychological splitting on the part of the receptionists to deal with it every day they come to work. They may experience themselves as doing "good" or the best they can, and everyone on either side of the boundary as too demanding and "bad."

Group relations perspectives contribute insight into to this scene of good and bad splitting, with chaos on one side of the front line and order on the opposing side. What is labeled the "front line" is in fact a group of employees who perform many different functions such as patient registration, making sure forms are completed by patients, collecting co-payments, and scheduling new appointments. They staff the phones, front desk, and back business area. As a group, they come to share many commonalities in terms of working together, and also in terms of how well they know and understand themselves and their work on this critically important boundary between the world without and the world within the clinic.

The poem and discussion and the use of "front line" suggest fight and flight are an underlying shared unconscious defensive system that, while sometimes clearly present, is also often undiscussable. The front line takes incoming fire from the patients and public and friendly fire from those behind the lines. In order to live a life at work under these conditions that include low pay, perhaps marginal technical support and training and loss of respect between high- and low-status positions, it is no wonder these critically important workers may feel that they are "under fire" from all sides—truly a no-win situation. Fight and flight are to be expected under conditions like this. And to be appreciated as mentioned earlier, the patients form a group that shares dependency not only on the receptionists but also on the entire, many times unfathomable, system of health care that lies behind the front desk.

Karen Horney's three directions of movement also provide insight into the scene portrayed by the poem. The receptionists and other frontline workers receive aggression from both sides of the battle line, as patients move against them with feelings fueled by dependency, fear, anxiety, and often ignorance of how the clinic as a system works. It just seems so impersonal when their health problems for them are so very personal. And when deficiencies in performing the boundary management function allow some chaos to filter through, this fuels the perception that the frontline employees are unable to do anything right, leading to punishing encounters (movement against) with the healthcare providers behind the front lines. Also to be appreciated is that patients begin their encounters with the healthcare delivery system by moving toward it to receive caretaking. And it is sometimes the case that patients give up trying to receive service and leave (movement away), perhaps moving to a new front line in another clinic.

Schizophrenic

> "Schizophrenic"—the word leapt out
> at us the way a tidal wave washes over
> a ship. A single word on his medical chart
> took on a life of its own, engulfed us all
> into the undertow. He disappeared
> beneath the surface of our own words.

Discussion

This brief poem is about the ubiquity of medical labeling—and labeling people in countless other circumstances in life as well. Medical diagnostic labels have not only a *scientific denotation*, but often carry with them a *moralistic connotation* as well. The latter is a way of putting distance between "us," the health professionals, and "them," the ill. Consider the consequences of being diagnosed with HIV. Stigmatic labels like "schizophrenic" are a way of banishing categories of people from shared humanity. It is a way of denying human kinship with sick and vulnerable people: "He's sick, not me (thankfully). I'm normal—not crazy." The pejorative, stigmatic label brands the patient as "other," dehumanized, degraded, and made into a (clinical) object. The patient disappears as a person and becomes only the objectified name of the disease, swallowing the person's identity.

Analysis

The poem and discussion once again underscore how powerful labeling is as an interpersonal defense mechanism. It is also important to appreciate how imprecise labeling of illness can be when one considers the varying definitions of the labels, the criteria for using them as a diagnosis, and the abilities of the person presuming to do the diagnosis. Sometimes things are not black and white but rather a shade of grey. Add to this reliance on labels that, once assigned, *become* the person who disappears inside of the label, thereby protecting others from having to actually know and work with the individual as a human being. How comforting!

Object relations theory with its denial, splitting, and projection that create a good and bad, black and white world helps to explain the powerfully seductive nature of clinical labeling and likewise labeling of all kinds in life. Splitting off and projecting one's distressing aspects of self and locating them in another person in mind as a representation, and in life as projective identification, creates this divided up good and bad experience of self and others. "I am not sick or vulnerable; you are."

Especially harmful is the taking over of the other person via projective identification, where the person is known beyond any reasonable doubt to fit the label. He or she is treated as though he or she *is* the label, distorting the other person's sense of self and violating his or her personal integrity. This is an insidious form of interpersonal aggression, that if not resisted may become incorporated and part of one's self, being taken over by not only the disease process and label but also the projections. The individual in a sense voluntarily assumes the "patient role." If the label fits, wear it!

Group relations theory contributes to understanding how a group may single out one of its members who, for example, comes to symbolize all that is wrong with the group. This amounts to fight and flight, where the group is in flight from awareness of its own problems and limitations and attacks a member as the source of this experience. The person's incompetence, deviousness, and self-serving behavior, to list a few attributes, are labeled as such, and thereafter the person carries this and these labels sheltering the group from assuming them. This can create serious personal disorganization within the individual, leading to distressing thoughts and feelings. The person has become an unwilling container for the group's projections. Similarly, other groups may be targeted in the same way. How very often one or more parts of a large organization are often thought to be the source of many of the entire organization's problems.

The three directions of movement Karen Horney discusses contribute to understanding the victimization of the patient, implicit in applying the label to the person who risks becoming little more than the label. Correct or not, the label has been hung around the person's neck, stripping away the patient's humanity. The implied intensity of interpersonal violence in the poem relates directly to moving against others as a psychological defense mechanism to allay the experience of anxiety. Assigning a label that then distances and protects oneself from others creates a sense of relief whether acknowledged or not. The patient may have been moving toward others for help, but then finds him- or herself enveloped by a clinical label (schizophrenic, AIDS, cancer) that takes over one's life, where movement away from others but also one's self—flight from the experience and reality—is an entirely reasonable reaction to what has just happened.

Medical Records

An ocean of patients' medical files,
Deep within the lower catacombs
Of hospital and outpatient clinic,
At the end of long, dark halls,
A place hard to find
Except for the familiar and hardy;
Here sit the staff ready
To file and retrieve history,
Ancient and modern,
To give patient and doctor
A past, something to build on
Besides the impression
Of the present moment,
The terror of ahistoricity
Where there is only
The blood pressure, pulse,
And temperature of now.
Medical Records wins few prizes
For the effort, but without
Them, we would know

Mostly "what" but rarely "why,"
And where to go from here.

Discussion

Nearly two decades ago when electronic medical records were just beginning to be used, I became friends with the director of Medical Records
at my family medicine department. Located on the first floor, Medical
Records is where all the old paper patient-charts are stored, and from
where they are retrieved when a physician needs them in the clinic or
teaching area. These spaces are filled with metal shelves of boxes and
row upon row of filing cabinets. To the observer this space is immense,
cavernous, packed, and often dark as compared to the brightly lit clinical
spaces. It makes an impression on you and a basis for a poem.
  Not only did Medical Records feel bleak and foreboding, but it was
also situated behind two large doors at the end of a dark hall at the back
of the first floor, near the exits. Many people elsewhere in the building had decorated their offices with paintings, photos, and soft lamps
to make their workplace cozy and home-like. This place felt desolate,
like a dungeon. Light needed to fill the darkness in some way in order to
redeem Medical Records from obscurity and invisibility.

Analysis

There are in organizations places that are dark and foreboding. Sometimes it is an executive's office where the resident within is punishing and
feared. Sometimes it a department ensconced behind its doors, where
entrance is not welcoming and a metaphoric darkness settles over anyone
who stays too long. And there are places within one's self that exist as if
in an ahistorical catacomb (the unconscious), always present influencing
thoughts, feelings, and behavior, but seldom if ever visited to discover
what is really there. A visit to Medical Records seems to have a lot more
to say about organizations, life at work, and ourselves than meets the
eye, perhaps due to the dim lighting and imposing nature of the shelves
lined with thoughts and memories best avoided. Opening the door speaks
to poetry as being a royal road to awareness to the unconscious. What
can one say of the stillness of the air, the scents of vast amounts of paper
slowly deteriorating, the light coating of dust, and the silence of the space
when one stands by the endless aisles of steel shelves?
  Object relations theory suggests we not only create other people as
internal representations, but we also create everything else as well. Why
would a small child be afraid of the darkness under his or her bed, or
an adult fear the nature of the deep night—or a strange and unfamiliar
place, sound, or group of people? We fill ourselves and the world of
our subjective experience up with sometimes unimaginable darkness and

threat that always seem available to us due to them residing in our ahistorical unconscious. We not only create as a free-forming self-dialogue what is around us as internal representations, but we also may transfer our past memories, thoughts, and feelings onto the present. This can create a present filled with fear that energizes interactions with others—our object relations. Think for a moment about the former brief story and its surreal scene. What is behind those massive doors?

The poem can also be understood by using a group relations perspective. As a group the Medical Records staff, while taking pride in managing the paper records, had to also deal with filing backlogs and misplaced patient records. Physicians learned long ago that completing medical records is no fun. They did not want to go to Medical Records to do their work.

Medical Records and the billing staff who are dependent on healthcare providers to document their work, easily become bad mental representations, encumbering the good physician with messy details so that all services are billed, and fraud is not alleged. Medical Records and billing staff fight back against incomplete records, while the physicians still flee from (are resistant to) completing them—a zero sum with all of the accompanying inter-group conflict. Electronic medical records have changed this, but some work remains to be performed often in the presence of the patient, where this encounter separates the patients from their caregiver. And there remain medical record audits to check the accuracy, correctness, and completeness of the physician's work. Escape (flight) from chart documentation is not possible.

Karen Horney's movement away (appeal to freedom) from that which is alien, frightening, and strange offers to reduce the anxiety that the poem evokes. What would it have been like to have been there, in the foreboding presence of the long rows of dimly lit steel shelves? The poem as a form of bearing witness is a movement toward others who care and understand, and who show empathy toward those tasked with filling the boxes with paper, maintaining their order, and guarding them from the chaos beyond the doors that lead to the "real" world. Also present is the implicit nature of Medical Records, where its staff members have a role that is felt to be moving against everyone else to complete the records, while all those others move against the Medical Records staff because they do not want to complete the records, having to dot every "I" and cross every "T" to stay legal.

Why We're Here

> Change accrues like ice
> Wraps itself around
> Tree limbs and branches
> Until they sag.

Some break from the strain;
Others somehow hold.
New rules, new routines,
New procedures, new technology—
Just when you've mastered one change,
Another comes along like an ambush.
After a while, it's almost easy
To forget why we're here:
To care for sick folks—
For a lot of the poorest ones,
We're the end of the line.
Sometimes we have to remember
To remember, that what we're here for
Is just to do the right thing—
That says the same.

Discussion

This poem bears witness to the dedicated work of physicians who serve the poor and indigent who are in need of care-taking clinical services. They treat people who are forgotten by the formal healthcare system. Their dedication and devotion are to be admired. Many doctors in these underserved areas may participate in free community clinics and events that provide care for those who cannot afford medical care within the formal system. They seem to remember why they are physicians.

Analysis

Understanding the nature of rural health care and care for the poor is, as we are reminded by the poem, a weighty matter that all too often creates a challenge that our society figuratively sags under if not breaks under. Those dedicated to the proposition of providing health care for the most vulnerable among us experience a sense of personal mission and accomplishment that many physicians working in high-volume practices in urban areas envy. At the same time, these dedicated caregivers are under-recognized and under-appreciated. The poem serves to bear witness to this fact.

Object relations theory directs our attention to splitting and projection that create different others to whom are often attributed good or bad qualities. The sick folks in rural and impoverished areas are underrepresented in the political arena and underserved by the healthcare industry. They seem to matter less. They are not so much bad representations in the minds of others as they are not acknowledged at all or simply have their human needs disregarded. They are then split off and segregated in many instances. They become disposable objects who may be ignored. The creation of "them" as objects allows others to treat them as disposable, relieving the anxiety associated with being aware of their needs. The poem speaks directly to this societal marginalization of these individuals as well as of those who seek to serve them.

Group relations perspectives make clear that these sick poor others are not part of our group, and their presence as a group makes them a presence that must be defended against. Fight and flight group dynamics have become a large part of our polarized society, split along rural and urban lines, conservative and progressive political ideologies, and poor versus rich. The poor, sequestered in urban landscapes or spread sometimes almost invisibly across rural America, are divided off from "us." Expressions like "white flight" and "red lining" in real estate, and building "The Wall" between the U.S. and Mexico, speak to the implied threat of these "other" groups that must be "kept in their place" and vigorously policed to protect the rest from the few. The poem also speaks to the slow change in bureaucratic organizations and in our society, that is burdened by laws, rules, and regulations long established to explicitly or implicitly keep the splits just mentioned in place.

The poem and discussion provide an almost alarming sense of awareness of Karen Horney's three directions of movement. These underserved patients seek out care when and where they can. They are moving toward healthcare providers in the deepest sense of dire dependency on provider compassion and skills. At the same time, these patients and the physicians who care for them are segregated (movement against) from the mainstream medical community and in fact from society as a whole. The healthcare providers become medical missionaries in a wilderness created by a society filled with neglectful disregard for the rural and urban poor who are being rejected and discarded, in what is very often a strong sense of moving against them. And to be appreciated is that those who embrace these two directions of movement relative to the poor may want to look away, hoping to block out awareness by moving away from those who have a presence that is distressing and who society disregards.

Toward Outside Experts

> Be polite.
> Listen.
> Be respectful.
> Don't get up and walk out
> while they speak.
> Use what you can.
> Eventually they will leave.

Discussion

The poem is inspired by the following story. I had been teaching rural family medicine residents in Oklahoma for two decades. A family medicine physician told me the story of a recent humiliating organizational experience he had. His indignation triggered my own similar experience, inspiring the poem.

At one rural hospital's Christmas party, the invited speaker, a physician-administrator from an eminent East Coast urban medical center, admonished his largely healthcare professional audience to accept managed health care (HMOs, PPOs, etc.) as the inexorable wave of the future. He told the group to make up their minds and that it was simply a matter of altering their thinking to conform to the changes that made them primarily responsible to the corporation rather than to their patients. To make his point, he showed a cartoon depicting a steamroller smashing one doctor in the asphalt, while another wisely sidestepped destruction. The caption read: "You can become part of the solution or part of the pavement." The physicians' response was uncharacteristic of prairie decorum, in which you politely listen to someone with whom you disagree, and then go about your business as you had been doing. Instead, several physicians got up in the middle of the talk and walked out in disgust.

A week later, one of the physicians who had been in the audience, wrote to me: "*Does this [cartoon and the presenter's haughty attitude] not instill a sense of helplessness? A sort of ultimatum? This doesn't smack of fascism, does it?*" It is as if what is not supposed to be happening—in the caring professions, of all places—is in fact happening. It is a matter of trusting—and mistrusting—one's senses and one's emotional response. The heavy boot of managed health care, it seemed, promised to crush all opposition and create in the rural medical community an atmosphere of dread, rebellion, siege, resolve, and anticipatory, inconsolable grief at the prospect of losing their way of practicing medicine.

There is an additional layer to the story: the frequent contempt that many *urban* physicians, and their health sciences centers, harbor toward their *rural* colleagues. An attitude of superiority on the part of many metropolitan-based physicians often finds expression in condescension when they give talks to physicians, medical societies, and hospital staffs in rural America. Such was the scenario of this story.

It is also the case that increasing numbers of physicians in the United States feel demoralized, robbed of their identity as professionals, and treated as disposable employees by the experts who manage healthcare delivery. Many physicians have become disillusioned. What had begun for many as a "calling" to care for sick people has turned out to be a grueling job of "healthcare provider," where seeing as many patients as possible and generating income have become the central corporate governing value.

The story of the poem is then based on the threat of professional death and being crushed under the wheels of "progress" and efficiency. One is "saved" as a physician if one adapts to the change and the managed care metaphor of the steamroller. The future of medical practice lies in what may be understood to be identification with the aggressor and a repudiation of those "softer" values and virtues that characterized the historical relationship between doctors and patients. Paradoxically, if one chooses to "live," one also chooses a spiritual as well as vocational death-in-life.

Analysis

Outside experts are usually professional consultants, but not always. Some individuals have either published regularly on a topic or have been singled out as those who have accomplished change or developed insight. Regardless of the particulars, outside experts are often relied upon by senior level executives and CEOs to offer advice and also to lead and facilitate organizational change. As outsiders, they often bring new perspectives and skills that are not available within the organization.

They also often have specific approaches that they apply to all organizations (their comfort zone), and they seldom have time to come to know the organization, its history, and its people. They may then fairly readily recommend or impose change that is not consistent with life at a specific workplace. We have on occasion heard consultants wonder why it is that the people in the organization are not using the new processes or tools or software that they so diligently brought to the organization.

This appreciation once again returns the discussion to understanding the psychodynamic nature of toxic organizations and work life. How do members of an organization see, understand, and respond to outside experts who presume to know but also seem to not know? In particular, object relations theory offers some insights in that few employees would have first-hand knowledge of the consultants sufficient to say they "know" the expert(s). The expert is then naturally created in everyone's mind, and equally naturally these images come to be shared, creating a consensus group *object that* is known to be the consultant.

Having worked as consultants, we know this is the case. We are often seen in ways that may, for example, resemble past consultants who wreaked havoc on the organization or possibly even made a fine contribution that everyone appreciated. The mental object is of course manipulated over time to fit new information about what the expert said or did or the latest rumor. It is also not uncommon for many to believe that the expert is better and more knowledgeable than oneself or any group member, fueled by splitting off of one's competency and projecting it onto the consultant. The expert, being aware of this, all too often accepts the projections and perhaps encourages them. Organization members come to experience them as an outstanding expert whose advice should be unquestioningly heeded.

Yet another perspective that contributes to understanding the presence of experts in an organization is Bion's notion of fight or flight. The alien other, the outside expert, may find that there quickly arises a strong resistance to the recommendations being provided. The organization and its members are fighting back and moving against the outsider. It might also be the case that flight ensues when consultants are brought in to restructure and downsize. Staying out of the line of fire may equal personal survival. Another possibility is that organization members, including management, assume a role of dependency, individually and collectively. At the group level, the dependency is expressed when organization members, after projecting their competencies, begin to feel incompetent, inadequate, and not up to the task of running the organization. They need expert help. Once again, they have split off and projected their self-efficacy onto the expert and retained a sense of not being able to manage effectively.

Dynamics like this are invariably present and must be appreciated by both outside and inside experts and the members of the organization. If awareness of these dynamics is not forthcoming, then there is likely going to be an unconscious dynamic of continually recreating the need for the external expert. We need help!

Reflections

Healthcare institutions are specialized kinds of organizations, the work of which is closer to matters of life and death, sickness and healing, than are most organizations. Their inhabitants must think and feel about— and try hard not to think and feel about—what most people in other workplaces mostly avoid. (In this way, people in military occupations share much in common with people in health care.)

The poems, experiences, and analyses in this chapter delve into the emotional world behind diagnoses, treatments, high-tech tests and machines, protocols, and rituals that live at the surface of health care. In addressing "what it's like to work here," we have tried to use scenarios that evoke the emotional undercurrents of life at work in health care.

In Conclusion

The poems and discussion in this chapter have been anchored in the lived experience of the workplace—that of healthcare delivery and, in particular, the patient and physician relationship. There are many aspects of healthcare delivery that often go unseen if not intentionally ignored. In striking a balance between business and the art of caring for patients, many hard-to-manage individual, group, and organizational dynamics arise that must be appreciated to exist, thereby allowing them to then be open to inspection and to the possibility of being addressed.

We now turn to a common feature and experience of the workplace— meetings. Meetings often consume an inordinate amount of time, often becoming stressful and unproductive. In Chapter 10 we explore the irrationality and psychological oppression that often underlie the official picture of meetings driven by explicit agendas.

Notes

1. Colman, A. & Bexton, H. (Eds.). (1975). *Group relations reader*. Sausalito, CA: Grex. pp. 281–312.
2. Diamond, M., Stein, H.F. & Allcorn, S. (2002). Organizational silos: Horizontal organizational fragmentation. *Journal for the Psychoanalysis of Culture & Society*, 7(2), 280–296.
3. Diamond, M. & Allcorn, S. (2009). *Private selves in public organizations: The psychodynamics of organizational diagnosis and change*. New York: Palgrave Macmillan.

10 Meetings at Work

Organizations regardless of size and complexity have *meetings* to cover a broad range of topics, ranging from social gatherings to meetings on planning, problem-solving, decision-making, finances, strategic planning, production, human resources, management, and marketing. Areas of professional sub-specialization have their own meetings. There are cross-functional meetings among specialized areas, and there are meetings of task groups and project teams. Lots of meetings are possible and may dominate much of how work is accomplished.

Meetings can be rewarding, but also not well planned, frustrating to participate in, unrewarding in terms of decisions and work produced, and most fundamentally they eat up a lot of time that might otherwise be put to better use. Meetings are often the subject of humor and complaining in organizations. It is little wonder that in many meetings, participants look at their smart phones and PDAs, check their e-mail and surf the Internet—under the table.

The poems speak to a darker, less productive side of meetings that may be alienating, threatening, and promote feelings of frustration, anger, and even fear. Most often there is an official, spoken or written, agenda. There are also usually unofficial, informal, secret, and even unmentionable agendas. Often these hidden agendas are about power, dominance, superiority and submission, loyalty, uncritical consensus-building, competition, mirroring of greatness, and control. These unofficial agendas sabotage and supersede the work of the group—and the tasks of the wider organization. The poems probe beneath this surface to attend to what is really going on.

Business Meeting Agenda

> Like the rest of us,
> he sat attentively along the perimeter
> of a conference table
> three inches thick and ten feet long.
> It took four husky men

to lift the table—
though as the room's centerpiece
rarely was it moved.

He lifted the one-page meeting agenda
from the table, stared at it
as if some god were silently commanding him.
From one end, he began to fold the page,
first lengthwise;
then from one end
he folded the flaps in
toward the center-crease.
He took the side flaps now,
folded them each twice along the diagonal
toward the thickening middle—

Wings! Long, sleek, slender,
wings they were!
This was no fidgeting I witnessed
from across the table
deep within the business
of our meeting.
He did not press the folds
firm to some airborne finality
or pick the paper fuselage up
between thumb and index finger.

His eyes, his ears, even his voice,
they held attentive all along
with the shifting speakers
and the conversation,
as if at the table
two of him were seated;
throughout the time
he barely glanced down
to watch his hands—
but he was free.

Discussion

This poem is a fantasy about an organization member who attends a meeting that he already anticipates would be tedious and run in a heavy-handed manner. While making a paper airplane might be considered as passive aggressive from the viewpoint of those in charge, from the view-point of the plane-maker attendee, it was an act of protest. Birds and airplanes—even paper ones—are symbols of freedom. The act of making the paper airplane might be seen as an assertion of personal autonomy in the face of group-and-leader coercion.

We all imagine doing something like this in lifeless, bureaucratic meetings in which the leader wanted the group to rubber-stamp his or her agenda. Many readers may have also felt something akin to this at times. How refreshing and life affirming is a fantasy that reaffirms I am still alive rather than spiritually deadened.

Analysis

The poem surfaces for consideration the duality of mind and body. The paper folder had to be there at the table listening to the meeting but also not there in a mindful sense—elsewhere and free. There is a deeply felt sense of alienation from one's self and work present in the poem and the discussion. This is all too often the nature of organizational life, dominated by powerful others who call the meetings, control the agenda, regulate what happens in the meeting, make all the decisions while asserting it was a group decision. There is a soul-deadening appreciation of organizational dynamics like this that suck the life out of committee members and the organization as a whole. These organizational experiences and dynamics are often played out in and are symbolized by all the meetings that are held that absorb time and energy, often to no one's advantage.

Object relations theory offers insights into the nature of the experience of sitting at the three-inch-thick massively heavy table, and the ever-so-life-giving potential of the paper plane. The table may be thought of as a creation in mind that receives projections of power, control, and oppression (a projective vessel), becoming a symbolic presence that is much less dangerous than the representation in mind of the powerful, controlling, and oppressive leader of the meeting. It is a safe object to manipulate in fantasy. How very often we find ourselves avoiding dealing with others and the accompanying projections and transference by placing and displacing the fantasies, projections, and transference elsewhere for personal safety. The table may be safely hated and despised, not unlike the notion of kicking a waste can. Much the same can be said for the paper plane that comes to symbolize an object invested with freedom and avoidance of being controlled and supressed by the leader's power as symbolized by the oppressive table.

Object relations theory directs our attention to dividing up people and the world around us into manageable bits and pieces, both in one's mind as representations and in practice. Defensively manipulating the world in one's mind relieves distress and anxiety and helps us to cope with realities that are not kind and nurturing. The poem and discussion speak to this sense of psychologically defending oneself against the power and control of the leader and the accompanying alienation from self, one's work, others, and the organization. We are perhaps only left with folding paper planes and leaving condensation rings on the table.

Group relations perspectives contribute insight into a group that sits at a massive table, obligated to submit to the leader's power and control. The agenda (that symbolizes control) is folded by one person (fight) but is likely vicariously enjoyed by others at the table much as in the poet's fantasy. Many at the table might prefer to be elsewhere (free) and may be understood to share a social defense against the oppressive experience (flight). These group dynamics represent "flight" from the leader, the meeting, the agenda, and even the oppressive presence of the table. Flight creates in this case the freedom from being consumed by a metaphoric black hole that absorbs talent, energy, engagement, creativity, and critical thinking, often leaving nothing behind to be observed. It was after all, "Just another meeting."

Karen Horney's movements against and away also shed some light on the meeting. The fight and flight basic assumption group may be reframed as movement against and movement away from—the leader, the members of the group, the agenda, and the larger alienating organizational context. The plane symbolizes a movement against the leader, the agenda, and the oppressive symbolic presence of the table. The folding, while observed by others, goes unchallenged by anyone, perhaps indicating that this individual is in fact doing something for the group, where its members feel a sense of aggression but prefer someone else to act on it. This is much safer. And the sense of being there and not there, paired with the idea of a paper airplane and the unrealized potential of flight from the meeting, provides a more than adequate symbolic context to understand movement away from the meeting, leader, and the oppressive nature of the table—a flight to freedom as Horney describes.

Art Form

The art of not being here—
a form as demanding
as haiku and fugue.
To look through
the parallel iron bars
before me
and walk the snowy pasture
with cows,
to fly aloft
with Canadian geese,
to escape the incarceration
of here—
while giving you
my undivided attention.

Discussion

This poem is about the paradox of not being spiritually present while being physically present at a meeting. It has close kinship with the previous poem. If control by the leader was the unstated wish, then the "way out" required to escape incarceration is the poet's response.

I have participated in meetings in which I created in my mind my exit. Imagining freedom from oppression takes a lot of work. Part of the work is creatively sculpting in body language the appearance of being present, while soaring high with Canadian geese.

Analysis

Meeting participants who prefer to not attend, even in welcoming settings, may escape into fantasy similar to the alienating context in the first poem. The word *boring* comes to mind. We have all been there and done that. The child gets irritable and demanding after listening to adults talk to each other for a while. Adults can feel the same way in meetings where the topic and discussion is of minimal interest or possibly minimally understood. There is then to be considered the leadership, the agenda, and larger organizational context, together with what each participant in the meeting and each member of an organization brings with them to the "table."

Object relations theory provides insights into how a meeting may for some be interesting, important, and engaging, and for others boring, leading to doing one's e-mail under the table. They are there but not particularly here. The experience of the moment is manipulated in one's mind to reduce the stress of being present. The experience of the child just mentioned may be transferred onto the present, creating a sense of impatience and irritability.

The events in the meeting and the people present are subject to being manipulated omnipotently in one's mind as mental representations. Others who are present are thought to be a certain way regardless of evidence to the contrary. They are effortlessly transformed in fantasy. One person, it may be thought, is smart or well-informed, while another is just the opposite and perhaps ignored or worse, dismissed as boring and irrelevant. Object relations theory combined with transference suggests that a meeting is never just a meeting—much more is going on than meets the eye.

Group relations theory offers perspectives for this poem, and the sense not so much of fighting back against toxicity resident in the meeting, but rather flight from the imprisoning bars to a snowy pasture where joy might be experienced. It is not uncommon to find subgroups in a meeting that have "punched out" and are not participating. They are present but gone. The members of the group join this basic assumption group that is seldom called into question by others or the leader. There may also at times develop a group similar to the pairing basic assumption, where there seems to be hope for better leadership, but little effort is expended to locate it and even less risk assumed to provide it. The would-be leader, it is understood, will not be followed, creating the basis for intuitive knowledge of the attendant risk attached to anyone bold enough to offer better leadership.

Karen Horney provides similar insights where the call of the snowy pasture is a movement away and an appeal to freedom, to perhaps be left alone as an individual to fantasize or as a small group left to chat about mutual topics of interest. Movement away is so strong in the poem that movement toward or against seems to be largely not available or accessible to members or subgroups in the meeting.

Stay Beneath the Smoke

"Stay beneath the smoke,"
the firefighter urged us
in his talk the other day.
"Down there you'll breathe
and not choke."
The more intense the fire,
I thought, the shallower
the band of breathable air.

How transportable a metaphor,
I further mused, to take to meetings
where the talk was thick
with threat and innuendo,
and where I had to crouch low
toward the floor of my soul
to avoid asphyxiation
from the heavy smog of words.

Discussion

This poem was inspired by a fire-prevention seminar I attended. It proved educational about responding to potential fires in the workplace and offered, as well, a rich metaphor about ways of adapting to endless meetings at work. Meetings can be spiritually asphyxiating. Suffocation of one's real self is an imminent possibility in meetings. Just as breathing is essential to life, it is as essential to the life of the human spirit at work. Staying beneath the Orwellian smoke of words, gestures, tones of voice, and PowerPoint slide lectures can prove to be a life-saving strategy to transport everyone out the emergency exit of symbolically smoke-filled meeting rooms and into fresh air.

Analysis

Meetings can sometimes make you wish you were not there, were not wasting your time, and were not so unproductive. There is also the type of meeting that seems to suffocate those in attendance where, for example, a speaker(s) might be said to suck all the air out of a room. The speaker and his or her agenda and Power Points fill the room to the furthest corner, sealing the doors shut in the process. No one can escape, and no one, it may be felt, can survive. It is not safe to interrupt, ask questions, or express a point of view contrary to that of those in control of the meeting. It is their way or the highway.

Object relations theory offers insights into how those present in the meeting are, in essence, turned into objects and warm bodies in chairs supposedly ready to receive the new ideas and strategies, or filtered information from the leadership about the organization—"We are doing great," it may be said. Just ask Enron's former employees. The leaders have likely split off feelings of self-limitations and incompetency and projected them onto their audience members as mental representations. I will lead. You will follow. The only question that may be asked when I say "Jump," is "How high?" The audience members in the room are not only thought to be less capable and competent than the leaders of the organization, but they are also continually treated this way, encouraging them to come to feel this way—the underlying dynamic of projective identification. The outcome is that those in the audience experience themselves as inferior, sealing themselves into the metaphoric room from which there is no escape. The soul-suffocating lack of respect given to them by management is poisonous.

Group relations theory contributes to understanding a meeting where not being asphyxiated becomes a personal triumph. The leader(s) of the meeting and perhaps of the organization may feel that he or she is in a fight to save the organization from the marginally capable employees as well as from competitors. The implicit or explicit abuse, contempt, and disrespect within the organization toward its members as played out in meetings, like that described in the poem, encourages everyone to feel under attack. Flight from this experience and the metaphoric room by the attendees who are trapped in this soul-stripping context finds a deep resonance in the poem. Also to be considered is the possibility of the audience fighting back against this experience, leading to a fight and fight group dynamic, where management is on the attack and the organization members attack back—resistance may not be futile.

Karen Horney's directions of movement are in evidence in the poem. There is a movement against those who attend the meeting on the part of the leader(s) of the meeting and perhaps management of the organization. Staying below the smoke to escape speaks to moving away in a dramatic way. And it appears there is little room in the poem's experiential space for anyone to move toward each other, although small sub-groups may emerge. It is worth noting that the purpose of the meeting is implicitly based on the assumption of moving toward each other.

Seeing Far Enough

Atop a skyscraper,
I sat in a meeting
that pained me to attend.
Looking west through the windows,
I watched the sunset flame,
then fade into night.
I watched the city lights
and thought of Christmas.
I could not see forever—
but I saw far enough.

Discussion

This brief poem is another attempt to escape the inescapable, about unlocking from within the door of a prison. The story of the poem actually happened this way in a meeting held in a large room at the top of a skyscraper. First, a lavish meal was served. Then, the leader served up a toxic, self-aggrandizing speech for dessert.

My eyes were the instrument of liberation from the confines of an oppressive meeting led by an ostentatious leader. Standing up and walking out was not an option, but my eyes could symbolically do it for me. Seeing the sunset and city lights are the opposite of and a reply to the pervasive darkness of a lifeless meeting, led by a self-congratulating CEO, in which the unstated agenda of submission, admiration, and loyalty was far more significant than the actual work the group performed after dinner.

Analysis

"Seeing Far Enough" encourages us the readers, to reflect a moment on experiences that the poem may evoke. Do we not all sometimes see the world through the eyes of a poet's free associations? The expression of taking the time to smell the roses speaks to taking the time to have the experience that brings us alive within. Having the experience of the poet and the accompanying free associations of the poet, and perhaps even a poem in mind, offers a sense of freedom from the confinement of the moment. We must take a moment to give some measure of thanks for *our* "seeing far enough."

Object relations theory is about relating to ourselves and others not only as objects but also as subjects. We can see a long distance and many different things by observing ourselves and others in meetings. We do this all the time consciously and unconsciously. We might notice a participant glancing down and imagine what sunset is approaching on his or her cell phone. Who is there? What is being said? I can only imagine. And what of the pair over there constantly whispering to each other or perhaps a few strongly engaged in listening and participating during a particular topic? And what might be imagined about a three-inch-thick conference table so heavy that it takes a crew of men to move it?

And what might or should we make of what comes to our minds as we sit listening, observing, and perhaps basking in a flaming sunset? Have we not experienced and imagined all of this in our free roaming minds, creating an object here and an object there that we may manipulate to relieve anxiety and perhaps provide a fantasy to distract us? And do we sometimes allow the leader of the meeting, the nature of the meeting, and others to take over and transform us from alive to bored? The unconscious dynamics of object relations offer many insights or perhaps a metaphoric window into the soul. We are surrounded by what we create in mind—fearing and enjoying it is a natural and even poetic experience.

Group relations theory is once again present where the group and the leader of the group are locked sometimes in a warm embrace and sometimes in mortal combat, as may also occur among subgroups in the meeting. Fight and flight are a common basic assumption group in many meetings where it can sometimes seem to be a war of all against all. Those who do not fight often are in flight sometimes to their cell phones under the table or out a window to a flaming sunset. The loving embrace, should it occur, may signal the rise of a dependency or pairing basic assumption group, where there is the hope of being taken care of by the leader and perhaps the group, or by a yet-to-emerge leader who most wisely never materializes.

Karen Horney's perspectives are also a way to understand the leader, the meeting, and the flaming sunset. The poet's gaze signals a movement away from the leader, the meeting, everyone present in the meeting, and the space the meeting is being held in. There is wonderment in the poem and its flight to freedom. Movement away also encourages thought about why this is a good option in a meeting. There is, it seems, a quality of confinement and oppression and movement against others either by the leader, by some members of the group, or by one's mere obligatory presence in the meeting. Movement toward others or toward the leader may spontaneously arise from time to time, offering some hope that feelings of dependency will be acknowledged and possibly dependency needs met.

But it seems in this meeting there is at best a fleeting possibility of moving toward others, and a plunge out a high window is preferred over being consumed by the leader, the meeting, the participants, and the space.

Business Meeting, Good Friday

> Business meeting, Good Friday,
> around a thick oak table,
> no veneer in this wood.
> We meet twelve to three
> in the afternoon.
> No sky blackened;
> no earth shook.
> We took note
> of more pressing business.

Discussion

This poem was inspired by an oppressive organizational meeting that took place on Good Friday, the most solemn day in the Christological calendar. The sacred significance of Good Friday was on the minds of many of those attending the mandatory meeting, which unfortunately included bullying by management that seemed especially unfortunate given the day.

Leadership in this toxic organization was heavy-handed, self-centered, oppressive, and indifferent to the feelings and concerns of employees and the people seated around the board table. The event seemed to be full of irony, paradox, and tragedy.

Analysis

In the workplace sometimes we hear that, "He was nailed to a cross," or "It is his cross to bear." Suffering in toxic organizations is all too common, as was the case in this meeting where a darkness-laden experience was filled with threat and laced with dominance and submission issues. Meetings are perhaps the single best way for a CEO or other leaders to impose their will upon everyone else—submit or you will become ritualistically sacrificed. Everyone explicitly if not implicitly understands this. Resistance is indeed sometimes futile.

Object relations theory points out the unconscious dynamics that create an all-powerful and dominant "other" and a weak and submissive "self." We split off and project our better selves and empowerment onto the leader, creating a magnification of the leader's power and greatness. This leaves us feeling diminished, and this in turn enhances the perceived differential. The leader does much the same in reverse, projecting weaker and deficient aspects of self-experience onto everyone else while retaining the powerful and effective experience. This "deal with the devil" brings darkness to interpersonal relationships and meetings. If these dynamics are not appreciated, then the deal is sealed without awareness of it having occurred.

Group relations theory draws our attention to group dynamics that create the scene in the meeting. The leader who called the meeting and set the place and time is authorized to do this, empowered to do it, but more important, is all powerful and can do it. Anyone who stands in the way may well be punished or possibly terminated. The group meets with this threat in mind, which is reinforced by the likelihood that during the meeting some in attendance will be bullied, threatened, and intimidated. The leader is prepared to dominate and control (fight for control), in turn expecting the group members to dutifully submit. The group dynamic becomes one of dependency, hoping their great leader will not be too abusive and perhaps even throw them a bone occasionally (take care of their dependency needs). Failing that, there may be a wish for another leader to emerge who may well be rejected by the group and discarded, since it was the hope for a new leader that was important.

The three directions of movement provided by Karen Horney also offer insight for understanding a meeting like this. The bullying and threatening are a movement against those who attend the meeting. And while it might be said that attending the meeting is a movement toward the leader, the sense of danger and brutality in the meeting surely translates into wishing to avoid the meeting, hiding out in the meeting, and as near as possible moving away from the oppressive leader.

Gulf

> From across the conference table's gulf
> you lean forward and say, "I feel guilty.
> I'm from a small town in South Dakota.
> I was supposed to go back and practice medicine.
> and here I am. Twenty years
> of feeling guilty is enough."
> We laugh or nod in nervous assent—
> big city, university, South Plains,
> what are we doing here? Our faces wonder,
> but we don't say.
>
> We're all from some-kind-of South Dakota,
> even if it's midtown Manhattan,
> where we once made promises we meant to keep.
> We can't say for sure why we couldn't abide.
> We just didn't, and our should-have-beens

and might-now-be's stalk us as coyotes their prey.
Their debt is hard to cast off, harder to pay,
when where we're from is also who we are,
not just were.
Is any sky as tall
as what a child saw in South Dakota?
I spoke with that child long ago
at the banks of the Ohio ten miles downstream
from Pittsburgh. He leaned toward me
across time's wide gulf and told me
about remorse
and gratitude.
We both turned and left
for the South Plains.

Discussion

This poem is about a poignant moment shared with a family physician colleague. The moment occurred after the conclusion of a department faculty meeting. Although my physician colleague and I were from very different worlds—rural South Dakota and a mill town in western Pennsylvania—we shared spasms of guilt and "what ifs" for having left behind—abandoned—our places of origin. Although both of us had well-established careers "elsewhere," there occurred occasional pangs of regret of having left our family homes. These few moments of shared vulnerability and intimacy were a stark contrast to the highly controlled, corporate-like, style of the meeting led by the chairman. The poem seems to acknowledge a deeply felt sense gratitude for the few moments of sharing that "softened" the hardness of the meeting and its toxicity.

Analysis

Much of the value of meetings seems to arise from the time spent as friends and colleagues before the meeting and after the meeting. This is easy to underappreciate and overlook. It is sometimes thought of as off-task and a counterproductive use of time. These periods before and after the meeting are a potentially rich time for renewing acquaintances, comparing notes, telling stories, receiving quick updates on events, and actually meeting the people who are there to meet. Perhaps it is the case that the agenda of the meeting and its leader is what is ultimately off-task and counterproductive, or maybe not. The time before and after of the meeting may count as much as the time in the meeting. Ideally, valuable *work* should get done in all of these groups (before, during, and after). They are not a "waste of valuable company time."

Object relations theory suggests that we turn others into objects in our minds. These creations need not be accurate reflections of who others really are in their own minds. Perhaps it is the case that others share our anxieties and guilt and shame for promises not kept. Or perhaps we are guilty, and they are not, at least in our minds. The poem reminds us that what we think we know may well get in the way of what we could know, and how wonderful might the moment be where we collapse this not knowing into intimate knowledge of the other. Object relations theory is a powerful reminder of our human nature and the many ways we cope with our anxieties and distressing self-experience. Often we create others as mental representations, to help us cope with these anxieties and the accompanying distressing self-experience.

Group relations theory perspectives encourage us to consider that groups and subgroups may, because of creating the others and other groups in mind, never be understood, appreciated, or known in any meaningful way. Perhaps they are also anxious and distressed by the organization's leadership and recent events, or angry and frustrated about how meetings are called together and led. We might never know, except for the brief chat before the meeting or possibly a longer visit after the meeting.

These dynamics lead to the basic assumption groups where fight and flight may be readily surfaced before, during, and after the meeting, as members of the group or subgroups end up being pitted against each other by the leader of the meeting. Who exactly should be blamed and scapegoated? Hating each other is often felt to be safer than attacking the all-powerful leader. The toxic nature of many meetings may lead to not having dependency needs met in the face of threat. The wish for a more nurturing and caretaking leader goes unmet. Given this, it is often the time before and after meetings when these basic assumption groups are more open to inspection and possibly even change.

The three directions of movement Karen Horney describes allow for a deeper appreciation of the times before and after meetings, where moving toward each other is safe to do by escaping the watchful eye of the leader of the meeting. The wonderment of the poem underscores this appreciation. Movement against is also present in the potential of a dominating and abusive leader of the group, aggressing everyone present without limitation. Who is bold enough to resist when the ultimate sacrifice might be paid? Movement away from a distressing, anxiety ridden, and counterproductive leader and from follower dynamics in meetings is underscored by this chapter.

Conventions

In June, the next June
is not soon enough;

one convention,
four airplanes
to and from.

Three days
of muted ecstasy,
seeing you once again,
time for what we call
visiting and catching up,
eyes locked in embrace,
like a telescope honed to its star.
The unsaid more palpable
than the spoken,
inducing in me
a sharp pang of arrhythmia.
Then there are the presentations,
unlike anywhere else;
here the undiscussable
is said out in the open.

At meeting's end,
we return to our lives.
At parting, our hugs linger.
We bid each other
to take good care of yourselves.
Then the longing sets in—
until June a year away.

Discussion

This poem is about commonplace, often-large academic conventions. Many kinds of people, including professionals, attend annual conventions, at which presentations on work in that field are made. This poem is inspired by a twice-annual meeting that I attend. The group tends to be fairly small, less than 100, but gathered from all over the world. There is a deeply felt sense of intimacy by the "old timers" and the "newcomers" who are welcomed and enveloped in the group. The poem is about the intensely emotional quality of the gathering, its official presentations, and then the emotion-filled parting at the end. In stark contrast with many workplaces, this meeting is looked forward to by those in attendance. They are joined together as professional colleagues and friends to catch up and learn. This atmosphere of community differs dramatically from many meetings, especially those in toxic organizations. It is this experience that is evoked in the poem and how much it contrasts with other meetings discussed in this chapter.

Analysis

Some meetings are actually looked forward to and in a sense hungrily consumed for their nurturance, support, and intellectual excitement. These meetings for people sometimes scattered across continents, provide an opportunity to renew friendships. There is a lot of catching up to do. The diversity of cultures and ages of the participants present allows for an ever-so-subtle passing of the metaphoric torch to the next generation. These types of meetings if anything point out for all to see and experience that meetings have their place in our lives. They can be constructive and fulfilling and looked forward to for the feast of fulfilling self-experience that they offer.

Object relations theory provides for the possibility of positive transference dynamics where the "bad" part of people, groups, and the meeting are largely split off and lost to awareness. I am good and you are good and it is good we are here together to have this experience. It is not as though there are no problematic elements to these gatherings. It is the case that those elements are most often denied, edited out, ignored, and otherwise done away with to create in mind an ecstatic sense of coming together to be together. We are surrounded by many good objects, processes, events, and a wonderful experience. When problems do arise, they are typically addressed directly with goodwill and a task-oriented, problem-solving attitude that avoids blame and us/them splits.

The group relations perspectives for this group and meeting suggest that fight and flight basic assumption groups are largely absent as are dependency and pairing. Although the intentional work group is thought to be a relatively rare occurrence in groups, they do occur. The poem and convention offer insights into the nature of an intentional group that is relatively free of basic assumptions and other defenses against anxiety. There is in general little stress, it seems, that promotes anxiety and defenses against it. All is well in this group. Everyone is welcome. The group fulfills members' needs, and the group in the moment is supportive of and sensitive to member needs.

Karen Horney's three directions of movement, when used to understand this poem and the convention that evoked it, provide insight into how a movement toward others can, when there is a lack of anxiety and defensiveness, allow for a deeper understanding of the poem and meeting. This consideration, while not ignoring the obvious needs being fulfilled in the poem, encourages us to examine the healthier, self-integrated, and *whole* object relatedness present in the poem that allows for meaningful and even non-defensive intimate attachment. Movement against others or away from others is not part of this scene or the poem.

There is a welcoming warm embrace and a fond lingering memory of the gathering to sustain one's soul until next we meet. The movement toward others lacks in many ways the compelling nature of dependency that is resident in the defensive nature of moving toward others. Rather, dependency and seeking out others has in the case of this meeting more the quality of an embrace as compared with a clinging, and a desire for as compared with a need for attachment. There is then a lack of compulsion and more of a sense of intentionality and self-integration.

Reflections

Throughout this book, we have taken frequent exception to the accepted cultural wisdom in business schools and organizations that workplace life is guided by techno-rationality, enlightened self-interest, and even pursuit of profit, productivity, and efficiency. Through poems, stories, and psychodynamically informed analysis, we have shown how unconsciously driven organizational darkness often sabotages the espoused virtues of official mission statements and strategic plans and prevails over them.

One recurrent place where this drama is played out is in meetings of every type and size, from small meetings around a massive boardroom table, to immense gatherings in amphitheaters and auditoriums, for the CEO or other upper management leaders to make ritual pronouncements and reports about the state of the organization and its future. Often irrationally driven undercurrents direct the course and flow of meetings.

Then, too, there are those rare meetings that become moments of grace and deep human connection. Both extremes are marked departures from the printed agendas and slick PowerPoint presentations.

In Conclusion

Our workplaces share much in common, and meetings are most certainly one of the commonalities. This chapter has explored what is likely familiar to the reader in that meetings are all too often problematic and induce boredom and a wish to not have to be present at all. We concluded, however, with a poem filled with a sense of joy and hope. All meetings are not bad, and we suggest that with some planning, work, and good leadership, most meetings need not devolve into the poetic experience of being there and not there, present and absent lost in fantasy.

In Chapter 11, we turn to yet another workplace commonality—the organizational space and objects that surround us every day we come to work. At first glance, tables, doors, and the space itself may seem innocuous, purely functional or instrumental, but this we suggest overlooks and denies the many ways space and objects influence and reflect our self-experience every day we come to work.

11 The Psychogeography of Work

Our organizations are composed of not only people but also physical objects like land, buildings, rooms, cubicles, furniture, office equipment, and supplies that create "material culture." Organizational artifacts are a part of how we perform work, and they are often also symbols of power and control. Where one's office is located usually becomes an emblem of status or lack thereof. Huge conference rooms that are elegantly appointed include the often-obligatory massive conference table and impressively upholstered chairs. These are all present to send signals about the significance of the organization and its leaders. They also make organizational members and outsiders feel a little less powerful and valued.

A building with an immense entrance lobby adorned with gold fixtures and an escalator that descends two or three floors is only there for one reason. We are made to feel small and insignificant by comparison with these architectural massifs, and we then may likely also feel small and insignificant relative to the organizational leader who put all these symbols there.

The poems in this chapter embody the significance of what we refer to as the *psychogeography* of the workplace. We use the term *psychogeography* to underscore the largely *unconscious* psychological significance of these places and objects. *Psychogeography* is a term that denotes the playing out on the stage of natural geography, national and international politics, group boundaries, human structures, and other physical features of the human landscape of unconscious processes, often rooted in childhood experiences.[1]

In organizations, the places where offices are located, how offices are equipped and decorated, whether one has an elegant company car or flies first class, and the quality of computer and printer one receives, are all material and technical elements of the workplace. They all also contain important psychological cues about personal, interpersonal, and organizational meaning. We may feel welcomed and embraced by a space or feel overwhelmed and insignificant. The poems consider objects in organizational space, and the space itself, as emotionally charged metaphors of often shared unconscious significance. Appreciating this is essential if we are to understand our sense of work and ourselves at work, especially in toxic organizations where the material is not often just that.

The Corporate Table

> Massive as an Arizona butte,
> the oak table rests upon
> a solid oak pedestal.
> Once the scene of
> clandestine meetings,
> the CEO's scathing rebukes,
> million-dollar transactions,
> it witnessed glory
> and ignoble defeat.
> A few years later,
> it became a good surface
> for lunch and coffee mugs.
> Its dense wood is inert,
> but if it could speak,
> what stories it could tell!

Discussion

The story behind this poem is as large as the organizational significance of the object that is its focus. It is about a common facet of workplace experience in large toxic organizations—a *table* in the CEO's vast office.

It begins with my first meeting with a new CEO, Tony. When he ushered me into his lavish office, the first thing that I noticed was the table at which we were to sit. We needed to discuss my role as a consultant with the company.

The table was placed in front of his large, wide desk. The table was a huge and massive square presence. It was uniformly a light tan, with rounded edges (bullnose), and was smoothly lacquered. It was beautiful and terrifying. Tony described his new vision for organization, his management style, and how he envisioned my role. Throughout our meeting the table was a mindful presence.

Tony was a command-and-control leader—top-down. He spoke, you listened. He ordered, you complied. Others characterized Tony as mean-spirited. If he didn't like someone or how work was being done, he sometimes publicly humiliated the offender. This behavior held as much for management as for staff such as secretaries. Many had been seen leaving his office in tears, fearing for their jobs. Like many new leaders who want to establish themselves, he wanted to dominate and when necessary instill fear: "My way, or the highway," so to speak.

For him, winning the competitive battle with other companies and cornering the market was what leadership was all about. His language was steeped in football and warfare. Many employees saw Tony as a visionary, traveling all over the world to make deals and create alliances to promote himself and the organization. Everyone else saw themselves as the worker bees, the "grunts," who did the day-to-day work "on the ground." They were simply there to "make it happen" and make him look good. The table one could appreciate seemed to embody Tony's grandiosity.

The honeymoon period with the board of trustees, shareholders, and upper management lasted about two years. No major "turn around" that had been expected was achieved. Symbolically, the table's size and mass seemed to have crushed the life out of the organization. Sometime in the third year he was summoned to secret meetings with the board, and suddenly he was no longer there. He disappeared. No one knew what happened. The company was looking for a new CEO, and the senior vice president stepped in as the temporary leader.

The table stayed, but at some point it was moved to the Information Technology unit, becoming a surface to put used computers and computer components on. There it sat amidst a junkyard of computers, monitors, wires, and other parts. The table, once the site of terror and grandeur, had been radically demoted and junked, kicked to the curb just like Tony. The table seemed to have taken on a life of its own.

A couple of years later, it showed up in a lunchroom. The transformed, even transmuted, imperial table had become an inviting surface for everyone around it. The resplendent, lacquered surface was now scratched and had rings from cold beverage cans.

No one spoke of the table. Rather, its placement and function(s) and meaning had simply changed. Those who "knew" the table and its history seemed to look upon its low rank with satisfaction. What goes around comes around! As a symbol of Tony's toxic behavior, it somehow deserved what it got. It was easy to imagine that the table merited its maltreatment. Displaced aggression can be a wonderful thing.

Looking back at the lives of the table it had served successively as an instrument of power, as a piece of junk in the computer junkyard, and finally as an inviting host for lunch and coffee gatherings. Sometimes a table is just a table, an artifact of material culture. Alternately, sometimes a table is a symbol, a metaphor of an expressive culture. And sometimes its meaning and function change over time. Tables sometimes have many lives.

Analysis

The poem makes clear that some objects like the table can be unconsciously imbued with meaning that draws primitive experience to consciousness. This in turn transforms and magnifies the object. In the poem this dynamic creates a foreboding sense of power and threat that weighed heavily on the poet's sense of self. The poem makes this palpably transparent and accessible. Certainly, many others experienced the table in much the same way, where the table is animated by the powerful and threatening nature of the CEO. Are we not all afraid of touching the same hot stove twice? The table, desk, office size, and décor all work as intentionally designed by the CEO—to suggest that power and intimidation exist relative to all who are bold enough to enter the office.

Object relations theory illuminates the unconscious nature of the table by encouraging reflection on the splitting, projection, and transference involved in creating a powerful and oppressive CEO as well as the table that evoke feelings of being confronted by a massive and powerful presence. Is it the CEO? Is it the table? Is it both? And as noted, it is many times much safer to manipulate an object in mind as compared with another who is potentially highly threatening. Splitting and projection direct our attention to our contribution to making the table more massive and with even non-existent attributes that further magnify its symbolic power. By splitting off and projecting our own sense of self as empowered, and locating it in the CEO and table as a symbol for the leader, we also diminish ourselves to metaphorically become the six-year-old who is dwarfed when sitting in a large chair and barely able to look across the surface of the table. The CEO has intentionally, and we have unintentionally, turned ourselves into the child.

Group relations theory also offers insights. The poem reminds us that sometimes fighting back as individuals or as a group against the CEO's power is dangerous and can lead to individual and group annihilation. Also to be appreciated is that many in the group unwittingly collude to make the CEO comparatively powerful and the group by comparison weak. The poem reminds us that even if resisting (fighting) the CEO is dangerous and perhaps futile, in the long run even the most powerful and threatening CEOs are expendable, and that the table can be transformed into an artifact that denigrates the former owner.

Karen Horney offers a different perspective. The CEO is powerful and dangerous as well as arrogant and vindictive. The nature of the massive table as intended by the CEO becomes a symbol for power and oppressive control. The CEO is willing to punish and humiliate others and enforce a rigid standard of servitude. This movement against others, when paired with the movement toward the CEO by others, may lead to pathetic submission and morbid dependency on the leader.

This sheds some light on how powerful CEOs are able to subordinate all those around them and how, through a process of selecting in and out of the organization, a relatively homogeneous group of sycophants and dependency-seeking others are created to minister to the needs of the CEO. All those sitting at the table are transformed not only by the CEO, but also by the symbolic essence of the table. Also to be considered, for some dropping out and moving away from this leader is the only way to cope with the menacing and punishing toxic organizational context. How very nice for some that the table came to symbolize an utter absence of the former glory, metaphorically setting everyone a little freer from the long shadow cast by oppression.

The Door

For the longest time,
I have kept knocking
on your door.
hoping that you
would open it.

You open it far enough
to see who is there;
then you close it.
I stand for a while,
then go away.

We repeat this
for the longest time,
until it occurs to me
that you will
never let me in.

Next time,
I stay away.

Discussion

This poem is a composite of many experiences, both as employee and as consultant. A door at work is no simple material, utilitarian thing about entrance, exist, closure, and opening. Rather, a door is imbued with meaning, both individual and group. A door is an instrument for manipulating the meaning of space: it "speaks" in many codes.

Consider a well-known example: A CEO's official "open door policy" of declared welcome may in fact be a deadly trap for an employee who takes the leader up on the offer. Instead of having one's views, concerns, and misgivings sympathetically accepted and considered, the employee leaves in tears of humiliation or without a job.

A door may be *used* as an impenetrable barrier to keep people at bay or as an instrument of privacy while one is working. A simple knock and the voice inside may say in a welcoming tone: "Please come in." Other times, a supervisor may burst in without knocking. As in the poem, the inhabitant of the space inside the door may peer outside with the door opened only a crack, only to close it with an implicit, "Go away. I don't want to see YOU." We have all stood at many such doors, real or metaphorical, and perhaps have eventually resigned ourselves to never gaining admittance and never trying again.

Analysis

Doors, if we stop to think about it, are an omnipresent aspect of our daily lives. There are doors everywhere, and they send many different messages to those on both sides. The presence of doors and their opening and closing signal both a barrier or an organizational boundary, and the opening and closing signal a time that is before it was opened and after it was opened and perhaps closed. When I the CEO open the door to you the employee, what is imagined will happen after that is filled with wonderment, awe, threat, and nervousness many times for both the CEO and the employee. It is then no wonder doors have so much meaning, including their use as defensive barriers against the possibility of what *could* happen if the door is opened after the knock at the door.

Object relations theory suggests that in mind and in fantasy we construct others and objects out of unconscious psychological dynamics that are defensive in nature. The stress in the poem of managing the door (whether it is closed, open, or cracked open with eyes peering out and in) suggests that physical nature of the door and the boundaries it represents pale by comparison to the unconscious dynamics of manipulating others and objects in mind. The person on the other side who is subjected to the knocking on the door at that moment may only exist for the individual outside the door in one's mind, and the recipient of the knock on the inside is left to imagine "Who is it that knocks at my door? Do I greet the knock as a welcomed visitor or a despised enemy?"

Splitting and projection might be said to metaphorically fill the air on either side, creating all manner of stress and anxiety, further enhancing reliance on a defense mechanism like splitting and projection. And of course, once the door is opened the transferences that accompanied the representations created in mind may well at least initially transform the nature of the interpersonal space with life experience from the past, including the last time the door was opened for the individuals involved.

Group relations theory suggests that in organizations groups must cross organizational *boundaries* all the time, whether they are in the form of electronic communication of all forms, mail, or actually traveling physically across boundaries to meet. There is an intuitive understanding that there are many doorways, and the actual door to the offices of another group is but one of them. Fight and flight basic assumption groups are often present in our organizations. One group (accounting, for example) may well be denigrated as bean counters by other departments (marketing, for example).

E-mails may become toxic. Phone calls can become combative. Hence the frequent anxiety when one sees an e-mail sent by a specific person or organization in one's inbox or hears the telephone ring. Still, the actual person is not here. Heaven forbid the combatants ever meet face to face. Doorways also suggest that many amazing creations and representations may be imagined about what is on the other side. Perhaps there is a kind and caring powerful other who will meet everyone's dependency needs. And behind every door there may also be the potential for a better leader who creates fulfilling work experience and organizational success. However, this door to the potentially better leader may never be opened.

Karen Horney's three directions of movement offer more insights into the power of the door in the poem. The door is used as a defensive barrier where admittance is regulated and controlled to protect the person behind the door who peers out defensively to see who is there. The door is then shut, locking the visitor out. This is movement against the visitor that rejects the visitor who eventually gets the message—don't bother to come back. The door also helps to understand moving away from others in that shutting others out is protective and minimizes stress and anxiety, the idealized absence of which might be thought of as the ultimate freedom. The movement toward others is represented by both individuals coming to the door, one to knock, and one to peer out. There is in this moment the possibility of mutuality and caretaking, but also the threat that the poem makes clear is there. Not you again!

Office Space

You say: I take up too much space;
You mean: I occupy any space at all.
Where I am is where and who
you wish to be—to expand, to sprawl,
into the office skin of me.

But you do not say so directly—
only that I must move swiftly
to smaller quarters,
more remote quarters
down the hall, down the stairs,
down to the in-fact-anywheres.

"Couldn't he just take his things home?"
you asked in committee, not looking at me,
then came later to offer private apology.

I move; you move me;
I keep out of your way.
I cannot keep out of your way.
I move further,
never far enough.

Space is parable
for both our dying,
and you'd rather
I go first—
but you'll only say
we're out of space.

Discussion

This poem is about a relationship between supervisor and employee, only the language of space and offices is used us to speak the unspeakable. The supervisor never says directly to the employee: "I don't want you around here. You should go away and get lost." The conversation about space and offices is a metaphor for telling someone who is unwanted to go away.

Space is, among many things, about *value*: what and who are valued, devalued, or without value—what and who are worthy and what and who are worthless. To be told by a supervisor or executive that "We simply do not have space for you, your group, or your project" is much of the time a *choice* about what and who merits space. We have all been told in different ways "There is no space for what you want to do" only to see other colleagues allocated additional space that was magically found. Space, like money, is largely about priorities (values) and in turn about the *power* to reward and the power to withhold from, actively aggress and reject another, both consciously and unconsciously. Space and other organizational resources can become symbolic tools wielded in toxic organizations and relationships where their sub-textual meanings are intuited if not clear (envy, hatred, shame).

Analysis

Money and space are two organizational resources that are readily available for executives, managers, and supervisors to manipulate. One person receives a raise and another for no apparent objective reason does not.

The size and location of organizational members' cubicles and offices also signal many things not only to the inhabitant, but also to others, and their assignment signals the ultimate power of the person in charge to decide where you exist at work.

A CEO at one plant hired a highly thought-of engineer who tried to limit the CEO's constant meddling into production matters he had no expertise in. The response was quick. The engineer's office was transferred from a large one in the executive suite to a closet-sized office at the opposite end of the plant. Get the message?

Object relations theory suggests that the beleaguered employee in the poem who feels minimized, disregarded, disrespected, and even disposable has been transformed into an object in the mind of the boss, which justifies and enables the abusive treatment. The employee has become an unfeeling, dehumanized object that may be abused and cast aside. Objectification is often a prerequisite before a human being is disposed of, as for example as organizational fat. And this employee might envision the boss as all-powerful, inhibiting any contesting of the treatment. Confrontation, it may be thought and felt, almost certainly means annihilation—out of space, out of here, just simply gone from work. Object relations and the manipulation of others in one's mind as representations inevitably fill the void left when authentic, trusting, and respectful interpersonal relationships deteriorate, becoming an undiscussable interpersonal blast zone.

Group relations theoretical perspectives suggest that fight and flight basic assumptions are a common element in the workplace. An individual may be targeted, turning all others in the organization into distressed observers who, as a group, do not want to become targeted as well. It is safer to lay low. Groups often passively accept bad behavior by powerful authority figures, usually out of fear of what would happen to the group or to a few individuals in the group who challenge what is happening. Personal survival as symbolized by a paycheck and benefits often takes precedence over doing the right thing. Rather than resist and fight back, flight both in one's mind and sometimes physically is the result.

When the authority figure is oppressive and dangerous, there are often group fantasies that the person will leave or be found out and fired, or that possibly a new leader or a consultant will emerge to make things better. In these cases, the basic assumption group of dependency, while perhaps a latent potential, does not arise to any extent because the oppressive and dangerous authority figure dominates the organization, group, and everyone as an individual. Surviving supersedes receiving compassionate care taking.

Karen Horney's tripartite perspective also speaks to the hostile nature of the space created in the poem. Movement against the individual and poet is the dominant aspect of more deeply appreciating the poem and its meaning in our daily lives at work. Everyone has had experience like this. The employee may wish to move toward the leader and the organization but is at every turn discouraged from doing so and possibly even punished for trying. The poem then most directly offers an escape of sorts from this punishing workplace experience. There is freedom from despair in the processing of the experience, in writing, and in poetry.

Rain Upon Our Corporate Roof

> Rain upon our corporate roof—
> we, the board, meet beneath
> its flat contour.
> Prairie sky stampedes
> above the acoustic tile.
> We sit dry around the mammoth table,
> but we must speak louder
> to defy the din above.
>
> "Talk louder! I can't hear you!"
> "Talk louder! I don't want to hear you!"
> "Talk louder! I can't bear to hear you!"
> Percussive tin prevails
> over our entreaties.
> Roof stampede, bison from the sky,
> roar across our plain! Send rain, plentiful rain,
> loud, pelting rain;
> send rain upon
> this corporate roof!

Discussion

This poem is a fantasy about being an employee of and consultant to toxic organizations in which meetings were run in heavy-handed fashion. The CEO or chairperson only wanted to hear "good news" about how the organization was functioning, producing, and making profit. The leader wanted the group to become a mirror reflecting back admiration and approval. The bearer of anything that would contradict this picture would be met with disdain, reprimand, and punishment.

In this poem, the sound of heavy, pelting rain eventually drowned out the vile sounds and lies that dominated the meeting. For those who must be present for meetings that become an exercise of control, narcissism, and lies-as-truth, at least it could be imagined that there is an escape via thunderous sounds of heavy storms on the roof of the building. Imagine a cleansing rain drowning out and flushing away the toxins that are an affront to one's ears—and spirit.

Analysis

The political scene in many countries is polarized between right and left. The air is filled with omissions, lies, and distortions that often seem to drown out reality and meaningful progress for one's country, culture, and life. Meetings run by high-ranking individuals such as CEOs are often dominated by hidden agendas, relegating the paper agenda to perhaps being folded into a paper airplane, at least in fantasy. The message is clear, and if not heard by some, punishment (behavior modification) may ensue. Getting with the program in some toxic organizations is essential for survival. Everyone comes to understand what is acceptable to the leader and what is not. Self-editing can become a soul-stripping experience and, at the same time, one that paradoxically threatens the organization's performance.

Object relations theory suggests that some meetings are attended by a lot of objects sitting in luxurious chairs, created in the mind of the leader to support an expansive sense of self and the accompanying demand for narcissistic supplies. Those in attendance must tow the line, heed the warnings, and conform, or perhaps be removed from the meeting (becoming a useless, disposable object), perhaps not being invited to attend in the future. The leader, as a result of splitting and projection, may for many become a highly admired object, while for others the leader may become a feared, reprehensible, and despised object invested with threatening and malevolent projections.

Splitting and projection often create charismatic, loved, and admired others, while at the same time voluntarily diminishing those who split and project themselves onto the others, stripping themselves of their sense of personal efficacy, worthiness, and productive abilities that are projected onto the leader. And certainly, the leader projects his or her deficiencies on those present, creating a sense of self without fault or limitations.

The meeting of a group with a toxic, abusive leader encourages considering the group relations perspective. The meeting contains a sub-textual context for all the objects in attendance to actively or passively aggress each other (the fight basic assumption) or disappear into the wallpaper (the flight basic assumption). Kind words from the leader are often readily embraced and remembered over time. Occasionally the leader may meet the often-ignored dependency basic assumption group needs. This makes any deviation by the leader from meeting these dependency needs a dismaying event.

And to be noted, some meetings may have one individual bold enough to take exception to the desires of the leader, calling into question information, decisions, and actions (temporarily fulfilling the pairing basic assumption group's wish for a leader to emerge). This individual may be said to speak for group members who, however, will not support or defend the person if attacked by the leader, but who welcome the effort at what might be said to be anti-leadership. In some instances, this fearless individual may be tolerated by the leader much like the notion of the court jester or fool who seems to live a live a charmed life challenging the king. In toxic organizations bold and fearless leadership on the part of a single individual may offer some sense of hope that things will change.

Karen Horney's three directions of movement also offer insights into this poem and the fantasized meeting that is grounded in the poet's experiences of toxic and oppressive leaders of meetings who must dominate everyone in order to feel in control, admirable, or at least feared. The scene described and the feelings evoked by the poem are where life in the meeting is drowned out by the din of the leader's personal needs to feel powerful and admired. This is a soul-stripping exercise of moving against others who are not expected to resist or strike back. The fantasy of a pounding and deafening rainstorm that creates white sound that drowns out the leader's words speaks to movement away and a flight into fantasy and the freedom that it brings. And also to be considered, in every meeting there are those who move toward the leader to secure safe attachment and some fulfillment of dependency needs. They gain by this, while at the same time sacrifice their personal integrity, and are possibly viewed as sycophants. Others know but seldom say anything. Better to leave this interpersonal contracting alone and listen to the rain.

Without Windows, Without Light

This place is without windows,
without outside light,
without outside air.
The seasons are changing,
but we would not know.

We work at our stations.
We imagine autumn.
We wear all varieties
of religious amulets
to simulate the sun.

This place is all brick,
dark glass, and metal.
It does not have windows;
it does not need windows.
There is nothing to see.

Discussion

This poem combines fantasy and reality. It is about countless hermetically sealed office buildings that are "worlds unto themselves." The experience of workplace life in contemporary tall, steel, and concrete buildings encased in glass can leave everyone feeling cut off from the world.[2] In fantasy, they leave the world behind. Those who enter within encounter hard, impenetrable, lifeless surfaces and highly controlled work environments. Many may well end up feeling contained within a workplace that is controlling, confining, and perhaps inhuman—not unlike a prison with no freedom, no light, and no air. The poem is then a study in often-bleak organizational psychogeography.

Analysis

There are in life inside workers and outside workers. Each work life is very different, including the heavier dirty work outside and the more boring and administrative work inside. The outside workers actually have to stop when it is raining. The inside workers in big buildings might never know it rained. For them, the world outside might as well not exist. There is nothing to see other than what may be conjured from fantasy. Working in an office with no windows, white artificial light, complete dependency on mechanical heating and cooling systems, and of course doors that are sometimes open and sometimes closed is an experience set apart from nature. The outside workers can only imagine what it is like.

Object relations theory suggests that inside the workplace, workers must find some way to cope with their partial sensory deprivation chamber. Reports from the outside world are always welcome. "That was a tremendous rainstorm!" "Did you see the truck accident on the corner?" Objects, door, rooms, and corridors take on a magnified presence in our minds. They can become invested with fantasies and transformed by manipulations in mind. Some places inside can be dark and foreboding, such as huge basements and sub-basements. We fill them with our selves and transference possibly associated with childhood fears of darkness and monsters under the bed. The executive suite of offices so nicely decorated can be so foreboding that no one wishes to enter. Those within these spaces become the objects of splitting, projection, and transference often associated with past experiences with remote authority figures.

These boundaries and surfaces become invested with the primitive psychological experience that Thomas Ogden suggests can be life-affirming in the sense of feeling a surface or knowing that because it is there, I exist.[3] Objects and space in office buildings become these surfaces of our life-affirming experience at work. They can take on a life of their own, filled with imagination, fantasy, and unconscious manipulation of "things." Sometimes this is good and sometimes it is bad. There might be nothing to see, and just as important, to feel, or experience as real.

Group dynamics at work take place within this sealed-off inside space. Group life can take on a surreal quality if we are not careful. Shared group fantasies, defenses, and basic assumption groups can without much effort take over how we work together. In particular, there may develop endless inter-group fighting, conflicts, and competition that contain toxic elements that detract from organizational performance. These dynamics are magnified by the sense of being self-contained and shut into an unwelcoming experiential space together. These elements become the context for individual and group dynamics that can feed upon themselves, including becoming a form of stimulation and entertainment in an otherwise oppressively boring setting. Small incidents may become big ones, and the end to one incident may contain the seeds of yet another conflict. Attack and counter-attack can become the norm. Flight from these dynamics to elsewhere within these self-contained environments does not seem to be a possibility, much like life in a prison.

Karen Horney's three directions of movement, while seemingly not relevant to space and object, do provide unique insights into how space and objects affect us. Some objects are attractive, desirable, and wanted, causing us to move toward them. The same can be said for spaces. Conversely, the experience of some objects can be distressing and even horrifying, encouraging us to move against them. Similarly, some spaces are so foreboding due to their nature or the people within them that avoiding and moving away from them is desirable. And also to be considered is that these inside spaces and the experience of them can also be made to feel safe, familiar, welcoming, and nurturing, providing for many people's dependency needs. There can be comfort from the security offered by a climate-controlled setting with good enough light. Once we decorate the space we call home, somehow it is changed and becomes welcoming. Our attachment needs are met.

Reflections

Organizational space is not emotionally neutral and strictly utilitarian. People including employees project their unconscious contents onto the physical space stimulated by their experience of the space. Organizational space and objects become filled with embodied meanings and emotions. Consider, for instance, the long-standing popularity of Scott Adams' satirical "Dilbert" cartoons (begun in 1989) about the Kafkesque experience of workplace cubicles.

Large office buildings and their interiors can become monuments to depersonalized relatedness—to other people, to the larger world. They are at once places in which to work, objects to work with, and powerful metaphors of conscious and unconscious significance. Organizational psychogeography is a large part of "what it is like to work here."

In Conclusion

We have explored space and objects from many perspectives in the hope the reader comes to appreciate more fully that everything that surrounds us at work affects our self-experience as well as our work. Many unconscious and out-of-awareness fantasies and manipulations in mind create a new and different sense of these objects and space that may be unique to each organizational member. The next time you approach an office door for entry—we hope you will take a moment, however brief, and allow the door and all its many meanings to come into your awareness.

Chapter 12 portrays the irrationality and despair in many workplaces through a one-act play about a consultant's experience of the organizations in which he works. The play intersperses his soliloquies with poems that serve as a Greek chorus commentary to the protagonist's testimonies.

Notes

1. Stein, H.F. (1984). The scope of psycho-geography: The psychoanalytic study of spatial representation. *Journal of Psychoanalytic Anthropology*, 7, 23–73; Stein, H.F. (1987/2014). *Developmental time, cultural space: Studies in psychogeography*. New York: Library of Social Science; Niederland, W.G. (1956). River symbolism, part I. *Psychoanalytic Quarterly*, 25, 469–504; Niederland, W.G. (1957). River symbolism, part II. *Psychoanalytic Quarterly*, 26, 50–75; Niederland, W.G. (1971). The naming of America. In M. Kanzer (Ed.). *The unconscious today: Essays in honor of Max Schur*. New York: International University Press. pp. 459–472; Niederland, W.G. (1971). The history and meaning of California: A psychoanalytic inquiry. *Psychoanalytic Quarterly*, 40, 485–490; Stein, H.F. & Niederland, W.G. (Eds.). (1989). *Maps from the mind: Papers in psychogeography*. Norman: University of Oklahoma Press.
2. Stein, H.F. (1982). Autism and architecture: A tale of inner landscapes. *Continuing Education for the Family Physician*, 16(6), June, 15–16, 19.
3. Ogden, T. (1989). *The primitive edge of experience*. Northvale, NJ: Jason Aronson.

12 Playing with Perspective
The Workplace on the Stage

This chapter offers a new form of insight for acquiring and understanding meaning at work. In Chapter 2 we discussed applied poetry as having value in terms of evoking awareness of our workplace experience, as a form of research, and as a way of representing data. In this chapter, the play (by Howard F. Stein) presented here along with its discussion offers readers the same *reflective approach* and *perspective* for understanding toxic organizations, life at work, and the many hard-to-comprehend nuances one finds in the workplace. Sometimes these meanings are consciously perceived, while at other times are known more in an unconscious sense—what Christopher Bollas calls the "unthought known."[1] You the reader will encounter many now-familiar poems in the play. You have read them before as part of an exploration of themes in earlier chapters. You will now re-read them as part of an imagined drama.

We begin by also changing our approach and start the chapter with the story of what led to writing the play in 1998, during the height of the downsizing, restructuring, and reengineering frenzy, and to the play's subsequent revision in 2018, for many the toxic times of the Age of President Donald Trump.

The Story Behind the Play *Irv, or the Consultant*

Beginning in the early 1990s, my long-standing approach to understanding organizations by using conventional scholarly, narrative, linear language seemed inadequate to the task of describing and analyzing downsizing as a movement and as a seemingly vast, highly destructive top-down driven (toxic) form of organizational change. A new idiom, *a new container*, was needed that became poetry, stories, and a play.

Many euphemisms emerged to describe these times—downsizing, rightsizing, reduction-in-force (RIF), redundancy, reengineering, restructuring, offshoring, outsourcing, deskilling, reinventing, redundancy, organizational flattening, horizontal and vertical integration, retooling, privatization, shareholder optimization, globalization, Lean Six Sigma Black Belt, autonomous self-managing teams, cost containment, lean management, managed health care, efficiency, survival, competitiveness, quality assurance, physicians as providers, patients as consumers. All these forms of supposedly rational "managed social change" or "managed organizational change" were enabled by an atmosphere of rampant deregulation. They quickly became part of wider cultural discourse. Behind the veneer of supposedly reality-based, rational, necessity-driven economic decision-making was an enormous human destructiveness, sadism, and pain that led to millions of broken lives, families, and communities as the layoffs ensued.

This broad cultural context led to my firsthand experience of these toxic dynamics that eventually led to the writing of workplace poetry to understand this experience. This included in some fundamental way "digesting" it to make it less toxic and personally destructive. During this time, I contributed to a year-long study of a hospital downsizing: *The HUMAN Cost of a Management Failure*.[2] I also helped to care for my suffering and traumatized community that was emotionally downsized by the bombing of the Oklahoma City Federal Building in 1995. These combined experiences led to two books on downsizing: including *Euphemism, Spin, and the Crisis in Organizational Life* and *Nothing Personal, Just Business: A Guided Journey into Organizational Darkness*.[3] The play *Irv, Or the Consultant*[4] emerged from my role as a consultant to organizations undergoing massive change and often ongoing trauma from which there was no escape, movement away, or flight from the toxic organizational dynamics that were filled with fight and movements against employees, who were turned into surplus objects and "organizational fat."

The play has been recently (2018) revised to acknowledge that "things" have changed, sometimes for the good, and sometimes continuing on with toxic organizational change. Two decades later, despite the ostensibly improved economy after the Great Recession of 2008, the various forms of "managed organizational change" have relentlessly persisted. Today, countless employees do more work to make up for their missing colleagues, earn lower pay, have fewer benefits (if any), and can count on less or no job security.

The Role of the Play in Locating Meaning in Toxic Organizations

The play, and how it incorporates poetry, represents a new, different, and creative way of looking at the relationship between poetry, narrative, storytelling, and the psychodynamic understanding of the depths of organizational life. The poems create a reflective "space" to better understand workplace drama. They become a "Greek chorus" to the protagonist's toxic workplace experience.

The play takes the form of dialogues, stories, and poems. These are drawn from, built upon, and sometimes contrived from the facts, observations, and analyses of firsthand experience of various realities of organizational life. Think of the play as a *documentary* in seven "scenes." The consultant-protagonist, Irv, offers a running response to and commentary upon what he is being told. The response and commentary take the form of poems. Irv's reactions are not only cerebral; they are also often emotional, even "visceral." In the play, "gut" issues in the workplace are surfaced for inspection and reflection.

The play is also an experiment in form. It articulates and evokes the "objective" facets of organizational life through the medium of the "subjective," the experiential. The dialogues may be recognized as an attempt to symbolize and work through what we might all experience as emotional responses or "countertransferences" to the traumatic wastelands that are created by managers and consultants in toxic organizations. These responses originate in your own experiences of past workplace traumas or ones being currently lived through. They represent and communicate organizational realities sometimes too fearful, threatening, and overwhelming to acknowledge except perhaps in poetry and plays. The play and poems may remind the reader of similar workplace experiences and provide a "time out" for "processing" them mentally and emotionally.

This play, then, is about the inner experience the American workplace of the 1980s, 1990s, and 2000s through 2018. It is about what work feels like—feelings about work that become part of work. It is about desolation and organizational toxicity. It is about *disposability*. It is about the sense of *futility* and *futurelessness*—at the same time that we hurl ourselves toward the future in the name of "productivity," "profitability," and "competitiveness." It is about nearly sacred "bottom line" thinking and the "problem of evil" that lies masked just below. It is about the *presence* of evil at work. The mood of the play is one of unredeemed desolation. My goal in the play is to evoke the palpable presence of toxicity at work.

The Play in Sum

This play is intended to promote conscious awareness of feelings and meaning behind words used as euphemistic smokescreens. We all know the words; we probably use them every day. They sound so rational, so logical, so inevitable, so real, so indisputable, so antiseptic, so tidy, and so business-like. They are a core vocabulary and constellation of a world toxic to organization members. They are both euphemisms and metaphors of the oppressive world of work where human disposability in the workplace prevails.

Director's Note

It might seem odd to the reader that this is *a play without action*. The entire play articulates *the inner world of Irv*. It is his rumination on decades of organizational experience. Perhaps a degree of working through takes place in Irv. A moment's reflection will reveal that the remembering and musing that Irv does is based on an enormous amount of action—traumatic, catastrophic action. The play in part represents and reenacts Irv's attempt to make sense of, and in a small way, to restore a degree of coherence out of, the chaos and fragmentation that are Irv's everyday experience in and of organizations.

IRV, OR THE CONSULTANT

An "organizational" play in eight scenes,
including prologue and epilogue
Dedicated to the memory of Maxim Gorky

Cast:

Irv, the consultant
Betty, the Chief Financial Officer
George, the Chief Executive Officer
Janet, the personnel director
Jack, the middle manager
Jerry, the plant division head
Joe, the CEO

Setting: The stage is empty, except for a stool near front of stage left and lectern (with lighted reading lamp) toward middle back of stage right. The background is drab grey cinder block. Stage lighting is dim. Irv is at the lectern; the other actors take turns sitting on the stool. (Alternately the stool can be replaced by a desk-and-chair set, as in an office setting in which interviews/consultations often take place. In this case, the actors [except Irv] might sit behind the desk and face the empty chair in which the consultant sits.) The music, as the curtain rises, is the Opening of Symphony # 5, Dmitri Shostakovich, First Movement.

A PLAY IN ONE ACT, *Eight Scenes, Including Prologue and Epilogue*

Act I, Scene 1

PROLOGUE

As the curtain goes up, *Irv* walks out on stage, sits on the lighted stool, and addresses the audience—much as Canio introduces Leoncavallo's opera *I Pagliacci* before the action begins. Throughout the play, this character will alternately speak from the stool and from behind the lectern.

(The music from the Opening of Symphony # 5, Dmitri Shostakovich, First Movement is playing as the curtain rises.)

IRV'S PROLOGUE

My name is Irving—or simply Irv. I am a consultant to organizations. I try to help executives and managers make sound decisions and to solve problems. But mostly, I listen. I nose around. I try to get just about everywhere and to talk with as many kinds of people as possible. I work in all sorts of places where people work—hospitals, factories, government agencies, corporations, universities, banks, just about every kind of business. People seem to feel comfortable with telling their stories to me. I've done this kind of work since the 1970s through 2018.

(Leaning forward toward the audience) I'm not here to tell you *my* story, though my story's certainly part of it. To tell you the truth, my *relationship* with people is the crucible in which they tell me their stories. I'm here to tell you about life at work. Most of the time, you won't see me. You won't even hear me. You'll see various people talking to me—sometimes cursing at me. But even when you don't see me, rest assured I'll be around in one way or another. Think of me as *your* consultant and tour guide.

So what are you in for? Consider this scene: A boss who is patently unfair to his workers tells you that "*Life isn't fair.*" You're not supposed to notice that he's part of life. His pronouncement doesn't apply to him, just to some philosophic abstraction called "life." He's this oracle looking down on mere, flawed mortals. You're supposed to believe that he's on your side, sympathetic. As if he would change things *for you* if he could. The main thing is to mistrust yourself and to trust him on your way to the gallows.

Well, that's the sort of thing consultant Irv comes up with during the course of his voyage in organizations. He says what everybody knows, but no one is supposed to say he knows—or even thinks. People trust him–I don't know why. They tell him things they tell no one else.

Well—enough of preliminaries! Let's get started. Let's roll up our sleeves and get to work!

(The stage light dims on Irv; Irv continues sitting on the stool during the scene change.)

Act I, Scene 2

(Computer company's *Chief Financial Officer Betty*, talking to consultant Irv; before she speaks, the music of toward the end of the First Movement of Shostakovich's *Fifth Symphony* is playing.)

Good morning, Irv. I'm Betty, the chief financial officer of the computer company you're consulting with. Am I glad to see you today! Irv, the strangest thing happened Monday. I was off sick Friday. I came in to work on Monday morning and the office next to me was cleared out. There was a desk, a chair, a computer, a couple of file cabinets and bookcases, a wastebasket. And that's it. Empty. I still can't believe it, and it's already Friday. It's like there's a big hole in this place. I knew the guy ten years. His name is Don. He was one of our numbers crunchers. A quiet guy, just did his work. It seemed like he was always here, always working. He is a computer whiz anyone in the unit could go to for a computer glitch. We aren't—maybe I should say *weren't*, since he's gone—weren't exactly friends, but we worked together a lot on projects. He was kind of part of the furniture.

It's so eerie. I'm numb over it. I keep going next door to look in his office expecting to see him. Maybe I'm imagining that he's gone, and he's not. But the place is *so* empty. I've heard of this kind of thing happening other places when people get RIFed. Here today, gone tomorrow. But I've not heard of this here. It's like he disappeared. Like he never was here. Irv, I'm not being sentimental about him. He and I didn't have something going—if you're thinking that. I just can't believe they'd do it—and the *way* they did it. I asked around the firm, and everybody gave the same story. Because it wasn't just him. It happened all over the place. About five hundred people RIFed in one day.

At 9:00 a.m. Friday, security guards showed up all over the plant to the offices and workstations of people who were going to be fired. They escorted them to the big auditorium over in the corporate conference center. They didn't even tell them why they had to go, except that it was an important announcement. After they walked them in, they left and locked the doors behind them. The way I heard it secondhand, the CEO then went in after everybody was there, delivered a little speech on how the company had to downsize radically in order to survive and be competitive. He told them not to take it personally—and thanked them for their service to the company.

The security police escorted them back to where they worked, helped them clear out their belongings, then took them down to Administration to hand over all their keys and receive their last paycheck. The police walked them to their cars, and that's the last they saw of this place. They weren't to come back. Gone. Just like that. I suppose they couldn't be trusted not to sabotage the computers or to steal equipment. I don't even want to think about the way it happened. It's like a roundup.

I asked around, and nobody knows where Don went. No forwarding address or telephone number. It's weird, Irv. Like he just disappeared. You wonder if you're next. You try not to think of it. Work harder, maybe they'll keep you. It's ridiculous, because you know it's not true. But you've got to believe that you're valuable to them (said with voice trailing off).

(Irv speaks/reads two poems from the lectern.)

Where Is the Blood?

Night at corporate headquarters—
The four of us who studied the company's downsizing
Walk silently through a long, dim-lit,
Blank, cream-painted corridor,
A place where phantoms dwell and wait,
A place where walls seem to close in on us.
We all look around,
As if we are looking for something.
After about twenty paces into this antiseptic cave,
I ask aloud, "Where is the blood?"—
My three friends say they were thinking
The same thing.

A consultant team, all in black suits,
Had recently studied the financial books
And recommended to the CEO
That they could save lots of money
And make the company look good to shareholders
By firing a thousand employees immediately—for starters.
"Mandatory downsizing to keep the company alive,"
"A necessary sacrifice for the sake of the company,"
The leader said to those gathered
In a locked auditorium before they were ordered to stand
In long queues of people processed
Impersonally, efficiently, in a well-oiled machine,
And finally escorted to the parking lot, never to return.

The four of us knew the story,
See it unfold before us again
In that cavern, as we walk and relive it.
The walls and carpet bleed,
Cover our shoes and clothes
In still-warm, thick, crimson blood,
Like in a horror movie.
The story hovers in the air;
Its ghost will not leave.
It speaks to us with great sadness;
Even the ghost could not rid itself of the memory,
Could not abandon the prison of knowing too much.
The four of us look at each other,
The story alive in all of us.

Bathed in fresh blood, we leave the building
And re-enter the night,

Carrying the hall's darkness with us.
We had been through the mass firing
Even before it happened.
We knew too much—
The blood will not wash off,
Not now, maybe never.

Survivor's Wound

If none will see
Atrocity,
Does the survivor
Have a wound?

If I screamed
And no one
Heard me,
Would I have screamed
At all?

My torment is double:
Holes in my flesh
And holes in time.

I speak for the dying
And for the dead:
Affirm, at least,
My scream!

Nothing happened,
You whisper back—
Nothing.
Your atrocity is
But a dream.

If none will see
Atrocity,
Does the survivor
Have a wound?

(Betty continues) Irv, we're supposed to be loyal and produce. Produce. I try to tell myself: "Hey, we're mature. I'm in control. What the hell, this is just work. Take it or leave it. I'll spiff up my resume and get it out on the market. I'll get one foot out of here before they can get to me." But then, come to think of it, where would I go that would still have good pay, benefits, and retirement? I doubt it. Companies these days don't look out for their employees the way they used to. Would I be worse off, Irv, than I am now?

So what do we do, Irv? Everyone's now scared for their job here. Who's better off, the survivors or the dead? When does the next shoe fall? And on whose head? We sure need some stress management workshops! But what will they change? It's like trying to relax on the deck of the *Titanic*. The way I cope is to go on a production frenzy. Just pretend it can't happen. And a feeding frenzy at the junk food machines. You oughta see how everybody's lining up there now. I shouldn't laugh. It's pathetic.

It's that office next to me that bugs me the most, though. I've never seen something so empty in my life. It's so bare. And I know what all was in there. I can still see it. It's like there's gaping holes in this place. If we're not careful, it'll all leak out and there'll be nothing left. It could turn into a desert without any oases. Irv, that's really what it's like now. I'm not exaggerating. (pause) We're living in our own ruins. (She stares out above the audience, as if she is seeing the destruction.)

(Irv recites/reads two poems from lectern.)

Office Space

You say: I take up too much space;
You mean: I occupy any space at all.
Where I am is where and who
You wish to be—to expand, to sprawl,
Into the office skin of me.

But you do not say so directly—
Only that I must move swiftly
To smaller quarters,
More remote quarters
Down the hall, down the stairs,
Down to the in-fact-anywheres.

"Couldn't he just take his things home?"
You asked in committee, not looking at me,
Then came later to offer private apology.

I move, you move me;
I keep out of your way,
I cannot keep out of your way.
I move further,
Never far enough.

Space is parable
For both our dying,

And you'd rather
I go first—
But you'll only say
We're out of space.

The Corporate Table

Massive as an Arizona butte,
the oak table rests upon
a solid oak pedestal.
Once the scene of
clandestine meetings,
the CEO's scathing rebukes,
million-dollar transactions,
it witnessed glory
and ignoble defeat.
A few years later,
it became a good surface
for lunch and coffee mugs.
Its dense wood is inert,
but if it could speak,
what stories it could tell!

Act 1, Scene 3

(The setting is now a corporate executive retreat, perhaps 40 middle management in attendance. The music accompanying this change of scene is the opening of the Second Movement of Shostakovich's *Fifth Symphony*. The speaker is *George, the* CEO of a division of a large multi-site company. He is reconvening the retreat group after a morning coffee break. Sitting very straight and formal, he looks around to get everyone's attention, then speaks in a serious tone.)

(As if recapitulating) The corporate executive retreat's going well so far. I remind you, for those that don't know me, I'm George, the CEO of your division of a large multi-site company. I hope you all had an enjoyable coffee break. Let's get back to work. I have a concern (pause), one that's a harbinger of things to come. A few days ago, I was in an upper management meeting with the CEO, the Vice President for Financial Affairs, the Vice President for Operations, and many other top executives of the home office. They started throwing questions at me I couldn't answer. I want to bring those concerns to you. They're looking at costs; they're looking at space utilization so that we can make it more profitable.

They asked me point blank why Irv's here in the unit, even why he's here in the company at all. They think it's a poor fit. They can't see that Irv contributes anything. (Hearing a sound from across the room, looking up, hearing Irv say something, then continuing) . . . *Irv, let me finish*. Please don't interrupt until I've given the whole story. (Looking directly at Irv) I know that you've received many performance awards over the years, even some national recognition for your work. I know you didn't go out and buy those plaques yourself. But don't you see how hard this is for me? Look at the position you put me in.

(Irv reads/recites a poem from the lectern.)

Imagine You

What do I do
When I can't imagine you?
I prepare for myself
A choice witches brew
Assembled and stirred
In a single pot.
And when I'm through
I'll have cooked for myself
A most fabulous stew
Made entirely from ingredients
I'd imagined as you.

(George continues) . . . What's that you're saying now, Irv? We've worked together here for ten years and, of all people, I should know what you do and why the company should keep you. Irv, you don't understand. Try to see it through my eyes. They put me on the spot. I wasn't expecting them to pin me down. And, to be honest, I haven't supervised your work directly for a long time. I just assumed you were doing your job.

(Angry now, on the attack) Don't make this any harder on me! The times are heartless. Profit's down, competition's cutthroat. Upper management is trying to keep the ship afloat. We're just trying to survive, Irv. We have to show that we deserve to work here. It's nothing personal, Irv. I decided to bring this issue back to our executive retreat because I didn't know how to answer them. Maybe you all can help me to explain what Irv is doing here.

(Irv reads/recites a poem from the lectern.)

Caulking the Wall

I speak with you—
I attempt to speak—
You say you are listening;
You say you are speaking.

But all I see
Is a wall of brick.

You spend the time caulking
As we continue talking.

I keep walking
Into a wall;
You insist there is
No obstacle at all.

(George addresses the group, looking around, while keeping composure, almost like a general addressing his troops) And it's not just Irv, ladies and gentlemen. It's thousands of employees and managers here like Irv. Upper management is in a mood to downsize a lot of us because they can't determine what many of us do for the company. After downsizing is reengineering and outsourcing some units. (More excitedly) I was at a loss to explain to them about Irv's situation. So I brought it back to our executive retreat here. (Now pleading) Irv, Irv. Help us to understand what you do, Irv. Please. Tell us why you're here. For heaven's sakes, Irv. Don't go silent on us. Don't just sit there. Help us. Help us, Irv! *Anyone, tell me why he's here. What does he contribute?* (Complete silence from the group, while ostentatious music from the End of the Second Movement of Shostakovich's Fifth Symphonyplays.)

(The light slowly dims from George until the stool is dark. The light shifts to Irv, who reads/recites a poem from the lectern.)

Speak Your Mind

I have for too long
Spoken in your idiom—
And yours, and yours—
Languages in which
I yearned to make myself understood.

You pressed yourself into me
By way of words and obligations
So much that you have replaced me
With yourself; you insisted
That I could not imagine myself
Apart from the words you stuffed
Upon my tongue; you said
I was not clear;
You never said you would not hear,
Nor could I recognize what you would not say.

I no longer remember what once
I wished to say—

Only that I wished to be understood
In a voice I might have recognized
As my own.

How could I have known you never intended
That I be welcomed
To your community of understanding;
That you asked only that I go away
Or stay and disappear
In your likeness?

And who can bear
To hear murder
In so mere a substance
As words?

Act 1, Scene 4

(*Janet, the personnel director* of a large hospital, speaking to Irv the consultant; music from the Opening of the Third Movement of Shostakovich's *Fifth Symphony* plays.)

(Matter-of-factly, as in a briefing) Hello, Irv. I'm Janet, the personnel director of the metropolitan hospital you are consulting with. Irv, let me start this consultation by giving you a little history. It'll help you understand where we're coming from. Our hospital is part of a consortium of a dozen specialty hospitals. In late 1994, it was widely rumored that some 400 people would soon be fired from the hospital system, and 400 additional unfilled hospital staff positions would be eliminated. One entire hospital building was soon closed. We found out that position transfers to other hospitals would not be permitted. In mid-January 1995, the entire hospital system learned through a leak in the local newspaper about this decision and how soon it would be implemented.

What we need you for, Irv, is to work with the department of human resources, the personnel department, and nursing administration of the hospital to assist a task force to prepare the whole consortium for this multi-phase RIFing process and to help us deal with the aftermath. You'll be here a while!

(Irv reads/recites a poem from the lectern.)

Progressively

For the longest time,
They only told me
My computer was incompatible
With the network,

Later with the printer,
Then with e-mail,
Soon with my own
Floppy disk drive
When I could not
Save even to myself

Which was why
I felt isolated but was told
I wasn't, I shouldn't, how dare I,
Weren't they trying?
Until they gave me notice,
Without explanation,
Saying only that, "You are
In violation of the law."

It was pointless for me
To inquire into particulars,
Since they were the law.
When I pointed out
Their negligence and flaw,
They would only repeat
Their refrain: "You are
In violation of the law."

When, for the last time,
I walked out the door,
I knew their equipment
Had finally been fixed.

The Box

without warning the security guard
appeared in his office
handed him an empty *box*
ordered him to put
all his personal belongings in it
and accompany the guard
to an auditorium for special processing
he was dazed but followed the command
after all the guard carried a gun
he quickly gathered his things in the *box*
and followed the guard
into the auditorium with many others
the guard locked the door behind him

the CEO entered and announced
that the company had a financial crisis
and had to downsize five thousand
employees immediately
the guard returned and ordered him
to bring his *box* to a long queue with everyone else
turn in his keys and badge and parking card
and everything else that belonged to the company
he brought his *box* clung to it
the guard escorted him to the parking lot
and to his car told him that he would
receive his final paycheck in the mail
in a couple of weeks and that he was
to leave and not return to the company
he held his *box* all the more tightly
sat in his car with his *box* in his lap
for several minutes before
starting the engine drove all over town
with his *box* all that remained
of his twenty-five years with the company
once he arrived home he sat in his
car with his *box* in his hands
he did not get out of his car
for a very long time unsure
whether he was alive or dead
he felt unreal alone with his *box*
the only thing in his life
that felt real now
a coffin of sorts
what would his wife and children say
what would they think of the *box*

(Janet continues, shifts in her chair, leaning toward Irv, with urgency in her voice.) Let me tell you what it's like as director of personnel here. I feel like it's my job to plan a funeral for somebody who's going to die but doesn't know it. As a manager I feel it's like World War II. The Nazis have come in and told us, "Point out all the Jewish people" so we can get rid of them. Then the Gypsies, then the Poles. That's what it feels like.

We're asked to plan a funeral and we don't know who's going to be attending. Irv, *this is my home* (spoken with tears in her eyes)! *They are my family!* Upper management keeps telling me that nothing's personal, that's how to get through it. But tell that to a nurse. Nursing is nurturing, and it's difficult for a nurse to let people go. So how does a nurse tell another nurse she's fired? I'm a manager. Irv, how do I work with a shorter staff and still be nurturing to them? If I survive this time around, how do I know I'll be here after the next cutback? I have vast concerns that I will not be employed here long, and I'm one of the people in charge of the program for the people who are being fired now.

You can tell from the look on their faces: people at the hospital are just waiting for the Nazis to come and demand the next trainload of Jews to ship to the camps. We've been through three downsizing displacement training workshops now. What will hospital restructuring do to us? No one tells us. Decisions come down from the top, and we're supposed to carry them out. We might be the next to go, no matter how well we do our jobs.

During each of the four downsizing workshops at the civic center, we held a job fair. We helped people to prepare résumés and to fill out forms to collect unemployment compensation. We had consultants give excellent career counseling; it wasn't just touchy-feely.

Irv, we were totally ignored by everyone in the hospital. It was as if we weren't there, as if the RIF hadn't taken place. Nobody talked about it; nobody talked to us. It's like they didn't want to know, even though people in our departments knew full well what we were doing all those weeks. Couldn't a doctor have offered to buy or bring the *pizza* (emphatic, anguished) for a lunch, for the staff or for displaced people?

We go around the hospitals, and the other employees act like they don't even know us. Nobody else sees what we do. They don't want to know.

(Irv reads/recites two poems from the lectern.)

Overdressed

Don't chide me
For wearing
So heavy a coat.

What do you know
Of the bite
Winter air makes
Upon my cringing skin?

How could you hear
What I might say?—
How would I know
Where to begin?

Downsizing

What is happening
Has not happened,
And if it has,
We do not want to know.

People I worked with yesterday,
Today are suddenly whisked away;
No one asks where they go—
Or even really wants to know.

There is no blood to show
For all their disappearance;
They just are
Not around anymore.

The signs all
Read the same—
On the highways, in the stores,
On the elevators, in the halls:

What is happening
Has not happened,
And if it has,
We do not want to know.

(Janet continues.) The atmosphere in Personnel is the absolute pits. You could cut the gloom with a butter knife. Personnel used to be upbeat, where you could go in the hospital to feel good. Not upbeat now. It is worse in Personnel than in other hospital departments. This is the place where we're supposed to be preparing for the future. There is a feeling of helplessness, hopelessness, powerlessness. You want to scream and say: "I'm affected, too! Not only the people who are no longer here. . . ."

There were no raises in personnel except for the *internal auditor* who showed—to the upper hospital management council in charge of the lay-offs—what could be done on the computer. *He* got a raise. "Just get them out!" was the message we got about the ones being laid off. "And we don't want to hear about it." No one got any pay or even a compliment for the kind of work we did. We staffed two-week-long "work fairs" in which we provided support and information for each group whose jobs had been eliminated.

Irv, it's overwhelming. Where do we even start when nobody really wants to know what's going on? I feel so bad for so many people. I got a call the other day from one of the nurses who had been RIFed. She said she was OK, that she was out looking for some part-time nursing for a start. She was worried about us. She asked how we were doing. I got the slightest twinge of jealousy. Is that normal, Irv? Just imagining the scope of the job here is mind-boggling. How do I keep above water myself? Irv, where on earth to I begin?

Irv, you. . . *you* can help us. (Desperation in her voice.) Tell them out there that we're all really working in *labor camps*. Employment is a myth. We're paid to work to death. That's it, Irv. I finally understand. But no one will listen to me. They'll think I'm crazy, or a troublemaker. But you . . . go, tell *them*! Please!

(The light slowly fades from around Janet. Light is only on Irv, who reads/recites a poem from the lectern.)

Without Windows, Without Light

This place is without windows,
Without outside light,
Without outside air.
The seasons are changing,
But we would not know.

We work at our stations.
We imagine autumn.
We wear all varieties
Of religious amulets
To simulate the sun.

This place is all brick,
Dark glass, and metal.
It does not have windows;
It does not need windows.
There is nothing to see.

Act 1, Scene 5

THE LIGHT SLOWLY RETURNS TO THE STAGE

(*Jack, middle manager* for a textile manufacturer, talking with Irv the consultant about an on-going saga at his company; the music is from the middle of the Third Movement of Shostakovich's *Fifth Symphony*.)

Good to meet you, Irv. I'm Jack, a middle manager at this textile manufacturer. Irv, there's something terrible going on here in our textile company. Like an infection more and more people are coming down with. Except the infection's supposed to be the cure. It's eating away at us, even though everyone's going around like we're perfectly normal—even better than normal.

About ten months ago, seven middle managers all resigned within a month of each other. They had all worked together and the rest of us here knew them all. They helped us get through some rough times when a lot of the upper executives were flying all over the place making presentations and showing how great we were doing. Except they rarely were home, and when they came home they had their fingers in everything. That's what's behind the word "micromanage," having to control everything and everybody. It's like they take over your thoughts and invade your body. That's what it feels like. Well, the seven who up and left helped stabilize the place for nearly a decade. They hardly traveled anywhere. They were home-bodies. They helped us to get through a day, a week, a month. They weren't visionaries, just hard workers. They were the grunts who did the detailed stuff. But they got chewed up and spit out. Promises were made—Irv, I don't know the details—and were broken. So were the spirits of these seven.

(Irv reads/recites a poem from the lectern.)

Thought's Geography

Before I have a thought,
You know what mine should be.

You can't seem to occupy yourself
Without first occupying me.

(Jack continues.) For months after they left, many of us referred to it as "the exodus." It felt like it. We missed those guys. We felt that they abandoned us. We tried not to think about them, just buried ourselves in work. We were supposed to pretend that nothing happened, that everything was just business. We were supposed to suck it up and make up for their work while we trained their replacements. How do you train someone to become a Rolodex that's worth a billion dollars in contacts? The men and women who took their places aren't bad, they're just not the guys who became our friends. We don't know whether to try to leave or stay here.

It's gotten bad for us. But we're not supposed to feel that. It's supposed to be like everyday's Thanksgiving, when the CEO, the CFO, and the various vice presidents put on white coats and chefs' hats and serve all the employees in line. But it isn't. The other day at a managers' retreat, the CEO—he loves to give Sunday sermons—gave us a pep talk. He said, "You know, I'm tired of hearing people talk about what happened nearly a year ago as though it were a tragedy for the company. People say: 'We call it The Exodus, The Leaving, The Bailout, The Jumping Ship.' It's as though they think we're worse off since they left. That's a bunch of crap. That's a myth. We've *benefitted* from their going. They weren't especially loyal, and I don't remember them contributing much to the organization. We're not survivors of some calamity. This is a big opportunity for us."

(Still quoting his CEO, Jack speaks now in a frenzied, triumphant voice, as though a general, leading a charge.) "I'll tell you: Some people call this an Exodus. From this day forth, we're going to call it *The*

Liberation! Union Textiles is in for a great future. And everyone here is privileged to be a part of it!"

(Irv reads/recites a poem from the lectern.)

Job Description

I'm the punch line
To your joke;
I'm the oxen
To your yoke.

I'm your Gentile;
I'm your Jew;
I'm the thought
You thought you knew.

I'm the question
You never ask,
Screen to your cinema—
That's my task.

(Jack continues.) Irv, I'm ashamed to admit it, but I'm scared by talk like this. The people who left Union Textiles had faults, but they weren't garbage. We're a company, and this is getting to feel like a football rally or preparation for war. It's not the way everybody in management tries to make it look. It's ugly, Irv, and a lot of us are downright depressed. And when we're not depressed, we're downright scared. It's like were a chapter from *Nineteen Eighty-Four*. This is America, the United States, Irv. This kind of thing doesn't happen here.

(The stage light slowly dims, as the speaker lowers his head into his hands. The light shifts to Irv.)

(Irv reads/recites two poems from the lectern.)

The Order

You order me not to dream
Except to dream your command;
You do not ask, just demand;
You stomp my dream
Beneath your heavy boots.

For what are you on the frenzied march—
To halt your dreaming, too,
By stomping on my face?
Is my dreaming's death
The keeper of your place?

The Wrong Ending

Rubbish is what he felt like—
garbage wrapped in newspaper
and taken out to the metal cans
near the mailbox.
After thirty years of service
fired without notice,
a company man his company disowned.
("Where did I go wrong?" he wondered.)
"Dead wood," "trim the fat,"
that's what the paper
said the next morning,
just one of three thousand let go,
all in the same day.
Thrown into the street—
garbage!

Act 1, Scene 6

(*Jerry, division head* in a large chemical manufacturing firm, talking with Irv; in a preliminary discussion about the consultation; the music leading into his soliloquy is the end of the Third Movement of Shostakovich's *Fifth Symphony*.)

(Somewhat formal, businesslike) Good morning, Irv. I'm Jerry, division head of a large, multinational chemical manufacturing firm. Irv, I want to talk with you about what a consultation with our chemical firm would entail. I've taken a look at the report from the petroleum company that you gave me. It gives me an idea of how you work, what you look for, and what some of the outcomes are. Overall, I like what I see, and I think you can help us to achieve our goals.

(Slowly) There's one part, though, that I don't understand. In one section, where you're talking about how people experience downsizing, you go on and on, page after page, about how awful it is for everyone involved. It's like reading a wall of words or running into this wall. I get your point, but (hesitation) why do you need to go into it for so long? (Protestingly) I don't get it, Irv. Please understand, I'm not questioning that RIFing's difficult to live through. But it's like you wallow in it. Or you describe how the petrochemical employees wallow in it. We've got to get over it and get on with the work of the firm.

Hell, Irv, I've had *my* share here during the twelve years I've been in the division. And I didn't go whining about it. For several years, in addition to doing my regular job, it's as if I had a full time second job trying to protect my employees and my whole unit from being wiped out. Some of the senior executives, and an earlier consulting firm, recommended dissolving our unit, RIFing several of the managers and employees, and merging the remaining ones with another division in the company.

(Irv reads/recites a poem from the lectern.)

That Look

I have seen that look before;
It tells where you think I'm from
And probably should go back to:
Minsk or Mars—some alien race
Of pigment or thought, *Ausländer*!

A travesty thrust into your skin.
Unforgiving eyes banish from sight
What might have been
Recognition of our common plight:
That in the night,
We all hail from Minsk or Mars,
And our marrow
Is dust and stars.

(Jerry continues, more animated, louder.) I can't begin to tell you how many hours, days, I spend on the phone, in meetings, firing memos, to try to protect my men. It's like we were in combat with our own! Day after day, I never knew what missile I'd have to dodge next and keep from blowing up here. It's like for three years I did nothing but justify our existence. Irv, I couldn't sleep. I put on thirty pounds. My home life went to hell—partly because I was hardly there, and when I was, I was worried sick about taking care of my people. How do you protect people when all the rules keep changing? I didn't know how to justify our existence. It's not as if we were making the company lose money. Nobody was more productive than our team. You could never anticipate what mattered to make a difference between life and death.

(Intensely, as if looking through Irv.) And it was hard for me to face them every day. What was I going to tell them? And how could I help. Sometimes the only thing I could do was to wait with them—and listen. Sometimes they'd ask, but mostly they'd just keep quiet and work like a bunch of desperate beavers to build their dam. I could tell from their faces that they were preoccupied. They were sullen, just not themselves. And sometimes I went out of my way not to face them. I'd just get off the elevator and bolt into my office and bury myself in work. The ordeal lasted so long. It's like we all went on permanent alert status.

(Out of breath, exhausted, he catches himself, stops, briefly laughs, looks directly at Irv, and says slowly.) *Look at me, Irv.* I'm doing the same thing I just accused you of. I'm going on and on about it. You must be bored stiff listening to all this. But this is the first time since the ordeal ended three years ago that I've had the chance to talk about it with anyone. We were too busy to think.

You can't imagine how horrible it was! And it lingers, even when you think you've forgotten about it. Somehow, you brought it all back. I didn't realize that it was still so raw. (He has a look of "recognition" about him; more relaxed, more at peace.)

(The light slowly fades on Jerry; the light shifts to Irv, who begins to read/recite a poem from the lectern.)

A Quiet Place

Have you found
A quiet place
No one can chase you
To or from?

Have you found
A quiet place
Where your face
Is not a mask?

Have you found
A quiet place
For your soul—
Where, though you're
Rent to pieces,
You're still whole?

Act 1, Scene 7 (final scene)

(*Joe* the CEO of a large retail store chain, sitting on the stool on stage; on the phone, talking excitedly to Irv the consultant; during his soliloquy, he holds the telephone receiver close to his ear, but gestures dramatically with it as well; the music is the beginning of the Fourth Movement of Shostakovich's *Fifth Symphony*; as he begins to speak a red light begins to glow upon the stage, increasing in intensity as Joe speaks.)

Hey Irv. Joe Here. I'm the CEO of the large retail store chain you're consulting with. So now you remember? Good. I had to call you. I know it's Saturday night. But you'll love this. Your consultation finally paid off. I listened, Irv. Hear me through.

Marketing's the thing. I want a workforce that's healthy. If they're healthy, they're productive, and we make a bigger profit. So: I want 'em young. I want 'em enthusiastic. I want to hold costs down. We got to make 'em think they work for a place that cares. We'll get the most out of 'em if they think they're getting a good deal on wages and benefits, even if they're not. The main thing's to get 'em and hook 'em.

Here's how, Irv. Get this: Americans go nuts over freedom. They're real suckers for it. Tell them their freedom's threatened and they'll rally around you. They're ready for war. (Softly, as if an aside.) If we just can link work for our company with freedom, we've got 'em hooked. They'll work their butts off!

(Irv reads/recites two poems from the lectern.)

On Forgetting Your Place

Have you forgotten
Your breed and rank?
How dare you aspire
Beyond your place?

Even in America,
We say, "Your grace,"
For sure to his back,
If not to his face.

Transformational Leadership

Ein Volk, ein Reich, ein Führer. ("One People, One Empire, One Leader."), Nazi political slogan

He arrived with a flair,
the new CEO,
like a god on a chariot,
this shaman of change.
He followed Nietzsche's dictum
that great creators must
be great destroyers,
Shiva in the flesh.
He drilled down his will
into the soul of the organization,
replaced their thought
with his thought,
until only his thought remained:
                one corporation,
                one mind,
                one will,
lockstep awe,
the culture a cult,
divine kingship returned.

His power glittered as the gold
        of productivity,
        of profit,
        of perfection,
a well-oiled machine
that submitted to one machinist,
to no one else but his glory.
        Beside him
        there is
        no corporation.
"There is only I."

(Joe continues, with agitated animation.) Here's the idea, Irv. A single slogan, a motto, that'll sink in like a branding iron. They'll see it everywhere in the plant. We'll have banners on the floors, in administration, in the cafeterias, at meetings, at the Christmas party, at the awards banquet. We'll save the biggest for over the main entrance to the building. In bold metal lettering. (Shouting now.) "*WORK WILL MAKE YOU FREE!*" We'll have parades like we're going to war! *Irv, we're gonna make a killing!* We'll pay 'em as little as we've got to, lure 'em into healthcare plans with billboards dripping with family life. Once they believe, they'll rather die before they doubt their belief. And it'll be everywhere, like the air and the sun. It will be like reality! Irv! What do you think of that!

(Click, or perhaps the sound of a click in the phone; the line goes dead) Irv, (hesitantly) Irv are you there? Well, the hell with you. I don't need you damn consultants. (He stands up and gestures defiantly.) I don't need any of you. I thought of it myself. *It's mine!* "Work will make you free!" Who would have thought of it! We'll have signs and posters everywhere. Children will carry them in parades. Everybody will buy it. *Suckers! Suckers!* (Raucous laugh, increasingly uncontrollable, while ranting.) What a buy-in! Work will make you free!! Free!! Work!! Ha Ha Ha

(An intense red light that had nearly baked the stage, now fades to a deep black-red, as the very end of the Fourth Movement of Shostakovich's *Fifth Symphony*, with its bombastic, boisterous, falsely triumphant music, surges to accompany Joe's raucous laughter. A somewhat dim light gradually appears on Irv, who is standing now in front-center stage.)

Act 1, Scene 8

FINAL SCENE, EPILOGUE

(The music of forced triumph finally ends. The stage is bathed in a dark, deep red. Light appears on Irv, standing in mid-stage, looking upward, reaching his hand outward, as if toward G-d.)

(Irv, mock shouting) Irv! Irv! Irv! Enough already with all the Irvs! (sigh, pause) Oi, do I have a headache (grabs both temporal sides of skull). (quieter) Tell me, God, who does *Irv* get to talk to? (restless)

What a noise Joe makes! (more sadly) Rave on, Joe. If it isn't his mouth, then it's his whiskey. They take turns boasting and huffing. (quieter) Sad guy. He's always lived for his banners and parades. (pause) Come to think of it, that's where we all live now. Slogans and froth.

What's a consultant supposed to do these days? (speaking as if about someone else) Why does Irv keep coming back for more? How does Irv even know what to say?

(Slowly, pensively) Tell me, God, are *you* listening? Nobody listens any more, so why should you? Why do I even think I am talking to somebody out there? I need to *think* I am talking to you, that's why. I can't do this all by myself. Tell me, what do you want with this Irv? Why do I keep with this consulting? The work is hard, the hours are long, the pay is iffy, and my health insurance isn't worth much. (pause) I bet Joe calls before I get to the office Monday morning.

(Irv takes out a piece of paper and reads a final poem.)

Office and Theater

I watch my bright-lit office
As I do *Richard III* and *Othello*
In a darkened hall.
I hold my breath—
Maybe this death can be averted.
If only I could leap on stage,
As with a therapist's flair,
Call "Stop! Do you not see
Where treachery heads?
Can we not halt history,
And with forgiveness,
Exit its thrall?"
But no—where betrayal begets betrayal
And obligation to avenge,
No one heeds, or draws a curtain
Till blood flows.
"Justice! Innocence! Vengeance!"
We cry—and cannot restrain ourselves.
We say we only watch,
But we also plot what we suffer.
We sail the ship Inexorable
To its triumphant sinking.
History is what consumes us;
We applaud the play as we drown

In the doom we contrive
As we await.
In this, our tragedy:
What we suffer,
We first wish;
The fate we curse,
We first rehearse.

(The light slowly dims; silence; the curtain slowly closes.)
END OF PLAY

Analysis

The forced optimism and celebration in the final moments of Shostakovich's *Fifth Symphony* gives the show away. The resounding, inflated music is a smokescreen for terror and despair. We wonder: how could Irv have endured more than four decades of boundless grief and rage? What do we, as attendees of the play, have to say to Irv that was not said in the play? The poems, some familiar and some new, and the dialogue, music, stage settings, and lighting, all speak to what has been the pervasive theme of this book—*the darker and toxic side of organizational life*. This side is often denied, observed uncomfortably with averted eyes, and heard through wishful thinking as something else other than what it is. The spotlight must be bright enough to permit this awareness and appreciation, or else progress toward a more thoughtful, reflective, and humane workplace will be left to endless reenactments of this tragic play.

The play offers the reader and its audience a fusion of music, poetry, and dialogue that once again seeks to create not only a sense of awareness, but more importantly also to create a feeling of awareness within that this too has happened to "me." It is okay to feel this experience, even if it's distressing. Irv the play and character encourage us to speak out loud, and even loudly, of these experiences and their internal dialogue, that sometimes leave us all demoralized and bereft of good self-experience.

This chapter is then the metaphoric last act of this book and of our efforts as authors to create conscious awareness of the darker and at times highly destructive nature of our workplaces. There are often not enough thoughtful listeners to these stories. We all need Irv.

When the play is viewed through the three theoretical lenses used in this book, more light is shed on how theory informs, enlightens, and increases our insight and understanding of the dark forces that often surround us at work. Object relations theory suggests that, while we may often projectively create the workplace in our mind with its powerful managers and executives, there are also considerable "data" out there in the *real* organization to *trigger* our internal defensive efforts that rely on splitting and projection, that may well magnify the power and fearful presence of executives and managers "out there." This at the same time reduces us to feeling much less capable and valued, as well as perhaps helpless and passive victims of their actions. The theory encourages us toward reflection to know better our own contribution to creating the horrific outcomes Irv listens to, as well as the psychodynamic nature of the powerful others who do much the same in their minds.

A notion like "two ships passing in the night" speaks to everyone being present and not present. We must be able to reach inward to create awareness of our defensive selves, and outward to be attentive to the defensive others, in order to achieve meaningful and authentic communication—ship-to-ship. Object relations theory is one insightful theoretical perspective that helps to frame this dialogue and the intra-personal and interpersonal poetry waiting to be created.

Group relations theory offers many insights into the play, starting with the often dark and intense fight and flight dynamics the characters and their dialogue speak to. What can be said of a small army of security personnel rounding up hundreds of employees for conveyance to a site of employment termination which, it must be added, is a soul-stripping and terrifying experience that must indeed be locked up in the guarded room, lest the terror spill out into the rest of the organization (although it is already there)?

Group and organizational dynamics are abundant in the play if not the basis of the play, where Irv not only *listens* but also *bears witness* to organizational dynamics that create eerily empty offices and the disappeared never to be seen again. Those who remain end up working even harder, hoping that work will not so much set them free but rather will sustain them in their job's life-giving paychecks and benefits. As a large group of survivors, are they not engaged in unacknowledged unconscious shared social defenses in order to believe the guards will not come for them next?

Karen Horney's tripartite model of defenses against distressing anxiety also casts light onto this stage. Management may well be cast into roles of arrogant characters who presume to know what to do, and who select drastic organizational change such as downsizing as the way forward to a brighter and more profitable future. This is movement-against-writ-large. And it must be said that the implementation of massive and repeated layoffs, restructuring, and reengineering necessarily carries with it a quality of sadism, where expunging from the workplace evil "organizational fat" is pursued with ruthless precision, sometimes enabled by capable consultants who Irv might have had occasion to meet and observe at work. And certainly, the plot of the play leaves one anxious to find the nearest exit, where flight from reality offers a sense of freedom from anxiety and from the stress of either being terminated or left to do not only one's normal work but also that of others who are no longer present—disappeared. There is, unfortunately and ultimately, no escaping this reality when management swings the terrible swift sword of downsizing and its accompanying instruments of personal and organizational destruction such as restructuring and reengineering.

Reflections on Irv

Irv is consultant to a nightmare, a nightmare without awakening. Perhaps Irv is one of the few who are awake, and terrified and devastated by what he sees, hears, and experiences. He becomes a listener and witness to people's unimaginable stories at work. He wishes he could be a whistle-blower, but who would hear the sound? He is in a world of the culturally deaf and spiritually numb. So, he "consults" the best he can and wonders whether he is doing anyone any good. He is *witness* to their unimaginable experiences and suffering; perhaps that is enough.

In Conclusion

This chapter condenses and recapitulates the entire book. If *Irv* is relentless in its darkness, so are so many workplaces as well. Here poetry, experience, and psychodynamic analysis add a depth that is most often overlooked and denied by champions of transformational leaders and managed organizational change.

The triangulation of poem-experience-analysis we have used in this book can be thought of as a form of warning that we hope will lead the reader to remember what has been stuffed far down in the mind because it is too painful. The resonance may, in turn, affirm the plausibility of the play, *Irv*, as if to say, "Yes, work was or is really like that."

We now turn to Chapter 13 with a wary eye on how this book maybe meaningfully concluded, not only in retrospect but also prospectively— what if anything can be suggested to contain and diminish the *darkness* witnessed by this book?

Notes

1. Bollas, C. (1989). *The shadow of the object: Psychoanalysis of the unthought known*. New York: Columbia University Press.
2. Allcorn, S., Baum, H., Diamond, M. & Stein, H.F. (1996). *The human cost of a management failure: Organizational downsizing at general hospital*. Westport, CT: Quorum Books.
3. Stein, H.F. (1998). *Euphemism, spin, and the crisis in organizational life*. Westport, CT: Quorum Books; Stein, H.F. (2001). *Nothing personal, just business*. Westport, CT: Quorum Books.
4. *Irv* has been performed:

   (1) at the Division 13 (Consulting Psychology), Mid-Winter Meeting, American Psychological Association, Phoenix, Arizona, 6 February 1999.

(2) in the Medical Humanities Series, Duke University Medical Center, Raleigh, North Carolina, 26 May 1999.

(3) in a Medical Ethics Workshop, St. John Medical Center Psychology Staff, Tulsa, Oklahoma, 17 July 1999.

(4) in a Consulting Psychology class, Wheaton College, Chicago, Illinois, 2000 (Prof. Michael Atella).

(5) in the Narratives Stream of the Second International Conference of Critical Management Studies, University of Manchester, United Kingdom, 13 July 2001; And it was published in Stein, H.F. (2007). *Insight and imagination: A study in knowing and not-knowing in organizational life.* Lanham, MD: University Press of America. pp. 171–191.

13 In Conclusion

Knowing and Feeling in the Workplace

"And poetry is the place you can come to when you have no words."
Joy Harjo, the new Poet Laureate of the United States, is the first Native
American to achieve that honor[1]

Poems, music, and art tell a story for which there are no words. They
make available and accessible nature and, in this book, organizations in
ways that are essential for the development of empathy, insight, reflectivity, and understanding. Better understanding of the organizations we
work within and that dominate our daily lives is essential if we want to
make them better and less toxic to ourselves, others, and the environment.
The work of this book, its poems, stories, and analyses, has contributed
to this "knowing" and "sensing" that are essential if organizations and
our workplaces are to become not only more efficient and effective, but
also less toxic to ourselves and, in a more spiritual sense, to our souls. We
now turn to exploring the value of using *lived experience* that is the basis
of the poems and stories in this book. What exactly have we the authors
learned from our efforts to triangulate toxic organizations?

What Has Been Learned?

Using lived experience to compose poems and tell stories has the advantage that they are not fictional—"It actually happened." De-identified
and fictional case examples are most often used to illustrate a point of
view or theoretical perspective. They are in a sense backward engineered
to make a point. The poems used in this book to study organizational
toxicity are "real" as only lived experience can provide. The accompanying contextual stories are equally real, providing a narrative for better
appreciating the poems. All of this actually happened. The toxicity that
is revealed is present as lived experience in all organizations.

Using lived experience yields "accessible" and "palpable" content
that allows the reader and listener access, empathy, and the co-location
of similar lived experiences. We are, within our organizations, often

surrounded by small and large toxic events, decisions, and interpersonal interactions. Answers to the question, "What's it like to work here?" can yield a panorama of discouraging and distressing stories about the workplaces people create every day they come to work. We have asked the question many times as consultants. Sometimes body language communicates more than words. The poems may indeed be a place where no words suffice.

Using lived experience to discuss organizational dynamics and toxicity can be stressful as past-lived toxicity is revisited. There is often no escape from affective memory. The distressing and pain-filled experience as well as the accompanying events become that which is known and not known.[2] This is the stuff of post-traumatic stress disorder and, if not treated, the basis for lifelong dysfunction. How else are we to understand self-harming for some after a massive layoff that suddenly transforms everyone into formerly valued employees without an income to take care of families? The movie *The Company Men* underscores this. The poems and indeed this book, we suggest, helps others to recover and examine these experiences of toxic organizations. You are not alone in this experience as the poems attest. In order to write this book, the authors had to do this important work of working through. We are the better for it.

Using lived experience can yield to a process of revisiting and working through, enabled by the promotion of reflection and the use of psychodynamic theories. The interpretations we have provided using the three psychodynamic perspectives have hopefully encouraged reflection and insight gathering. The three perspectives are different from each other, but at the same time this is the purpose of a triangulation. We are trying to locate where we are, and using different vantage points is essential in terms of exploring the underlying psychosocial dynamics at work that create toxic organizational experience. This work, we also hope, encourages exploring the use of other perspectives as well as acquiring reflective insight into what are inevitably complex, hard to understand, and sometimes hard to live through aspects of life in our organizations.

Using lived experience allows a much deeper accessing, awareness, and appreciation of the dark side of work life and the many toxic aspects of organizations. This book has been a study in the lived experience of toxic organizations in the United States and increasingly globally. Throughout the book, rather than paint with broad strokes on the canvas of sociological and economic theory and quantitative research methods, we have stayed close to day-to-day life in workplaces. That focus has been on the *molecular* (subjective, intersubjective) structure of workplace experience. Our triangulation of applied poetry, stories, and psychodynamic analysis is the portal to that often elusive, if not invisible, inner world.

Organizational Toxicity–In Perspective

This book has conveyed at a palpable level a sense of organizational darkness that includes feelings of chronic vulnerability and lack of a sense of safety and meaningful inclusion, an enduring feeling that "There is a target on my back," and an unabating feeling of helplessness ("waiting for the next shoe to fall"). These feelings arise within a larger context of executive, managerial, and shareholder pressure for greater productivity and profit that seemingly inevitably leads to lower wages, few benefits, no loyalty from management, and no job security. Feeling vulnerable and marginalized comes with the turf. "Organizational toxicity" is in some ways a mild term for the pervasive sense that one is being spiritually violated and poisoned in a polluted workplace.[3] Better understanding of these toxic dynamics is the first step toward change.

Approaches to Understanding Toxic Organizations

In this book we have argued that applied organizational poetry, stories, and organizational psychodynamic thinking contribute to a deeper understanding of organizations as simultaneously intersubjective, experiential, transferential, and containing unconscious structure. For many psychodynamic organizational theorists, researchers, and consultants, psychoanalysis—with its focus on free association, transference and countertransference, metaphor, language, and storytelling—becomes a vehicle of both conscious and unconscious deeper understanding of being human. All of these perspectives and dynamics have implications for understanding our contemporary workplaces. They led us to our methodology of triangulation. The themes of the chapters are a mosaic of organizational life. Through the use of this approach, we have tried to immerse you, the reader, in the world of work as we have come to know it. We have offered *our* world at work and hoped that this would *resonate* with *your* work experiences. We hope this has promoted reflection and insight about the experience of work and organizations. Our effort at triangulation has perhaps co-located "our" truth of lived experience in toxic organizations.

The three vantage points of the triangulation "speak" in distinct but, we hope, complementary voices. The juxtaposition of the triangulation with the mosaic of workplace subject areas has allowed the creation of a narrative that provides some sense of order and coherence to the often-chaotic nature of work experience. This narrative has peeled back layers of knowing and understanding the workplace to reveal its more fundamental effects on those who inhabit it. These many workplace experiences made accessible by the poems and illuminated by the accompanying stories and psychoanalytically informed perspectives have provided a rich theoretical context for better appreciating our lives at work as employees, consultants, or organizational researchers.

Beyond Poet and Poem

The discussion of applied poetry in Chapter 2 underscores the underlying complexity to using it as a method to study the complexity of often less than rational organizational dynamics. The book has surfaced for inspection how the work of a *lone poet in isolation* could possibly "connect" with readers who have different workplace experiences. Is it reasonable to generalize from one poet's poems to countless American workplaces? After all, from an *outsider's* vantage point, poetry is a singularly individual personal creation. The poet stands apart in reverie, locating the words and metaphors that communicate what is imagined. How does a poet in such circumstances bring light to organizational darkness for others in their own workplace circumstances? It turns out that the poet is not alone in the darkness.

Since an applied poet is conceptually part of a larger group process, the poet is emotionally and metaphorically neither solitary nor alone. The applied organizational poet occupies such multiple roles as organization member, participant observer, consultant, and researcher. The poet in linking these roles serves as a kind of emotional "lightning rod" for the unconscious life of organizations and the broader society. The poet in using words and images reveals the hidden "unthought known" that everyone knows at the unconscious level but does not yet know they know.[4]

George Devereux offers yet more insight.[5] The poet feels what everyone else feels. The poet creates a poem within intrasubjective space but also within the potential space of relational intersubjectivity. The poet imagines in the intersubjective interpersonal space between poet and the other. Like imagination itself, a poem is thus at once personal (intrapsychic) and relational. The applied poet not only wishes to "express" and to "articulate," but also to communicate with others who perhaps can both validate the poet's experiences and have their own experiences validated as well. The poet's striving to be aware and understand helps those who hear and read the poems to find companionship in locating meaning in their workplace experiences.

It then turns out that the seemingly solitary applied poet is not solitary at all, but rather speaks to and speaks for countless people in American workplaces who have experiences similar to the poet. The applied workplace poet *gives voice* to all organizational members. The applied poet provides, as Harjo notes earlier, images, words, and metaphors to express the raw, inchoate experiences of employees, managers, and leaders who participate in the same organizational—and broader—culture.

Put a different way, *consensual validation* between the applied organizational poet and reader or listener takes place through the resonance of the author's experience with the reader or listener's own experience: as if to say, "I've felt like that, too." In the resonance between these two widely separated metaphorical "tuning forks," both poet and reader participate in a subject-to-subject relationship. The applied poetry of the workplace dwells simultaneously within them and between them. From the theoretical perspective of what Thomas Ogden calls "the third"— where what "is" is neither entirely inside or outside—applied workplace poetry functions as a "creative third," rooted in the counter-transference of both poet and reader or listener.[6] Workplace poetry truly "works" when both poet and reader or listener are reading or listening with what Theodor Reik felicitously called "the third ear."[7]

Lessons Learned

Reflection on the work of this book by way of conclusion encourages us to underscore several noteworthy aspects of doing this work.

Bearing Witness to Organizational Darkness

Workplace applied poetry as bearing witness to organizational darkness is a recurrent theme. The poet, as an organizational observer and participant observer, bore witness, viewing employees and managers as subjects, not as objects. The poet's sense of ethical urgency in part drove the necessity to write, "This really happened." There was not only a sense of urgency to write the poetry, but also to convey it to others to validate *their own* experiences of emotional abuse, terror, and psychological trauma. Applied poetry can become the "royal road" to the inner life of the irrational, toxic workplace, and in turn to bearing witness to its destructiveness.

The Triangulation of Applied Organizational Poetry, Stories, and Theory to Expand Consciousness

The triangulation metaphor and method provided broader and deeper significance to increase the understanding of the workplace, what Diamond called "the unconscious life of organizations."[8] The relationship between the three "nodes" of the triangulation is a *circular feedback loop*. Each complements and amplifies the other. By the time one has read the poem, the story, and the analysis, one returns to the poem enriched, enlightened, and with deeper understanding and feeling. One can begin the process anew, but will not, upon returning to the beginning of the journey, read the same poem the same way. The same holds true for reflection on one's life experiences at work.

It is equally important to note that this book makes *two* methodological contributions to understanding organizations and consulting with and leading/managing them. First, the use of applied poetry as an instrument and data of organizational research offers a new and deeply grounded approach for better understanding the toxic nature of our workplaces. Second, the method of triangulating poem, story, and psychodynamic insight as a tool of organizational understanding, explanation, consulting, and leadership underscores the complexity resident in understanding workplace toxicity and is uniquely suited to this task.

Looking Forward: Implications for the Workplace

This book and its experimental exploration of sensing, knowing, and understanding organizational life and one's self at work has offered triangulation as an approach to becoming more aware and reflective about what ultimately are complex and ever-shifting organizational circumstances and experiences. This context leaves organizational members uplifted some of the time and, regrettably, diminished just as often.

Organizational theorists, researchers, and consultants are cautioned in their use of quantitative methods that ignore the *experienced* realities of organizational life revealed in this book. Reengineering and redesign of business processes are only part of the solution to making our organizations more efficient and effective. Leaving out the humanity of organizational life is done at the risk of having newly reengineered processes resisted, disregarded, or discarded. "We already tried that."

In sum, we hope this book has been able to shine a metaphoric light on the darker side of organizational life, a reality that must first be acknowledged to exist in order to create the possibility of more humane and fulfilling organizational experience. Applied poetry that is linked to the context that inspired it and opened for inspection using psychodynamically informed perspectives is one way forward.

We conclude the book as we began it—with an applied workplace poem drawn once again from lived experience that we acquired trying to practice what we preach. The poem speaks to the concept of a "good enough" leader as one way to envision creating less toxic organizations.

Good Enough

He sits at the large table,
his hands gently folded in his lap,
his eyes riveted on the group
with whom he is consulting,
listens attentively with every corpuscle
of his body, now and then asks questions
or offers a comment, a leader
who follows his group as well as directs,
who tries to live up to his motto of
openness, inclusiveness, transparency,
collaboration, respect, and trust.
He sees everyone at the table
as an expert and tells them so,

always keeps a white, magic marker board
handy to record everyone's ideas
so that they can see them for themselves.
For him, the white board belongs to the group,
not to him alone. He invites their participation
in searching for solutions to the problems
they together had identified.

He admits to the group that he is as fallible
as anyone else around the table,
encourages no-fault change
soothes anxiety by helping everyone
to feel safe, expects no one
to be perfect or to have to be right.
Members of the group begin
to think out loud with no fear
of punishment. The answer to the question
"Who is to be blamed?" is No One,
no guilt, no defensiveness,
only work on fixing the problem.

He is a good enough leader,
which turns out to be good enough
to get the work done,
and to make everyone feel valued in the process.
Sometimes a consultant is a good enough healer.

Notes

1. Harjo, J. (2019). PBS news hour interview, September 19. www.pbs.org/newshour/show/u-s-poet-laureate-joy-harjo-on-opening-a-doorway-of-hope-for-indigenous-artists
2. Bollas, C. (1989). *The shadow of the object: Psychoanalysis of the unthought known*. New York: Columbia University Press.
3. Gabriel, Y. (2005). *Organizations and their discontents: Miasma, toxicity and violation*. Paper presented at Critical Management Studies 4 Conference, July 4–5. Cambridge, UK.
4. Bollas, C. (1989). *The shadow of the object: Psychoanalysis of the unthought known*. New York: Columbia University Press.
5. Devereux, G. (1980). *Basic problems in ethno-psychiatry*. Chicago: University of Chicago Press.
6. Ogden, T. (1994). The analytic third: Working with intersubjective analytic facts. *International Journal of Psychoanalysis*, 75, 3–19.
7. Reik, T. (1948). *Listening with the third ear: The inner experience of a psychoanalyst*. New York: Grove Press.
8. Diamond, M. (1993). *The unconscious life of organizations*. Westport, CT: Quorum Books; Diamond, M. (2017). *Discovering organizational identity*. Columbia, MO: University of Missouri Press.

Index

Printed in the United States
by Baker & Taylor Publisher Services